ROCKER
Scars & Strikes

ROCKER
Scars & Strikes

John Rocker
and
J. Marshall Craig

© 2011 by John Rocker and J. Marshall Craig

All rights reserved. Published 2011
Printed in the United States of America
RMC Publishing, LLC
1550 Spalding Drive
Atlanta, GA 30350

No part of this publication may be reproduced, stored in a retrieval system, or transmitted in any form or by any means, electronic, mechanical, photocopying, recording, or otherwise, without the prior written permission of the author.

Library of Congress Control Number: 2011943553

ISBN 978-0-9847419-0-8

Cover illustration by Morgan Publishing. Back cover photo by McGinnis Leathers. All other photos, unless otherwise credited, are from John Rocker archives or the source of the photo is unknown; credits will be amended in future editions once brought to the publisher's attention. Design by Morgan Publishing, Atlanta, Georgia.

For My Father, Jake

Thank you for all the sacrifices you made and the inspiration you gave and in many ways will always give. I owe more to you than you will ever know.

Miss ya everyday. I love you Dad.

TABLE OF CONTENTS

Acknowledgments	ix
Preface by J. Marshall Craig	xiii
Introduction by John Rocker	1
Chapter One: A Day In The Life	6
Chapter Two: Pregame	14
Chapter Three: Playing The Lottery	23
Chapter Four: Just Another Salmon	53
Chapter Five: The Gods Giveth and the Gods Taketh Away	96
Chapter Six: Myth of Free Speech	103
Chapter Seven: My Nation 'Tisn't Free	116
Chapter Eight: Stealing Home	124
Chapter Nine: Speak English	147
Chapter Ten: A Few of the Kings	157
Chapter Eleven: A Few of the Stupid Moments	183
Career Stats	197

ACKNOWLEDGEMENTS

As with most stories that are worth telling there are many people who deserve a degree of gratitude for their roles in creating the situation(s) by which such a story could be told. In my perspective I've had what I think to be a rather unique life full of its fair share of highs and lows. I would like to take time now to thank the ones responsible for the highs as well as those who stood by me during the lows. For the most part you are the same people.

First and foremost I would like to give a full share of gratitude to my mother and father, Jake and Judy Rocker. You instilled in me the crucial values of honesty, hard work, determination, resilience and sacrifice. These things you taught me have proven to be the most crucial in finding the happiness I have sought. In many ways these things became a part of me by watching what you did, not necessarily what you said. I learned about sacrifice from seeing all of the times you came up short, so that I didn't have to. I learned about honesty when you told me the truth, no matter how tough it may have been. I learned about hard work, Dad, when I saw where you grew up and then thought about everything you had been able to provide for us. And I learned about determination and resilience during all those times I saw both of you press forward when the easiest thing would have been to just turn around. Mom, Dad, without these cornerstone values I would not have had many great experiences nor the ability to write this book, and for that I am eternally grateful.

I would also like to properly thank my high school baseball coaches, Jim Turner and Greg Moore. In addition to improving my skill level on the field, each of you took a special interest in me as a person and had a genuine concern for my future. You both understood the difficult decisions I was confronted with at a very young age and always did your best to bring clarity through the clouds. Thank you for being such strong men of character for an impressionable young mind to observe.

I would also like to thank the Atlanta Braves Baseball Organization for giving me the ability to say, "I fulfilled a childhood dream." There is no way to ever put a price tag on something like that. Many people have such dreams, but few will live to see their fulfillment. Thanks to you, I am one of those few. You drafted me at the ripe old age of 18, and gave me the 10 best years of my life. You gave me lifelong friends, a lifetime of memories, and a championship ring. In return I simply say, "Thank you."

Lastly, I would like to thank all of the people who have stood by me and with me, in front of me and behind me, through all of the years and all of the ups and downs. You know who you are, but it's still nice to be appreciated. First and foremost I would like to thank the Smaha family. Ched Smaha has been my closest friend since the second grade and this third-generation Lebanese family has always been there for me as if I were one of their own. From them I have seen what it means to be a true friend.

I would also like to thank a host of others who have unselfishly extended their friendship and encouragement, and in doing so have made my world a much better place. I would like to take this opportunity to extend my personal gratitude to Ryan Klesko, Javy Lopez, Otis Nixon, Leo Mazzone, Bobby Dews, Bobby Cox, Glenn Williams, Bruce Chen, Odalis Perez, Bobby Bonilla, Walt Weiss, Ozzie Guillen, Andres Galarraga, Brett Boone, Ted Nugent, Dennis Martinez, Jeff Cox, Joe Sambito, John LeRoy (RIP) Wes Helms, Dave Burba, John Burkett, Damian Moss, Ellis Burks, Jim Thome, Steve Woodard, Eddie Perez, Orel Hersheiser, Chan Ho Park, Alex Rodriguez, Alan Butts, Mark DeRosa, Marcus Giles, Ron Gant, Norm Charlton, Kim Cooper, Jack Morgan, Jeff Marshall Craig, Terry Mulholland, Chris Mohr, Doug Johnson, Ray Cox, Keith Brooking, Richard Spear, Toni Millikan, Tom House, Dave Tomlin, Gregg McMichael, Mike Remlinger, Mark Shapiro, John Hart, Derek Foote, Adam Butler, Wes Culp, Rich Spiegel, Andruw Jones, Pascual Matos, Jacob Shumate, Bill Fisher, Stan Kasten, Mel Roberts (RIP) Randy Ingle, Bruce Dal Canton (RIP), Rudy Seanez, Russ Springer, Chino Cadahia, Kevin McGlinchy, Frank Fultz, Dr. Dave Radichesky, Jennifer Cagle, Austin Wolff, Bailey Wolff, Jerry Nyman, Alan Embry, Gabe Whatley, Kevin Millwood, Dr. Ernest Easley, Steve Rickman, Larry Whacks, Eric Von Haessler, Rich Caserotti, Mark Farriba, Andre Reed, Chuck Finley, Johnny Morton, Staci

Sutton, Candy Maldonado, Carlos Baerga, Kevin Mench, The Ballinger Family, Alicia Marie, Brad Clontz, Dan Tyre, David Webb, Paul De'Agnes, Mike Procaccini, Robert English, Doris English, Donna Manor, Mel Manor, Jimmy Manor, Jennifer Manor, Debbie Hornback, Alan Hornback, David Hornback, Dawn Bloye, Kevin Bloye, Chris Van Zant, Ben Acree, Jameel Mamdani and the millions of Atlanta Brave and Major League Baseball fans. I would like to acknowledge all of the times and circumstances from which you could have turned your back. You chose, however, to build me up instead of tear me down and that means more than any of you will ever know. Thank you.

I have spent the last several paragraphs giving some much due credit to those I feel rightfully deserve it. I think it's a safe assumption to make that most of us have a number of people in our lives that we give recognition to concerning their involvement in our own personal success, happiness, etc. These inspiring people and the encouragement they give us can only go so far, however. Their intentions are always the best, but at the end of the day when it's all on the line and you reach that place where success and failure go their separate ways there is only one person you ultimately must be able depend on, and that person had better be you! I have had some terrific people in my life that have inspired me, motivated me, comforted me, loved me and will always "be there" for me. But as much as these wonderful people have to offer, when the time comes to determine my fate on any level, I can honestly say that I ultimately want that fate to depend on me. So in closing, I would like to say that over these 36 years through the highest of highs and the lowest of lows I would like to give myself a small bit of gratitude for never giving up on me. In the darkest of times there is always comfort in knowing that you can depend on you.

John Rocker

PREFACE

You don't know John Rocker.

I mean, really, you may have been in the packed stadiums or caught him on television at the height of his career pitching in a World Series for the Atlanta Braves, or in the American League playoffs for the Cleveland Indians. Maybe you caught him with one of the other various teams he was with during his career. And no doubt you've heard or read controversies over some of his public comments.

Hell, maybe you once even sat beside him on a New York subway!

But the REAL John Rocker is going to surprise you. In fact, there's a lot surprising here: First of all, you've likely picked this book up because you're generally a fan of baseball; you're a fan of the Braves, of John, or you're one of Rocker's detractors – there aren't many people in between.

I am not a sports fan. I had no idea who John Rocker is and, believe it or not, until one Sunday afternoon at a mutual friend's house in Atlanta I'd never even seen a baseball game. Nor had I been aware of his controversial public statements. But Rocker sat me down and we watched a College World Series game together. He explained a few things about what was happening on the screen. That was and still is to this day the first and only baseball game I've ever watched. I've still never seen a hockey game, a football game and, though I personally play tennis ... have never watched Wimbledon or the U.S. or French Opens. Just not wired to watch,

I guess. I hope that makes me the perfect person to help John tell his story, because I am in no way blinded by the stardom, the hype, the history; nor am I tainted by all the garbage that's been written about John or negatively influenced by how badly he's been treated by media.

This book is the real John Rocker. Don't get me wrong. He is controversial and freethinking, opinionated and doesn't shy away from writing exactly what he thinks. You may agree with some or all of the things he likes to talk about — or you may strongly disagree. But he listens when I speak and I listen when he speaks. So what if we have a differing opinion on certain subjects? What's important to John is that there is dialogue — people freely expressing their opinions. I discovered very quickly after getting to know him that he has a very competitive nature and drive to succeed; this is one of his strongest traits. Of course, there's a lot more to a man's story than a few things he's said in public. And the measure of a man far exceeds his mistakes, his victories, glories and successes; it is comprised of the whole: And John Rocker is a smart, reasoned, kind and — like most of us — very forgiving unless crossed in a manner that's unforgivable.

When I was approached to help John tell his story and I looked into what the press had said about him and, indeed, what he had said in the press, I was inclined — ever so briefly — to not even meet him, to be honest. I was put off at what had been reported. Still, I was impressed by his athleticism and intrigued that no matter how he'd been portrayed in the press; he never went silent or stopped doing interviews.

I think John would say the same thing about the prospect of meeting me — though he says he admires my work, he was also highly suspicious of a California liberal co-writing his book. An IMMIGRANT California liberal at that, who has no interest whatsoever in sports!

I decided, however, to give the man a chance, just as he decided that it wasn't a waste of time to have me fly out and meet with him for dinner in Atlanta. I mean, sports fan or not, I thought it might be interesting to meet a guy who nearly accumulated more saves for the Atlanta Braves than any other player in the team's history.

I spent more than 20 years as a reporter myself and instantly I saw through the veneer — this dude got burned, and burned badly — the Dec. 27, 1999, issue of Sports Illustrated in particular — and I knew I wasn't about to step into a room with the devil, that the guy had been given really, really crappy treatment by media. Sports Illustrated burned him with a piece that was a construct primarily of Rocker's indiscriminate direct quotes — so the writer set out to burn him, did it and turned Rocker into, as some have said, a "beating boy for the press, for society, for 'Saturday Night Live,' for late-night TV."

And don't just take it from me — in a lengthy academic journal article for the Online Journal of Sport Psychology, for which Rocker and the writer of the Sports Illustrated piece both participated, scientist John Stiles concluded that Rocker had been treated unfairly and was the victim of a very well-done hatchet job. Years after the damning article, a prominent CNN commentator who is also a Sports Illustrated columnist, and who is clearly not a fan of Rocker's came out with his admission that, "… the media … had blown the story out of proportion (true)."

John and I hit it off immediately. We joke with each other about our differences but these are the differences which have brought us together rather than separate us and, ultimately, that's one of John's messages. It's one of his beliefs: The differences in people, varying cultures ARE a good thing for America. It's, as he points out, one of the primary traits that makes America the greatest country on the planet.

John's got some very strong and controversial views on how cultural and language differences should be presented and exist in American society. Personally, I agree with some of them and disagree with others. But ... ultimately, isn't John correct in that this country is largely based on the very principle that everyone is entitled to his or her opinion?

I've never met a man so persecuted and gone unforgiven by so many for what he's said — some of which was clearly said – but when taken out of their intended context and reported with an obvious bias can bring about extremely unfair results.

Yes, he says what's on his mind – but he'd never deliberately hurt someone's feelings unless he is attacked first. I find that refreshing; I know every word out of John Rocker's mouth is the truth. He doesn't lie, doesn't pull any punches and is exactly the man who he appears to be — which is far different than the man portrayed in media.

Yeah, he said some stuff that was just silly and ill advised. You show me one perfect person who's never said something he or she hasn't regretted later, or at least regretted saying publicly or in mixed company. C'mon, that's human nature.

In that way, he's like the actor Michael Richards (from "Seinfeld"), who lost his temper after being repeatedly and viciously heckled at an L.A. comedy club and said some things he KNEW would upset the people bullying him and shut them down. Yeah, he went over the top but he was defending himself. They couldn't take it, lawsuits started flying and Michael's acting career has been destroyed. This is where "political correctness" is so flawed and even as a liberal I agree with John.

I've already lost "friends" in my liberal rock and roll/ movie world who are appalled that I'm helping John with his book. Wow. That level of hypocrisy from people who should be open-minded is staggering to me. I kinda want to ask them if they've ever been censored the way they wish John could be. That might be a bit too much perspective for them, however.

So why am I helping John with this book? Why did John want to involve me, instead of heading to some famous sports writer who can recite every World Series stat from the last 25 years?

He wanted a blank slate, as it were. He DIDN'T want somebody who knew everything publically there is to know about him and who was going to come to the table with the possibility of a pre-conceived notion of who and what he is. And after hearing his story, I wanted to help him tell it. I've done books with rock stars; written my own novels and even a World War I non-fiction history ... I'm a storyteller. And in my opinion John's got a great one. Make no mistake, this is a collaboration. I did NOT "ghost write" a book for John Rocker — he is on his own an accomplished writer and there are whole chapters where my only input was cosmetic finesse to his story. And so far, it's a story of a remarkable man who's led a remarkable life and achieved the dream of millions of American kids by making it to the big leagues not too far removed from high school. It's about a kid who hit the heights of stardom, but who tragically wasn't allowed to leave the game on his terms, – but who was ultimately forced out by not just giving it his all, but by giving MORE than his all and causing irreparable damage to his arm and body. John gave so much to his teammates, his team, and his fans, that he literally pushed his body beyond its limits — something I consider the mark of an honorable man. And he continues to conduct himself in the same way in business and especially charity work in his post-athletic career.

You don't have to like him to respect him; you don't have to approve of his political views to appreciate him. But I can tell you that if you meet him, chances are you'll like him a great deal. He tells his stories with tongue firmly in cheek and he likes to joke around and tease people he's close to and considers friends. Unfortunately, in stark black ink on a white page, that subtlety is easily lost and implies quite the opposite of John's intent.

Let me tell you a quick story: One day an acquaintance of John's brought his son by — I don't know, he couldn't have been 10 years old — who loves baseball and greatly admires Rocker. John spent quite a bit of time with the boy, signed a baseball and a few other items for him and, then, much to my surprise, asked the kid, "Would you ever like to be a Big Leaguer?" Of course the young boy sheepishly said yes. "Well you know," Rocker responded, "at any one time there's about 750 players in the major leagues. Someday, there's no reason one of them shouldn't be you. Why can't that be you out there? ... it's gotta be somebody."

It was amazing! And you gotta know — you GOTTA know! — the next time that boy went out and threw a ball past a batter, he had John's words racing through his head. Really, how cool is that. In my opinion, dude gets a pass for anything he's said in the past just for that little moment, and I suspect Rocker has those little inspirational moments with other people all the time — the difference being there's never a reporter around or TV camera capturing all that great stuff.

Rocker's a genuine and honest man with a point of view. And if that is viewed as dangerous or a threat to someone, then this country really has changed, and for the worse.

So tighten up your laces: I'm going to help try to put you in John Rocker's shoes ... and since getting to know the man, I don't think many of us would walk a much different path than the one he continues to tread.

J. Marshall Craig
Santa Barbara, California
October, 2011

INTRODUCTION

Hello there! By the obvious fact you are reading this preface means you have picked up my book. So let me formally introduce myself. My name (fortunately or unfortunately depending on who I'm talking to) is John Rocker and one of the first little secrets I would like to let you in on is that stereotypes are there for a reason; they don't just create themselves. So with that in mind, I am going to stereotype you, the reader, into one of four possible categories: either you love me; you hate me; your opinion of me is indifferent, but are still curious to see what outrageous, bizarre, ridiculous, crudely insightful things I may have to say or, you have absolutely no clue who I am. To those of you in group four I would love to meet up and hang out sometime. Anonymity truly is bliss, and it's also one thing I've not had the opportunity to experience much of over the last decade. For those of you in groups one through three please be patient while I spend a few minutes bringing the late 90's cave dwellers up to speed.

Depending on whom you ask, opinions regarding me exist all over the spectrum of public perception. To some I'm the fierce competitor who they once loved to see come charging out of an Atlanta Brave, Cleveland Indian or Texas Ranger bullpen, eyes bulging, nostrils flared, scowl draped firmly across my face dead set on trying to knock the bat right from the grip of any opposing hitter I faced. My goal was to throw my fastball clean through your Louisville Slugger. Sometimes it worked; other times it didn't. Over the years many have told me how much they admired the intensity I often brought to what can sometimes be a rather sleepy game.

To others I'm the idiot who came charging out of an Atlanta Brave, Cleveland Indian, or Texas Ranger bullpen, eyes bulging, nostrils flared, scowl draped firmly across my face like I was some side show circus performer. Over the years maybe you haven't had much to say to me directly but you've definitely let me hear your boos from the bleachers, vitriol in the media, and I'm sure I've been responsible for more than a few profanity-laden-tirades directed at your flat screen TV.

To some I'm the guy who once picked a fight with an entire city.

I didn't mean to bruise the Big Apple — I really didn't. But when Billy Crystal during his opening monologue in the October 20, 2001, broadcast of the Concert for New York, referred to the pre-9/11 days, as "it is not like the good old days when the only guy we hated was John Rocker" I have to say I was somehow honored. You probably didn't mean to, but you called me a "fellow American" in that moment, Mr. Crystal.

To a few, I'm the guy who grew tired of being verbally abused by the most foul, hateful, threatening, lewd language anyone could ever imagine. The guy who became sick of the despicable behavior that he was constantly subjected to, and became even more frustrated at that disgusting behavior being constantly romanticized in the media as if it were just merely some colorful characteristic the city was known for like Philadelphia and cheese steak sandwiches or Buffalo and wings. I've enjoyed hearing comments from many of you over the past years letting me know how much you enjoyed watching me give it back to the ones I was getting it from and how refreshing is was to see someone who wasn't willing to just lay there and keep taking it.

While to others I am and probably always will be simply known as "that guy." That guy who during a man vs. city fisticuffs let his naivety, inexperience and immaturity get the better of him in a lone Sports Illustrated interview that will be forever embedded in sports infamy. For it was in this interview that a green, less-than-well-traveled kid learned the hard way how a few letters which make up a few words when properly positioned on a page in just the right context at just the right angle can create whatever perception that is desired. Unfortunately, for me that perception became one of homophobia, racism and intolerance.

All in all over the last decade nearly four thousand articles have been written with me as the primary subject. Most of which have been nothing more than glorified plagiarism insisting upon claims arising from a solitary article that to this day stands alone in its content. Despite the candid testimony from dozens of friends, teammates, and coaches of every race and many different nationalities totally contradicting the media's adamant accusations the broken record continues to play.

Truth is, I'm much more complicated and intricate than a single scathing profile created by the crude sentence fragments of some "sporting" magazine. And we should all understand human beings are extremely complex creatures, to say the least. An attempt to place neat tidy labels on people with one-word definitions would not only be absurd, it would be ignorant. Hell, sometimes I even have a hard time defining myself, and I'm sure I'm not alone. Maybe the next time I find myself wondering why I did or didn't do something, why I said something, why I didn't say something, or am just generally confused as to which direction I want my life to go; I'll just ask a journalist. At least they "claim" to have me all figured out. Maybe a college degree in journalism should also be awarded with a minor in psychology.

I don't know about you, but I consider myself to be somewhat of a variable. I'm not completely this way, or totally that way. I don't think anyone is. My thoughts, opinions, likes, and dislikes may vary according to circumstance, experience or mood. In my opinion there are very few issues or situations where someone is going to react or feel the exact same way every time. For over a decade now, however, media has done their best to simplify me for their own convenience into a clean, succinct package using the simplest labels with the most basic definitions.

I look forward in the coming chapters to tearing off the neat labels and tidy packaging and revealing who I am as I and people who have known me for decades see me. I can't speak for everyone, but it personally confuses me when I consider the dozens and dozens of close friends of all races and nationalities who have persistently defended my character time and time again yet media in their relentless pursuit of the sensational have continuously penned thousands of articles contradicting the words of those who are and have been the closest to me.

Now don't get me wrong, I fully understand and appreciate the fact that I can be very opinionated and outspoken. I wouldn't change that about myself. I feel, however, that as citizens of the greatest country the world has ever known not only is it our right to use the power of our opinions, but it is our obligation. A privilege not exercised is not a privilege at all. Change and growth in our society comes in large part from the ability we have to voice our opinions. I have been severely chastised for the majority of my adult life for simply exercising a privilege which all Americans are entitled and in theory should be no different than yours.

Now I will be the first to admit that the depiction of me as portrayed by Sports Illustrated should leave every reader appalled and disgusted. The comments as presented were harsh, cruel and unnecessary. I've never been accused of being a genius, but I am smart enough to fully comprehend how that article was received. I am, however, smart enough to remember the conversations from which much of that interview was written and the massive context from which many of those infamous quotes were surgically extracted.

I'm looking forward in this book to addressing the same social and political topics for which SI vilified me all those years ago, because although professional baseball was my calling; politics has always been my passion. The opinions are still the same. The context, however, will be drastically different. This context will contain the full, necessary conversations, which Sports Illustrated thought could be vulgarly summed up in few vague, off-handed sentence fragments. After reading these full conversations you may realize that your opinion is still different than mine, or you may realize that we are a lot more alike than you would have ever imagined or admit to for that matter. Either way is right because the ability to openly discuss opinions and debate differing ideas is perhaps the strongest link in the foundation of this great country.

During the last decade of the "John Rocker Story" one side has obsessively beaten that dead horse with sound bites, sentence fragments, and sensationalism in an attempt to justify their self created persona and self imposed judgment of me. Every responsible reporter should attest, however, that the cornerstone of credible journalism is to be fair and balanced. So far I haven't experienced much "fair" and I haven't seen much "balance." I think that every rational, intelligent person out there, however, can fully agree that there are always two sides to every story. Most of you have heard ad nauseum for over a decade what media has wanted you to hear. It's now time for you to hear another side of this story. My side of the story.

I think in the overall scheme of things this book is being presented from a unique perspective. I've actually been in part "talked into" telling my story by a guy – J. Marshall Craig – who is a liberal Canadian immigrant who resides in Santa Barbara, CA. Jeff is also in the movie and music business, and ironically is not a sports fan by any stretch of the imagination. As he told you in his preface, this hippie bastard had never even seen a single pitch of a ball game until I sat him down one day in Atlanta and commented a College World Series game for him. In my mind Jeff and his background presents the perfect virgin slate to help me tell what I want to be a truly unbiased account.

So as it now stands, in one corner we have the left-wing liberal, immigrant hippie, J. Marshall Craig, and in the other corner we have the redcoat Republican, "let's go huntin'" Southerner, John Rocker. And we've gotten together to write a book bringing into play our own unique perspectives. Looking at our collective backgrounds you would think this relationship would bare a strong resemblance to say that of maybe George Jefferson and Archie Bunker (who I've actually been referred to as the modern day version of, which I find a bit funny).

During the course of writing this book, however, I have truly enjoyed swapping ideas and engaging in debates on various issues with someone who is coming from a completely different side of the fence. He has shown me a few angles and perspectives that maybe I had never seen before, and I would like to think I have done the same for him. One thing I have always enjoyed is discussions, debates, conversations etc. on everything from social issues and politics to who is going to win the next BCS National Championship. Unfortunately, I think much of the forum for honest, open public debate on many important issues has been grossly impeded by our media's insatiable thirst for sound bites and the sensational. It could just be my cock-eyed optimism getting the better of me once again, but I hope that in some way this book can add some perspective on a few topics of consistent national debate without the intrusion of media sensationalism.

Most importantly, however, I want this book to simply be about a kid from somewhat rural Georgia who beat the odds and reached a place he could once only dream of. He encountered a unique situation along the way and gained some very distinct perception and experience. Now at the age of 36 I look back at where I came from, where I am now and all that's happened in between and there is only one line I can think of to truly sum it all up. So to steal one from the late, great Jerry Garcia, "What a long strange trip it's been." And away we go; I hope you enjoy.

John Rocker
Atlanta, Georgia
July, 2011

CHAPTER ONE

A Day In The Life

It's a cool, crisp late October morning in Manhattan. The days are getting shorter as the sun emerges over the East River. The city begins to awaken with its ritualistic melody of taxicab horns and police sirens.

I'm still in bed, wide-awake. Too awake, in fact: My reality is finally setting in and I'm slowly beginning to realize its magnitude. I am in a place where all baseball players — young and old — have dreamed of being, New York City, in the fall. In the more than 125 years of baseball history, if you're a baseball player and you find yourself in Manhattan as the leaves are changing, it can only mean one thing: You're playing in the World Series against the legendary New York Yankees.

It's the calm before the storm. Ten hours before the first pitch of the 1999 World Series on Yankee turf. I've worked nearly my entire life and made many sacrifices to find myself in the exact position I'm in right now. The journey to this day began over a decade ago. Butterflies? How about turkey vultures? My head is a tornado of thoughts: I am one of the miniscule few to actually realize my ultimate childhood dream. In just a few short hours this will be the biggest game/ series I have ever played in, on the grandest stage imaginable.

An entire career can be created or destroyed in just a few short games where so much is at stake. The label of hero or goat can be cast in an instant and last a lifetime on any pitch, during anybody at bat.

Focusing on the magnitude of any game such as this one can paralyze even the greatest of players. As I slowly move about my room early this morning I begin to realize I must mentally reframe my situation. Today has to be just another day at the office; same routine; same thought processes; same mentality.

I have to purge my brain of all those romantic, grandiose thoughts from my childhood fantasies — and I have to keep them at bay for nearly half a day or risk becoming a total head case.

As I put my daydreams back to bed, I slap myself back into reality with a stern mental pep talk. I have to — I HAVE to — make this day just like any other day on the road before a game. This means my usual room service breakfast of a three-egg omelet and a bowl of oatmeal at the Grand Hyatt's bargain price of about fifty bucks. As breakfast is on the way, I decide to turn on the TV to try and settle my painfully anxious mind.

Bad idea.

Who knew? Being in New York City just hours before the last World Series of the Millennium, television is NOT something that's going to take your mind off what's coming down. Every TV channel from public access to the Home and Garden Channel is talking about the upcoming series — and only the upcoming series. I sit there and begin to flip channels as self-proclaimed "experts" talk about how the fate of my team, the Atlanta Braves, could rest solely on my performance, which will come just a few short hours from now. One guy undermines my talent and questions why I haven't been released yet while I click channels, and another commentator predicts that the Braves don't stand a chance unless "John Rocker" comes through in the clutch.

No pressure, right?!

I finally snap to and realize television is not helping.

Breakfast comes. I eat in silence. I keep reminding myself it's too early in the day to be thinking about the game. Knock it off! Maybe I'll take a shower and walk around the city for a bit, do some shopping. That should keep me occupied and slow down the formation of that ulcer in my stomach.

I finish breakfast, get dressed and head downstairs, hoping for a leisurely, relaxing walk around the city. Another BAD idea. As I make my way through the lobby of the team hotel heading for Lexington Avenue, I notice my first problem. Did someone forget to tell me the Rolling Stones are also staying in this hotel? Or was the Pope preparing to make an address from the lobby and no one told me? There must be 400 baseball-card, glossy-photo-wielding autograph seekers standing outside, just waiting for a signed piece of history. Now, on an ordinary day, signing a few cards and photos is no big deal — but in this moment I'm trying my very best to forget that this is no ordinary day.

With each signature come predictions, comments, questions and even some suggestions from the peanut gallery about that big ol' elephant which seems to be following me around. The more I try to treat this like an ordinary day, the more I'm being blatantly reminded it's anything but ordinary.

After about 15 minutes, I make it through the gauntlet of autograph seekers. With the exception of a few stray pen marks, everything seems to be intact. I make my way to the corner and flag down a cab.

As I head to 5th Avenue to take my butterflies for a walk, I notice the entire city is alive with World Series fever. I've played in New York many times, and there is always a certain energy that's present, but there is nothing like the penned-up anticipation of that place in October when it's World Series time.

As I walk down the street, it seems as if half the people I see are having conversations about the big series and the other half just ask me directly: "Eh Rocka, how yous guys gonna do tonight?"

The atmosphere from the East Village to Harlem, Queens and everywhere in between is enough to give me goose bumps and make my hair stand on end. This atmosphere, however, is doing nothing for the anxiety I'm trying to keep in check.

Looking back, I have no idea what I did or where I went that day, what stores I went into, who I talked to, how many autographs I signed or how many boos or cat calls I tried to ignore as the hours passed. But I do remember that internal alarm clock going off: It's 3 p.m. and the hour of reckoning is drawing near. It's time to start getting proactive in meeting my fate. According to my regular daily road game schedule, it's time to get going to the ballpark. I step to the corner of 57th and 5th to hail a cab. A man wearing a Yankees hat picks me up. "Yankee Stadium," I say.

The normal 25-minute ride from mid-town Manhattan to the Bronx seems to take two hours. The driver has a local sports talk radio show on. I hear my name mentioned a couple of times but by now I'm locking in and really don't care; I was done stressing. My worry has now been overcome by excitement!

"This is actually happening," I tell myself.

"Tonight will be the fulfillment of a very long journey."

The ultimate stage — Yankee Stadium: Ruth, Maris, Mantle, DiMaggio ….. Rocker? I have to take a minute and convince myself that somehow I'm worthy. All of the incredible moments and great players that have been a part of this stadium, and soon I would be forever intertwined into the history of this magical place.

The cab turns a corner and there it is sitting on the horizon: Yankee Stadium. It wouldn't be long now. I'm so filled with anticipation I could probably outrun the cab the remaining half-mile; but I manage to keep it together.

Remember, "It's just another day at the office. Act like you've been here before." The anticipation is killing me.

As the cab pulls up to the player's entrance, it is an absolute mob scene. Media trucks as far as the eye could see line both sides of the street. Fans are piled 10 deep behind police barricades, hoping to get an autograph or a handshake from players as they file past, heading for the stadium entrance. It was borderline chaos. To hell with that, it WAS chaos! But I wouldn't expect or want anything less from the die-hard Bronx faithful. I had no idea it would be like this, but it makes me smile in amazement at the circus atmosphere this game creates. And we, the players, are the main attraction when the carnival comes to town.

Once inside, it's down to the belly of the beast and into the visitors' clubhouse for the beginning of the "work" day. After the bedlam outside, it was time for me to give up my fantasy that this was just another day at the office and come to the realization that I'm involved in something very special. I'm certain the clubhouse will be an equally chaotic scene of disarray as I just witnessed up on the street. Actually, disarray would be an understatement. As I walk, or, more accurately, push my way into the clubhouse, I think to myself, "Every reporter on the planet must be here."

There are so many reporters in our clubhouse there is no hope of privacy. I'm guessing there are about a 100 journalists inside — about 10 times the normal amount of media and about four times more than the number of players. You put that many people into a room that's barely 1,500 square feet and I scarcely had room to tie my shoes.

The undressing and dressing ritual for most players is the same day in and day out – at least it was for me. Not today, however. Not with an extra 100 microphones, recorders and note pads walking around. Today it's more like, take my shirt off, do an interview. Take my socks off, do an interview. Take my pants off, do an interview. Stand there naked, do an interview. You get the picture. The word "pushy" doesn't even begin to describe what's going on.

Now I'm dressed, I've fed the piranhas, and it's time to head outside and absorb the stadium atmosphere of my first World Series game. In a novel the size of War and Peace, Tolstoy couldn't describe all of the thoughts, feelings, sounds, and emotions that I feel emerging from the darkness into that stadium. Out of the tunnel, up the dugout stairs and into the brisk October afternoon. The facade of Yankee Stadium climbs high into the sky like a giant tidal wave ready to crash down from all sides. Set against the crisp, blue sky of a cloudless New York afternoon, it's truly a thing of beauty. The stadium facing is lined from foul line to foul line with red, white and blue bunting, signifying a worldwide celebration of baseball.

As I reach the top of the dugout stairs, I finally catch my breath and walk past a few dozen more reporters into the outfield to begin my pre-game routine. I can scarcely remember grass so green as I stride past third base to join my teammates down the left-field line. I thought colors like that were reserved only for our dreams. The lone interruption in that mesmerizing sea of green is the symbolic World Series logo commemorating the last World Series of the century. What a truly unforgettable scene. The 200-foot walk that day into shallow left field is truly one of the greatest feelings I think I will ever experience in my life. Everything was just as the baseball Gods intended.

It's just three hours before the first-pitch. The fans are steadily piling in; fifteen or twenty thousand by the middle of batting practice at 5:30. The energy in the ballpark is starting to increase with each passing minute. Most fans arriving that early are looking to get a World Series souvenir — and chastise the visiting team with some degrading remarks they think will somehow help their beloved Yankees prevail. But I try to ignore it all: Getting ready to play the biggest game of my life has now become my primary focus.

Before I know it, batting practice is over. On the way off the field I stop for a few last quick pre-game interviews, and then up the tunnel to a closed clubhouse for some final preparation. Whether it's getting a little basic treatment in the training room or having a last-minute meal, game time is only an hour away and the jacking around is pretty much over. As everyone is getting their game face on, Pat Corrales, the bench coach, comes through the clubhouse to alert us that introductions will start at 7:50. It won't be long now, and those butterflies I've been trying to tame all day are about to fly out of my throat.

At 7:30, players begin milling toward the dugout, wanting a few final minutes to loosen up and swallow the ambiance. We walk out onto the field, displaying a calm demeanor, but a blender of emotion is churning within. The stands are full now. The blue sky has turned dark on this short autumn day. The crowd is becoming restless as a chant of "Let's Go Yank-ees" begins to pop up in small pockets around the stadium. The storm is on the horizon.

As the eight o'clock hour approaches, the players and coaching staffs of both teams come to the top steps of their respective dugouts, awaiting their introduction into baseball history. The PA announcer comes on at 7:50 p.m. sharp and welcomes everyone to the World Series. A thunderous cheer goes up from the fifty-thousand-plus on hand. An equally uproarious boo is heard with the announcer's next comment: "I would like to introduce tonight's visiting team. The National (Boooo) League (Boooo) Champion (Boooo) Atlanta (Boooo) Braves (Boooooooo!). Anyone who says that a home-field advantage is overrated has never played a World Series game in Yankee Stadium. As our introductions continue the fans grow more and more hostile as each visiting player is announced, wanting desperately to skip the formalities and get to the glorification of their hometown heroes.

"Now, I'd like to introduce to you, your American...." And that is pretty much all I hear. From the lead-off hitter to the 25th man on the roster, a person would need extraordinary hearing to have made out the name of a single player wearing pin stripes in the Bronx that night. Yankee fans are exceptional during the season, but in the playoffs and World Series, their enthusiasm and vigor is unmatched. (I mean fahget about it!)

It's 8:01 p.m. lineup cards have been exchanged; the Yankees have taken the field; and the lead-off hitter is preparing to dig in, as the umpire points at Game 1 pitcher, Andy Petite, and says, "Play ball!"

The anxiety and anticipation is over. It's time to perform on the greatest stage in baseball. In my world, the greatest stage that there could ever be.

As the first pitch is thrown, I find myself front and center, 400 feet away in the visitors' bullpen. Not exactly the best seats in the house to watch a game, but as long as I had a uniform on, I wasn't about to complain. You can't fully appreciate the exertion that goes into simply watching one of these games until it's over and you find yourself completely, physically and mentally drained. Every pitch could be the turning point of the game, or even the series, and each inning is fought just like the ninth of a one-run game. No one is giving away anything. All 27 outs are earned by both sides and whether you're in the game or not, and you feel like you must do your part to help earn each one.

I am in my most intense "cheerleader mode" for the first five innings. Watching from the edge of my seat as I pondered situations I may face later on in the game. At the end of the fifth inning, I get up and began moving around; stretching out, warming up, going through my usual routine. This may be a two-inning night for me if the game stays close. Something I'm not used to, but obviously would have no problem contributing if it would help the team get a leg up in the series.

The game wears on, 5th inning, 6th inning, 7th inning, the score remaining close. I could see the handwriting on the wall. I would make my World Series debut in just a few short minutes. Was I prepared? Had I studied the scouting report enough?

"Relax, stay focused; you're fine."

By the 7th inning the bullpen looks like an anthill that had just been stepped on. Everyone is going through their last bit of preparation before they may be called on to pitch, with the hopes of their teammates and millions of fans resting on their shoulders. Tonight is certainly not the night to have "one of those days." No matter what the situation, anyone who gets the ball must be perfect.

It's the bottom of the 7th and we're up 5 to 2. Two outs and Tom Glavine, after pitching a heck of a game despite having the flu gives up a three- run home run to Chuck Knoblauch. All of a sudden the bullpen phone rings. Everyone nearly jumps out of their shoes. I think even a few fans within earshot were startled. Bobby Dews, the bullpen coach, runs over and catches the phone on the first ring. After listening for a couple of seconds, Dewsy barks out, "Remlinger, you've got the 8th."

Immediately our bullpen catcher, Alan Butts, jumps behind the plate as Mike rushes to the mound. There's not a second to waste. Going into this game, of all games, without being ready is not an option. Whoooh ... Pow! Whoooh ... Pow! Faster and faster.

"Two outs!" someone yells.

"Two outs!" Dewsy repeats.

"You ready, Mike?" I ask.

"Yeah!" he answers.

Seconds later, "Three outs! Let's go, you're in."

The air raid drill is over. The bullpen calms down, if only for a moment.

I assume the position back on the edge of my seat, and join my teammates in mentally coaching Mike through the biggest inning of his life.

"Great Job, Rem!" we all yell, as Mike retires the side in order. No scares, no false alarms to irritate the ulcers in all of our stomachs. But with one thought I relax and then the next moment I think, "Is it my turn now, or will Mike go another one? We're in the American League; so they won't have to pinch hit for him, but Bobby is not going to wear him out tonight and ruin him for tomorrow."

Amidst all of my justification and rationalization, the phone rings and yanks me back to reality.

"Rock, you're in. You've got the 9th."

A few seconds of paralysis hits me before the adrenaline takes over.

I quickly spring out of my seat, role the limbs and torso around.

Ball, glove, mound, it's time to get going.

My World Series debut is just three outs away.

On the mound, rapid fire, arm feels good.

"Buttsy, get down," I motion.

Fastballs away: one, two, three, four, five.

"One out!" Someone yells.

Fastballs inside: one, two, three, four, five.

"Two outs!"

Breaking balls. Everything looks good!

"That's three"!

"Rock; you got it."

I air out a couple of fastballs for good measure and then it's time to get in there.

I've made my last preparatory throw.

The pinnacle of my career is at hand.

Ninth inning. World Series. Yankee Stadium.

I turn to make my signature charge to the mound.

Heart is pounding.

Thoughts are racing.

Spikes are clicking against the cobblestone walkway as I rush toward the culmination of my childhood dreams. The bullpen door flies open. I'm at a full sprint as the vastness of Yankee Stadium appears in front of me.

The blinding lights.

The deafening noise.

The swirling thoughts.

The raucous crowd.

Then suddenly …..

The crowd fades to gray.

The stadium noise blends into a hypnotic hum.

As I race toward the mound, I realize that I have reached the end of a very long journey.

And then … unconsciousness.

I honestly can't tell you one hitter I faced that night or how a single pitch sequence unfolded. I think that's what happens sometimes when we want something so badly, something that seems so unachievable, when the reality finally occurs, it collects into nothing more than a blur of memories.

I guess that's just part of the cost.

CHAPTER TWO

Pregame

ome people will claim they were "born" to do something — whether it's being president, a doctor, a lawyer or a professional baseball player. I personally don't think it comes that easily, though of course there are exceptions. What I can say is that I was born to want to play baseball, that's for sure.

When I was a kid growing up in Georgia, I certainly had my hopes, my dreams and my determinations. And as most athletic kids usually do I had my "icons." Whatever sport I was playing, I would imagine myself to be that person. Whether it was making a three-pointer, running for a touchdown or hitting a homerun the person in my mind was who I was grooming myself to be. As I can best remember it, on the peewee league football field (or the playground) I was either Bo Jackson or Herschel Walker. When basketball was the season I saw myself as the 5'8, 12-year-old, white, "human high light reel" Domonique Wilkins, and on the baseball field I wanted to be George Brett. To a boy with pretty much nothing but sports on his mind these obsessions can run deep. Obsession and imagination are a far cry from reality, however. To bridge such a gap in anyone's life and mold a person to make such grand fantasies tangible takes a nearly insurmountable amount of hard work, determination and experience.

Everyone, no matter where you come from or what you're destined to be in life, can look back and remember events and fortunate happenings that have a pro-

Did somebody leave the car doors open? Nice ears.

found effect on who you will ultimately become. One of those moments happened for me in Kansas City, Mo., when I was 14 years old. That summer my father took the whole famdamily to Kansas City for five days on one of his business trips. One of the evenings was a night out to see the Kansas City Royals play. As I've just told you, at that time there were no two bigger sports heroes in my mind than Bo Jackson and George Brett. Well, as it just so happened during that time they both played for the Royals. You can imagine my adolescent excitement! As I remember the evening, we arrived at the ballpark and found our seats, which were field level down the right-field line. They weren't bad seats, but there were certainly better seats in the house. After the first couple of innings had passed I noticed my Dad speaking with one of the ushers. I really didn't pay much attention to what was going on until the usher walked up and asked me to come with him. Without any questions I got out of my seat and began to follow. When the usher stopped he pointed to an empty seat in the first row right behind the home dugout.

"I understand you're a big Brett and Jackson fan," he said. "You can probably get a little better view of them from here."

I sure could! To this day in my mind's eye I can still see George Brett on first base and can picture Bo Jackson running in from right field and down into the dugout directly in front of me. What an impression that brief moment made on my young psyche! Fourteen years later, wearing a Cleveland Indians uniform, where do you think was the first place I looked when I walked onto that very same field, before I played my own game against the Royals? I could still remember exactly which seat I had

Slinging one for the tribe.

sat in all those years before. When each of us looks back to one event or a series of events that played a significant part in helping shape the person each of us eventually becomes, we often realize that many of these events may have been subtle at the time. But as we get older and the bird's-eye view of life emerges, I think certain experiences from our past begin to take on a significance which gives us a better understanding of exactly who we are and how we got to where we are in life. That evening in Kansas City became one of those moments for me and to this day is one of my fondest memories.

Events that left that kind of impression on me when it came to shaping my dreams of playing Major League baseball were very few and far between, however. As I mentioned earlier I grew up in somewhat rural Georgia and where I lived we didn't even have cable TV until I was 18 years old. During the years where I should have been choosing a baseball star to emulate and analyzing his every move, I was basically living in media isolation. My knowledge of the outside world was limited to the local paper and the Big Three broadcast networks, ABC, NBC, CBS, and sometimes a very snowy picture of TBS so long as the "rabbit ears" antenna were properly positioned. I can remember most summer evenings my father and I fist fighting with our television in an attempt to maintain a discernable picture; so we could watch the then-lowly Atlanta Braves drop yet another one. Hey, it was baseball though, and I loved it!

So while most kids were camped out on a daily basis in front of a "cable" TV soaking in the highlights narrated by some ESPN reporter, I had to hear second hand who hit the game winning home run in the previous night's Cubs game. I had to imagine what the celebration must have been like after Nolan Ryan's 5th no-hitter. As much as I am a fan of the game, its history and many players from every generation I'm definitely disappointed that I was unable to witness so many of its great and memorable moments. Often times visually experiencing something creates an idea, from that idea comes desire and desire most often gives birth to motivation. Despite the lack of visual experiences

My first little league team, the "Pirates" I'm the one in the conductors hat on the back row, far left.

throughout my younger years, however, I certainly never lacked motivation or determination for that matter.

I would guess my real motivation to succeed at the game of baseball began about the time I realized that I actually had a talent for it. I think most of us would agree that it's much easier to become motivated to achieve when you stumble upon the realization that you actually have an aptitude for something. I think I was first made aware of my talents in somewhat of a subtle way as I began to recognize that more and more kids on my Little League t-ball team refused to play catch with me. About half way through my first year the only people who would throw with me before our practices were the coaches and soon they even began to complain about sore hands and busted mitts. It was about then the comprehension began to emerge that I must have been born with the ability to throw a baseball. At that age, however, realizing you have a talent is one thing; knowing what to do with it is quite another.

My fellow Little Leaque buddies and I decided we would name our all-star team the "Bad News Bears". I'm sure it was funny at the time.

So, I guess I just did what any nine-year-old kid would have done: I just kept playing. Any chance I got I was all about playing some baseball. I didn't care if it was a four-on-four pickup game on the play ground — I just wanted the chance to try and throw a pitch by someone and then hopefully take one deep over the azalea bushes (which was an automatic homerun on the playground).

The pinnacle of each of my early years, though, was that one Saturday in March when my Dad and I would go down to our local little league park to sign me up for that year's season. On that day I knew it wouldn't be long before our first organized practices would begin to be followed shortly by those games I so much looked forward to. Now, I can't speak as to the atmosphere of other little league programs around the country, but there were some pretty extensive bragging rights at stake on each and every game in my home town little league. As I'm sure it is in most places at that age, the majority of the kids you play with or against either go to your school or you at least know them from around town. So as it was every year as our little league season began the classrooms and playgrounds were full of weekly 4th-grade trash talk followed by bragging rights to the victors.

As I sit and reflect on those times, I can say without one shred of doubt that those were perhaps the purest and most enjoyable times I have ever had the pleasure of experiencing. I think life can be funny that way. Some of the greatest things we ever experience can never be truly appreciated until they're gone, and we have no way of realizing how special they actually are while we have the ability to enjoy them.

Well, as it generally does, time kept rolling by. With every passing year my love for the game grew exponentially. I wouldn't have admitted that I was becoming obsessed with the game, but ... I was becoming obsessed with the game! Gradually, my room became a shrine to players who only played games on cable, and my shoe boxes began filling with baseball cards. I had never seen many of these players perform, but had heard the stories or read the articles, and putting a poster on my wall or a card in my album was my way of paying homage. Every meager dollar I was able to muster was usually invested into four or five bubble-gum baseball card packs at the grocery store. During the car ride home it was like a mini Christmas morning as I would tear into each pack hoping some of my favorite players would be inside. Once the cards were looked through, dissected and studied, they were put into one of several albums based on whatever organizational method I was using at the time, or they found their way into shoe boxes for safe keeping. To this day I still have every one of them — probably around seven or eight thousand, I'd guess.

My "hobby" was a full-blown obsession by the time I was 10. The collecting, the organizing, the studying would certainly appear to be all the required neuroses someone must possess to be considered a formidable enthusiast. For me, however, it was one way I found to fuel and in some way even created my growing fire to become a Major League ball player.

By the age of 14 the dream that I had been hit with enveloped me. Like I'm sure a lot of kids do at that age, I became obsessed with the idea of playing Major League baseball. I'm a firm believer that the bigger the dream is, the greater the desire, and the more obsessed one has to be to ultimately achieve it. But at the age of 14 the moon seemed a more reachable location than a Major League diamond and with that in mind I became one fixated little guy. Any book out there by a favorite player or magazine article about a favorite player I tried to get my hands on. I wanted to know everything about the game of baseball. What were the thoughts, the feelings, the experiences of these people that I so desperately wanted to emulate? As I would read a quote by my favorite pitcher it would become a mantra for the next game I pitched. One of my favorites came from a Sports Illustrate article on Roger Clemens — with whom I would later share an agent.

Roger's quote, which I would repeat over the years during my own performances, simply went, "I was out there throwing fastballs and upper cuts." Slowly but surely the mentality began to form and the flames of desire intensified. By the age of 15 becoming a Major League player was not a dream anymore; it was a lifestyle. The thought process began to emerge that something had to be done on a daily basis to somehow prepare myself to fulfill my fantasy. I remember coming home dog tired after high school football games and going through my 25-minute shoulder-strength and stretching routine because it had to be done every day. Some days I would wake up an extra 30 minutes early before school to go through it again — because it had to be done, every day. In addition to all the responsibilities of school, home and whatever sport I was actively playing at the time something "baseball" had to be done everyday.

Some days I could only muster 20 minutes' worth of some varied preparation while other days would consist of playing a game followed by an hour and a half of a strength-and-stretching workouts just to go home and sit in front of a Braves game with a bag of ice on my arm, followed by reading myself to sleep with the "Mental Game of Baseball." To some this might seem a bit over the top for a kid who probably should have been more interested in chasing girls on his Friday nights, but what can I say. As I look back now on the other side of the dream it almost takes my breath away. I sure am glad at the age of 14 I didn't fully understand the magnitude of what I wanted to achieve. I'm glad I didn't know the odds and percentages of not only a minor league player ever participating in a Big League game, much less a 14-year-old high school kid. But I guess in a way that's part of the beauty of having a dream like that. You really don't care what the odds are.

As I began to mature, my physical abilities slowly began to catch up with my mental desires. As a high school freshman I worked my way into the varsity team's number one starter by mid-season. By season's end my numbers weren't obnoxious, but they certainly were respectable for an under-developed, immature kid who would disappear if he turned sideways.

A mantra I often refer to recites, "Confidence creates success and in turn success creates greater confidence, but you must first have confidence before you can have success." I can't definitively say that the success I enjoyed during that freshman campaign gave me all the confidence I would need to ultimately catapult me to the Major Leagues, but it certainly made me a believer in myself, which on any level and in any endeavor is a must.

That season certainly didn't start out that way, however. I remember early that year during our first few workouts being a bit intimidated by a number of things I was encountering for the first time. The field we played on was by far the largest I had ever been on, and I was deathly afraid of being embarrassed during batting practice if I couldn't hit the ball as far as some of the older players. I had always been a pretty good hitter, but at that age, especially during batting practice, you always want to show off your "pop". It was definitely an ego thing for all of us testosterone-filled young'uns out there, and the guy who displayed the most power certainly felt good about himself while the weakest swinger would definitely carry around a bruise on his ego. The days leading up to our first workouts that spring were a little nerve-racking for me. Would I be able to hold my own with the older players or would I end up as the butt of senior ridicule and be told to "come back when you grow up a bit, kid"?

I thought I was pretty good, but what if my perspective was skewed? What if the people I had been playing against the last several years weren't that good and I was not a good player, but just less bad than my competition had been? These were the thoughts and fears that obsessed my 14-year-old brain in the days leading up to my grand debut with the mighty varsity team. As I look back I can't help but laugh at myself a little for what a huge deal I thought all of this was, and I guess in my own little world at the time it probably was a huge deal. I'm sure my immature mind somehow saw this opportunity as somewhat of a "first step" in realizing my grandiose dream, and that this immortal high school varsity baseball team would be my first "proving ground" of sorts. I think I can safely say in the days leading up to my first competition against much older players, and even during the first few weeks of workouts, I was short on that much needed confidence.

Jim Turner and my assistant coach, Greg Moore after one of our high school games. It looks like we won.

As I say, and as I firmly believe, you need confidence before you can have success. It's unfortunate that at 14 years old I didn't know that fake confidence — although not ideal, is still confidence. It took me years to learn that there is nothing wrong with fake confidence. What's that cliché? Fake it 'til you make it. I've gotten a long way in my life with those six simple words.

Nevertheless, during the first couple of weeks of my freshman campaign I was having some trouble coming into my own. The older players could drive; some of them had beards; they could get into R-rated movies and buy cigarettes, for God's sake! I wasn't even done with puberty yet! In addition to the intimidation factor of some of my teammates, I continued for some time to find this huge ballpark a bit daunting as well. Up until then I had only played on fields that were barely bigger than the ones little leaguers play on. My new field was almost the size of a Big League diamond and it took me a while to gain my bearings.

Early on there was a lot I had to become comfortable with as far as my surroundings were concerned, but mostly I had to become comfortable with myself. I trudged along for a week or two feeling around for that light switch in the dark. I wasn't embarrassing myself, but there was certainly nothing to brag about either. Then one day I found that switch. I've always been amazed at how one event, one moment that may seem insignificant to almost everyone around you, can affect the confidence level and opinion of oneself to such a degree that there is an almost instant metamorphosis. That happened to me on one swing during batting practice in early March of what until then had been a very doubt-filled season.

I had always been a pretty good hitter, though in the early going that year people wouldn't exactly stop what they were doing to watch me swing; but I wasn't a total embarrassment either. Yet I didn't believe I was quite measuring up to what I and most other people were expecting of me. During batting practice some days I would swing as hard as my skinny little arms were capable of, only to have the left fielder and shortstop fight over the fly ball. That is definitely one emasculating feeling — especially to someone trying to impress all the really cool seniors.

One typical day we were going through our normal practice routine when I was called in from the outfield where I had been shagging fly balls to take a few rounds of batting practice. This was pretty typical as far as the daily practice schedule went. I jogged in from the outfield, grabbed a helmet and a bat and waited my turn to step in and take my swings. If memory serves me correctly I believe the standard routine was for each player to get four rounds of eight cuts. As I stepped to the plate to take my first round I felt about like always. The first few pitches came in and I sent them back out with moderate authority. At this point I don't know if it was a subconscious confidence that came over me or what, but with each pitch I hit I began to feel stronger and more solid than I had felt at any time before. As I climbed back in to take my second round I became conscious of the fact that something was different about me that day. During this second round of BP I began to hit the ball with a command and authority that was significantly different from anything else I had ever displayed. I began getting a few shouts from the outfield as I short-hopped the left-field fence on a couple of swings. Hearing that encouragement, my adrenaline began to kick in. I had just hit three or four balls farther than I ever had before. I know it was just batting practice, but at 14 years old seeing how far you can hit it is 90 percent of the fun. As my turn came around again I noticed some of my teammates had stopped what they were doing to check me out. I stepped in for my third round with a level of confidence and aggression that I had been missing. My first few swings picked up where my last round had ended. Now even those "cool ass" seniors started to take notice and began chirping at me a bit. Then, on about the 5th or 6th cut one of those "short-hop" balls from the previous round just kept carrying. I felt like Carlton Fisk in the '75 World Series trying to coax his game-winning homerun over the Green Monster in Fenway. I stood there at home plate with some beat-up helmet on my head, one of only three team bats we had in my hand, and begged just like Carlton did that day in '75 for a tattered high school batting practice ball to clear the 325-foot sign in left field.

Looking back two decades later and having had more than my fair share of defining experiences since then, I can honestly say that the exact moment I watched that dingy baseball drop on the other side of that chain-linked fence a change took place. It was the change one experiences when all of the doubts, fears and anxiety most of us carry around concerning our own ability to succeed are wiped away and replaced with the confidence we will ultimately need to achieve whatever dream we desire for ourselves.

I finally felt like I belonged.

CHAPTER THREE

Playing the Lottery

Few times in our daily lives do we consciously realize that a mental, emotional or physical transformation has occurred. When these events do take place, however, they are rarely forgotten and the changes they evoke can sometimes lead to the "awakening" we have been waiting for — even if we were not aware of the need to be wakened. No one who witnessed that (seemingly) meaningless home run during a meaningless high school practice in the spring of 1989 could have known that specific moment had instant significance. That is, no one but me.

I have no doubt that minute blip on the radar screen of life was forgotten by everyone who was there that day probably before dinnertime. I, on the other hand, walked off the field that afternoon carrying an entirely different opinion of myself, which I have come to learn, is about 90 percent of the recipe for success and/or failure. Although a bit cliché, a mantra I repeat to this day is: "whether you think you can or you think you can't; you're right."

On one day, during one precise moment, my perception took a giant step towards becoming "right." I can't say that from that day forward everything just fell into place because it certainly did not. I can say, however, that this moment gave me my very first taste of the confidence I would ultimately need to satisfy my growing desire to achieve a nearly impossible dream. Although the doubts and fears weren't totally eradicated (which I don't think they ever totally can be), at this point I had some ammunition to battle these feelings when they decided to crash the party.

Little by little, month by month, slowly but surely, I began to transform mentally, emotionally and physically as I concentrated on my dream daily. My mindset became a permanent focus that something had to be done every day to get me closer to the top of this tremendous mountain I was attempting to conquer. From that one auspicious batting practice, events began to cascade which fueled my fire of self confidence, and by the end of that freshmen year I felt like I was on my way to becoming the player I dreamed of someday becoming. By year's end my dominating thoughts were not ones of doubt and worry, but of satisfaction, motivation, and confidence. In my opinion there is no greater motivator than success. Whether that success is actual or anticipated, ultimately what should keep us inspired each and every day is the achievement of new or continued successes.

With this new feeling of satisfaction and accomplishment came another and very important mental first in my developing mindset. This new "first" was the feelings and emotions that are created when either self imposed or outside expectations are actually lived up to. In my opinion there is no better feeling than to engage in a task where preconceived expectations exist and then deliver. In the years to come a large factor of my personal motivation was to envision myself on the day after the season was over, having the ability to go somewhere quiet; take a deep breath and feel totally satisfied at having done the job which was expected of me, and most importantly, having done the job I expected of myself. As the span of that freshman year came to a close, although not possessing the self-awareness, I had begun to establish the mental and emotional base that would be crucial to the future success I desired.

With a firm foundation of confidence beginning to grow under my feet things began clicking for me on the field. Although still very inexperienced and unsure just how good I needed to be to one day get paid for my services, with each passing week my assurance gradually became more tangible and I believed that I was at least on the right track. After playing throughout the summer and working hard during the winter I came into the spring of my sophomore

JT's "final breakdown" of the 92 season.

year eager to continue my march toward the dream. By mid season things were going well and I began to get a small bit of attention from a handful of local pro scouts.

On the one hand this interest provided a great deal of encouragement that in fact maybe I did have what it took to see my dream become reality. On the other hand it became an immediate wake-up call alerting me that the moments of truth were drawing near. It wasn't going to be to much longer before the fate of my dream would be determined.

The first notification I received on just how much better I was going to have to get came on a cold rainy March Saturday in Albany, Ga. A local scout for the Pittsburg Pirates invited me to come throw at a pre-draft workout at a small minor league stadium that I would eventually play on years later during my time in the South Atlantic League as a member of the Macon Braves. On this day, however, I was still just a goofy 15-year-old kid who had worlds to conquer before I eventually returned to that field. As I arrived for my workout I naturally began sizing up the other invitees. Within a couple of minutes those ominous seniors from my freshman year would have been a very welcome site compared to some of the studs I would be working out with — and competing against. The majority of the guys I was observing were there at the Pirates' request to receive a private evaluation in consideration for the upcoming June draft. After one good look around, my first thought was, "what the @#$% have I gotten myself into!" But I psyched myself into some sense of serenity for my first litmus test. As I began throwing in the bullpen, the scout who invited me walked up and told me I would be facing three hitters.

"Let me know when you're ready," he said.

I'll never forget the first guy I faced. Picture Michael Clarke Duncan's character in the movie "Green Mile" — something like that! I can think of six different types of compact car that are smaller than this guy was! As he lumbered up to the plate I shook my head again. "What the @#$% have I gotten myself into!"

At this point, however, there was obviously no turning back. This "beast" of a man was 60 feet away wagging his little bat at me; it was time to get a dose of reality. With the next 30-plus pitches to this monster and two other hitters I did the only thing I knew to do. I absolutely came unglued on each pitch. Every pitch I threw that day had everything my scrawny body could muster trying to impress those hitters, the scouts, but I think mostly I was just trying to impress myself. After the dust cleared and I retied my shoes and straightened my hat, much to my surprise I had actually held my own. I didn't dominate anyone, but for a skinny under-developed sophomore facing guys who were being considered as possible June draft picks, I had just passed my own critical acclaim. I had now seen the bar.

I had not reached it and certainly hadn't gone over it, but that March afternoon in Albany I saw how much further I needed to go.

From that day forward I took on an adjusted approach to attaining my ultimate prize. There now became goals within THE GOAL. I had seen my weaknesses, my shortcomings and the process became to mend these deficiencies gradually, one by one. I think that is where a lot of dreams get put on the back burner or derailed all together. Too many times people get overwhelmed with the magnitude of whatever aspirations they may have. These aspirations may be to become a doctor, a lawyer, retire at 40, own a successful business or whatever. I've seen many people so inundated by the perceived magnitude of a dream or challenge that they never even begin the process of accomplishment. In reality success is rarely measured by a single victory, but instead is the result of many, many smaller victories. I now had a list of small battles to fight so that the next time a compact car wearing baseball spikes came to the plate I could dominate him!

Over the next two years my level of commitment, although still intense, now became much more focused. The hodgepodge of Major League players that I considered myself to be a pseudo fan of narrowed to just a small few that I could relate to and saw myself emulating. I started molding myself into the form of those who lived my dream as their reality. With a new determination I began a much more concentrated effort to learn all I could about the approach my specific role models had concerning the mental, physical and conditioning side of playing baseball at its highest level. Gradually, my moderately ignorant, scattered-gun approach to success began to be replaced with a more pointed and "heightened" level of understanding and dedication. Of course it hadn't evolved to the degree it would be when I eventually reached the professional level, but I did begin at this relatively young age to learn all I could about conditioning, mechanics, and mentality and began to apply my learning with an obsessive effort.

As my junior season rolled around it had been nearly a year since the decision to approach my challenge with a more precise effort had been made, and during the season's early going it definitely appeared that I was on the right track. The first game out of the shoot that year was a seven-inning no-hit shutout where I recorded 15 strikeouts. In fact in the first three games that year I only gave up four hits and one run. Things were certainly going according to plan. That is things were going according to MY plan. I've found it to be interesting over the years that just about the time things may be following the plan that in our infinite wisdom we have laid out for ourselves, "life" has a funny way of coming along to remind us that something called "reality" is out there and it hasn't been informed of our own specific schedules. Just as the previous two years had produced important firsts in a couple of areas, my junior season came along with a first of a somewhat different sort.

It was a Saturday-afternoon game in early April. I was playing center field that day, so I was a little more relaxed than usual. It was almost game time and I asked one of our coaches to throw me a few, so I could take a few extra hacks before the game. As I began to hit everything seemed normal, just like the thousands of other swings I had taken in my life. Then on one non-descript cut, out of nowhere, it was like someone jabbed a rusty butter knife deep into my left shoulder.

"What in the hell was that?" I thought as I crumbled to one knee grasping my throwing arm. I stood back up with a stupid, confused look on my face. My coach immediately asked me what was wrong.

"I don't know," I said.

"I just got a real sharp pain in my shoulder and it felt like the thing popped out of joint or something."

I stood there for a few seconds not knowing quite what to make of what just happened, so like any head strong 17-year-old would do, I told my coach to just keep throwing. I dug back in and began taking a few more cuts. On about the third swing WHAM! There it went again! This time I went down in a heap, dropped the bat and screamed like a little girl. After a few seconds I composed myself again and yelled, "What the HELL? Good God that hurt!"

At this point I think my coach was just as confused and almost as worried as I was. "What's going on?" he asked.

"I have no idea! It's like my shoulder keeps popping out of joint!"

Now I had seen guys have their shoulders separated and it's a pretty gross site. The arm hangs down about four or five inches below where it's supposed to be and there is a wide gap between the humerus and scapula. My arm didn't look grotesque like in a separation, but something similar was definitely going on. "Are you OK to play?" My coach asked. "I think so. I'll give it shot."

So with an uncharacteristically timid and cautious demeanor, I walked out of the batting cage and jogged out to center as the rest of the team took the field. On the way out to my position my arm began to really hurt, and I noticed there seemed to be a significant loss of strength. As I started to play catch with our left fielder, each throw was followed by a piercing pain just above my left biceps. Suddenly, my bewilderment morphed into dread!

"Oh my God! What the hell have I done?"

Later in my career I had a similar injury and became a full-blown anatomy major on the inner workings of the human shoulder, but at 17 dissecting frogs in biology class was about the extent of my anatomical knowledge. So I did what anyone who lacks a certain detailed understanding would do: I worried my ass off. By the time the inning was over, I was a mental mess. I jogged in from the outfield believing that my short-lived career was all but over. I immediately ran to my coach babbling God knows what about the pain, the weakness etc. etc. I'm sure I sounded deranged. Too bad most high school medical kits aren't stocked with Valium. I certainly could have used a heavy dose. After a few minutes though my coach was able to sedate me with some words of experience and wisdom and recommended I take the rest of the day off.

The balance of the weekend was absolutely agonizing as I awaited my orthopedic appointment on Monday afternoon. I was sure the doctor was going to tell me I was deformed, crippled, washed up, finished, and on and on I obsessed totally oblivious to the one key factor that I had on my side: I was still a very young guy. This dynamic, or lack thereof, became painfully apparent to me some 15 years later when a similar injury would ultimately end my career.

There would be no such dire news on this day, however. As the doctor looked over my MRI exam result, I was diagnosed with a torn labrum caused by the subluxation of my shoulder capsule — What? Ok, for all those out there who are also academically challenged and just said, "what?" — as I did — here is a quick explanation. The labrum is a piece of cartilage that is attached to the top of the humerus bone where the humerus meets the scapula (where your biceps and shoulder merge). Additionally, subluxation is a condition by which a joint such as a shoulder or hip comes partially out of the socket and then pops back in. It is not nearly as painful or gruesome as a separation, but it will definitely get your attention and can cause some moderate damage in the process. Naturally, my initial thought at hearing the doctor's explanation was, "this can't be good, not for now or for my future." Looking back nearly 20 years later, however, I still find it entertaining how situations that seem so pointedly straight forward at their outset can produce such a profoundly different result from the one that seems so obvious at their inception.

In short, I would not have become a Major League closer had it not been for this injury, the physical condition which allowed this injury to occur or the need for surgery that it created. I know this may seem like a very odd comment, and while I was listening to my diagnosis the words I just wrote would have seemed more than laughable; they would actually have seemed absurd. No matter how smart we think we are though, life always somehow seems to be one step ahead. The condition that I'm referring to is the "looseness" of my shoulder capsules. From what I've read and been told over the years a thing like that is predominantly hereditary. Either you have it or you don't. The fact that my left shoulder capsule was extremely loose/flexible allowed it to subluxate when I hit; therefore causing damage to my labrum; it also, however, allowed that capsule to generate the kind of rotation which would ultimately enable me to throw in excess of 100 mph. That may seem a bit confusing, but here is a fact that may add some perspective. The average human shoulder can rotate approximately 110 to 120 degrees (when you hold your arm at a right angle even with your ear that is 90 degrees). The average Major League pitcher has a shoulder that is capable of rotating in excess of 160 degrees. Translation: the more rotation, the more speed the arm is able to generate and therefore the faster a baseball can be thrown. In other words having loose/limber shoulder capsules is a must to becoming a Major League pitcher. To a degree something like this can be improved over time, but for the most part it's just a gift.

Besides the discovery of a genetic "gift" this situation also thrust me into a fast forward time warp to acquiring the detailed knowledge that would be needed to reach my ultimate goal. Thanks to a loose shoulder capsule and a torn labrum; by the age of 17 I could talk shop with just about any orthopedist or rehab specialist concerning pitching specific strength training, mechanics and the inner workings of a human shoulder. The old saying goes, "Every silver lining has a touch of gray." The bigger picture, in my case, was that my gray lining had "a touch of silver."

At the end of my diagnosis the doctor informed me that my condition wouldn't get worse, but without surgery it wouldn't get any better either. His advice was to take a few weeks off, begin an in-depth rehab program and if I could tolerate the pain keep pitching. So that's what I did.

As instructed, I took a few days off to let everything in my shoulder calm down a bit, and then began a five-day-a-week rehab and strength program at the Piedmont Medical Center rehab facility under the surveillance of ex-pitcher turned rehab specialist Scott Hefner and his staff.

As I have already eluded, I had been seeking to quench my thirst for knowledge of all things baseball for years. One very important area that I had a particular interest and a great need for was in cultivating a pitching/baseball specific conditioning program. Not that 17 is considered "physically mature" by most standards, but even by typical standards I was a bit underdeveloped. In fact, most conversations that I would have concerning my future baseball possibilities generally centered around my need to "fill out" and physically mature. Despite these recommendations, during my quest, which was now in its third year, I had yet to come across a conditioning program to satisfy my glaring deficiency.

Within 10 days of receiving my prescription for a heavy dose of rest and rehab I had a workout routine and bounty of knowledge that not only assisted me in overcoming my injury, but was integral in transforming my scrawny, underdeveloped body into one that scouts could realistically see wearing a professional uniform. In fact, many things I learned during that stint I continued to use throughout my career as part of my training, stretching and conditioning regimen.

It certainly took many years to put all this into a proper place on the scale of significance. Of the many lessons life has taught me, I probably gained the most perspective from this initially terrifying experience. During its outset, this event had me throwing in the metaphorical towel on my adolescent fantasies. In the years to come, however, I was able to acquire some perception and realize that the injury had an enormous impact in ultimately molding me in a mental, physical and emotional way into the player I desperately wanted to become. Life's lessons come down a multitude of avenues; don't always assume you know exactly where every road is going just because you asked directions.

The balance of my junior season didn't go according to script, but it did turn out much better than my once-panic-filled mind would have ever anticipated. I followed doctor's orders and took a four-week siesta from playing and focused exclusively on my new strength and conditioning regimen. By the end of my hiatus I wasn't pain free, but I did feel a level of solid strength. Seeking assurance from my doctor I asked if it was OK to pitch, even with the pain while also seeking certainty that my injury would not get any worse from throwing. I was assured it wouldn't and was free to resume my pursuit at Major League stardom.

By the time I returned to the team the season was winding down. There were just a few games left for me to knock off the dust before the state playoffs began. As soon as I was cleared to play, my coach gave me the ball and threw me out there against one of our in-town rivals. As it turned out my first game back was a two-hit shutout with 12 strikeouts. There is no way I can know for sure, but I imagine the sigh of relief that exited my body after that game probably created a small atmospheric disturbance! At least for now, the dream seemed to be intact.

A few days later my team began its march toward a state championship as the high school playoff season began. Over the next few weeks, although still pitching with a good deal of pain, I had several more strong outings, and after a few close wins we suddenly found ourselves vying for a state title against one of our biggest rivals, Stratford Academy. Stratford had a very strong club which fielded three players who would be chosen in the following year's June draft. One of them was a third baseman by the name of Russ Branyan, who I would eventually play with as a member of the Cleveland Indians, and who has enjoyed a very successful Major League career.

During the weeks leading up to the state finals my outings were strong, but the nagging of that torn labrum seemed to be going from bad to worse. Once again my adolescent angst began to get the better of me and I started to panic.

"What if the doctor was wrong?"

"What if my shoulder IS getting worse?"

My obsession prompted another doctor visit seeking an updated diagnosis and some professional hand-holding. Almost annoyed, my doctor assured me there had been no further damage, but with increased use there would be increased inflammation and irritation. Again, I was encouraged to keep going out there as long as I could tolerate the pain.

This appointment and diagnosis came just a few days prior to our state championship "show down" with our cross-town foes. The night before the championship game, which would have been the first in school history, my coach timidly asked me if I felt "good enough to go tomorrow."

The answer I gave, without even realizing, unveiled yet another important characteristic of the player I was slowly morphing into. I think my response had something to do with either a bullet or a compound fracture not being able to keep me off that mound tomorrow.

On the surface such an attitude might seem heroic or even valiant, but this "fight 'til your dying breath" mentality ultimately cost me my career.

I can recall many years later warming up in the bullpen to face Major League hitters and not having the arm strength to even get the ball to my catcher on the first few throws. Yet stubborn and hard headed to the end, I would refuse to call back to the dugout and tell the manager I couldn't go. Eventually my shoulder sustained so much damage that not even the legendary orthopedic surgeon James Andrews and his magic hands could put humpty dumpty back together again. Ultimately, there is a fine line between "heroic" and "stupid." Sometimes it's better to just live to fight another day.

At 17, however, I didn't understand that the human body actually has limits; so even with a bullet wound and/or compound fracture I WOULD pitch this game. The next day arrived with tremendous excitement. This was by far the biggest game I had seen in my budding career and in my small-minded world it was a huge deal. Even though we had a number of outstanding players on the team, I felt that my teammates largely saw me as the one who had gotten us there and I wasn't about to let them down. As game time rolled around I began my warm up routine praying to God that my shoulder would hold together and get me just twenty-one more outs.

One of the most important things for a starting pitcher is the way he (or she) prepares for their next start. The preparation schedule between starts is significant, but the last 20 minutes before the first pitch is thrown is often vital in determining how a pitcher will ultimately perform. Veteran pitchers can usually slough off a poor warm-up session by leaning on the knowledge acquired from years and years of experience. Young pitchers, on the other hand, can have their psyches severely damaged during a poor warm-up session, and taking the field with bruised confidence can often lead to a short game-time experience.

As I stepped to the bullpen mound just minutes before the first big game of my life, I wouldn't admit to anyone (most notably myself) that I felt like ... crap. As far as I was concerned, I didn't see any bullet wounds; I didn't see any compound fractures ... and there was only one person who was going to be pitching this game and that person was me. Young, dumb and full of ..... ! What's that cliché? Well whatever it is, that's what I was.

As I started hurling pitches at my catcher, using terms like "bad," "poor," or even "what the @#$%!" would have been complimentary compared to reality. I probably threw more wild pitches during that warm-up session than ones my catcher actually caught. I was doing my best to try and blame nerves for most of it, but the truth was my shoulder just hurt like HELL. It was way too late to turn back now, though. We were five minutes away from the first pitch of the Georgia High School Association State Championship game and I had let my mouth write a pretty big check that now my ass had to cash.

For all intents and purposes I guess I was loose. As I walked out of the bullpen, my coach asked me one more time if I was sure. Hiding the terrified/pissed off look on my face I replied, "Don't worry, I got it."

To this day I don't know who or what "divine" entity infiltrated my body from the time I left the bullpen to the time I stepped on the mound to deliver the first pitch of that state championship game, but whoever or whatever "it" was threw a helluva game that day. I managed to pitch my high school to its first state championship while racking up a dozen punch outs and yielding only two hits. I think I even got Branyan a couple of times that day, although it's very doubtful he would remember it that way.

The victory pose shortly after winning the 1992 State Championship

If anyone has ever heard me give an interview, especially around MLB playoff time, I will often use the expression "Big-Game player." Its one key dynamic that I feel must exist on any team if its players expect to win a championship. This type of player is not necessarily the best guy on the field, but when a big game or series roles around and the "hardware" is at stake, this is the guy you want on the mound or at the plate.

Guys like Mark Lemke, Derek Jeter, John Smoltz, Jim Leritz, and Mariano Rivera immediately come to mind when I think about who a few of the Big-Game players were in my era. I also consider myself to some extent to have been a "Big-Game" player. I know in a number of areas I was not at the level of a Smoltz or a Jeter, but I like to think that 22 scoreless playoff innings and a September ERA around 1.00 has got to put me in the mix somewhere.

As I flash back some 20 years it may seem like a far stretch to compare a high school championship and its "big game" significance to the stage of a World Series or LCS. In my opinion, however, becoming a Big-Game player (and remaining one!) is not always about talent but more about the mentality which must be created and must be cultivated. That specific game and all of my personal dynamics surrounding it, in my opinion, was the initial catalyst from which my "Big-Game" mentality eventually evolved. For many of my teammates and friends this would be the last time they would ever put on a uniform. It would be the last time they would ever have the chance to be a winner. As I saw it their memories were in my hands. Even then I understood what a serious responsibility that was.

To the best of my understanding a birth took place during the days leading up to that game, a birth that years later would ultimately mature into a mentality where I actually relished being the "last line of defense" on some of the biggest stages in professional sports. At that age I would have traded eternity for a life as a Major League ball player. My place in heaven would exist in the old Astrodome for game three of the NLDS; bottom of the 10th in a 3-3 tie, bases loaded with no outs and a hot-hitting Carl Everett at the plate. The mental march to succeed in that situation began with a busted shoulder; a high school state championship and 15 friends whom I just couldn't let down. Whoever we finally become and where ever we eventually end up in life, it all has to start somewhere. Now as I spend time writing this book, I can't help but wonder what unforeseen realizations this experience may expose a decade from now.

I was on cloud nine for the next few days. For about 72 hours all was right in my little corner of the world. I'm sure I took it all in, enjoyed being the "big man" around town, but then, like an open-handed slap during a deep sleep, reality jolted me back into consciousness. I still had a surgery I was going to have to deal with. My shoulder had been running on fumes for the last several weeks, and it wasn't just going to fix itself.

Now although the severity of my injury had been downplayed to a large degree by my orthopedist, no surgery can ever be taken lightly. The simple fact that whatever ails you can only be mended with a scalpel, stitches and anesthesia is always cause for some degree of concern, and despite the efforts of everyone around me to temper that concern I was still an emotional wreck.

The days leading up to the operation were filled with pre-surgery rehab and enough neurotic questions to frustrate a trivia champion. I was listening to what everyone was trying to convince me of, but there was no way to shake my fear of the horrible possibilities of the unknown. Hindsight always existing in a much clearer perspective, my neurosis proved to be just as overblown as everyone was trying to tell me. As advertised, the surgery took no more than an hour and I was home by lunch. I wasn't exactly looking for someone to arm wrestle when the anesthesia wore off, but with my new-found virtual Ph.D in physical therapy, I did find myself on the football field getting ready for the upcoming season in just over a month!

As my senior year began the mental, physical and emotional armor that I needed for the final push to the next level seemed to be intact. The year had been filled with many unforeseen and terrifying challenges, but as I've said, without that trial by fire I don't think the tangible and intangible factors needed to get to the next level would have evolved. Obviously there was still much to accomplish and overcome in a number of areas if I was going to eventually arrive at my destination, but for the time being the scars on my left shoulder carried enough knowledge, experience and perspective to give me the foot hold I needed to make that next leap.

In my opinion there is no better feeling than setting a goal, mapping out a game plan to accomplish that goal, sticking to that game plan, and then witnessing the successful fruition of achievement right in front of your eyes. It's a scene, man! I recommend you try it some time. To say the first few months of my final year as a prep student were exciting would be a gross understatement. In a broad assessment the only thing that was more exciting than those first few months were the final few.

By the beginning of this, my determinative year at success or failure, it was appearing that the road map I had put in place as a 14-year-old had contained all of the right twists and turns. Although things began in a somewhat subtle fashion, by the second month of school the jig was up. As of mid October that year I was getting nearly a letter a day from some of the most respected Division 1 college programs in the country. Letters from schools such as LSU, UGA, Pepperdine, ASU and South Carolina came as regularly as junk mail. Each letter was usually an invitation for what is known as an "official visit" and most times would be followed up with a personal phone call from that program's recruiting coach. Word had also spread to a number of professional scouts in the area. It wasn't long before many of my school nights weren't being spent studying for the math exam, but instead entertaining phone calls and sometimes-personal visits from an Orioles scout, the Auburn pitching coach, the UGA recruiting coach, a Red Sox scout, a Braves scout … all looking to me for the answers. What was I going to do this spring? How did my shoulder feel after surgery? Did I want to go to college? Did I want to enter the draft? Did I want to go to college in the South? Did I want to go to a big school? Did I want to go to a small school? By the end of many of these visits and phone calls I felt more like a terror suspect than a high school senior on the cusp of realizing his dreams.

As I've said, in my opinion one of the best feelings a person can realize is seeing the successful fruition of a planned course of action. There is another side to this scenario, however. It is the "Oh @#$% what the hell do I do now!" part of it all. The butterflies of opportunity along with the pride of accomplishment were growing within me every day. As I became more and more inundated with flattering offers and requests, a new emotion began to consume me: the emotion of fear. What do I do now? What if I pick the wrong school? What if I go to an LSU or a UGA only to find out I'm not good enough? What if I get drafted? Should I skip college? What if I don't make it? What if? What if? What if? Dear God!!!

Some people will say I'm crazy, but I think it's an undeniable fact that there are just as many people who fail to reach their goals from a fear of success as from a fear of failure. They subconsciously sabotage themselves because the "what if's" of success almost seem worse than the "what if's" of failure. There is anxiety on both ends of the spectrum. The truth is, however, fear is nothing more than an emotion created by our hypothetical thoughts pertaining to the possible outcome of a specific situation. This "fear" is simply the byproduct of the doubts we manifest concerning our own ability to succeed. In short, learn to control and manipulate your thoughts and you will control your ability to succeed.

That explanation may seem a bit hokey, but as a Major League closer with failure potentially lying at the end of every delivery, learning to overcome and manipulate thoughts of doubt and worry is a must. Year after year I would get the same mundane questions from some boob reporter before every big game or series. They would always want to know: "Are you nervous about tonight's game? Are you worried? Do you feel there is a lot of pressure on you?"

Time and time again; I would answer the same way, "The only worry or pressure that exists is the worry and pressure which YOU create!"

I referenced my "heaven" a few paragraphs earlier. At one point in time that place actually existed. It was game three of the NLDS in 1999. The Atlanta Braves were playing the Houston Astros in the Astrodome with the best of five series tied at one game apiece. I was in the bullpen pacing back and forth listing to the 50,000-plus on hand get louder and louder with every pitch Russ Springer threw. Russ was a great pitcher, but was uncharacteristically off that day and by the time

I saw Bobby Cox heading out to the mound and gesture me in from the bullpen the bases were loaded, no one was out, the score was tied 3-3 in the bottom of the tenth, on the road, in front of 50,000 inside a DOME! Pressure? What the hell do you think?

With a typical mindset I would have been cross-eyed from fear, anxiety, angst, nervousness; you name it. I wouldn't have even been able to remember which hand to put my glove on much less keep a 3-3 score intact with the winning run 90 feet away and no one out! Reframing this situation was a must! I could have let the fear exist. I could have allowed myself to become paralyzed with doubt as I obsessed about all the possibilities, which could result in a negative outcome. I could have done that. I could have let fear dominate me, and in turn guarantee that at least one of those fears would manifest in some way and cost us the game. Or, I could reframe those fearful thoughts in a way that would give me the best chance to get the result my team needed.

In a situation like this though how could I possibly remove all the fear, doubt and anxiety knowing one minor mistake could cost us a playoff victory and potentially a playoff series? What could I possibly do?

I simply said, "@#$% it!"

To this day I can still remember plastering a determined look across my face and charging in from the visiting Astrodome bullpen thinking to myself on the way, "@#$% it. Those aren't MY runs out there. I don't care. I won't get the loss. No big deal. There's still tomorrow's game."

Of all the big games and big situations I pitched in that was undoubtedly the finest job of mind manipulation I ever did on myself. Obviously, the outcome of that game was tremendously important to me. I had the hopes of my teammates, coaching staff and every Atlanta Brave fan perched squarely on my shoulders. I absolutely couldn't dwell on that, though. I couldn't allow the fear and doubt that accompanies such an understanding to exist if I wanted to get us out of that inning.

What's that?

So how did it all turn out?

Well, Carl Everett hit a weak ground ball to Ryan Klesko that went 3-2. Tony Eusebio hit a sharp two hopper up the middle that Walt Weiss made an unbelievable diving play on, got to his feet and threw the runner out at home; and Ricky Gutierrez struck out swinging on a 2-2 slider down and in. We went on to win the game in 12 and took the series the next day. That game and series win propelled us on to the National League Championship where we beat the New York Mets in six. Moral to the story: Don't let fear exist; it could cost you a National League Championship.

As you might imagine it took many years of reading, studying and conscious effort to get to the point where I could mentally keep it together in a situation like that. Seven years earlier, however, fear, doubt and anxiety called the shots. Week after week I would consistently find myself being pistol whipped by my thoughts. As the weeks dragged into months I became extremely talented at the art of neurotic obsession. By January the baseball season was just around the corner and I was being reminded by nearly everyone I came in contact with that my time to procrastinate was quickly running out. Conversations no longer began, "Hey, John," but "Hey, so what are you going to do?" There seemed to be a black cloud of doubt constantly following me, and with each passing day it got lower and lower.

In December I began trying to be somewhat proactive in answering the questions surrounding my baseball fate. Despite all of the attention from the pro scouts, I had always seen myself as bridging the gap between high school and professional ball with a career at the collegiate level. So with that much of my decision having been loosely made; I began making official visits to my top choices.

As with most things in life, nothing can just be simple. College recruiting is certainly no different from the athlete's nor the school's perspective. With the hundreds of college programs in existence and the dozens that may be courting a particular individual, a player can only choose five schools to make an "official visit" to. Of course there is nothing stopping you from visiting as many schools as you would like, but only five are permitted to give you the full tour of their facilities, dorms, campus as well as make introductions to coaching staff and some of your new potential teammates. It's a very inefficient system, but those are the rules they've put in place to assist an indecisive 18-year-old with making his or her decision as tough as possible.

After a couple of months and what seemed like an infinite number of conversations with family and friends, I timidly cut the field to five and scheduled my visits. My initial frontrunner was the University of Georgia, but visits were also set up with the University of South Carolina,

Ched Smaha, Jake Fincher and myself stop for a quick pic shortly after a game against our cross town rivals, Startford Academy on the day I signed my scholorship to the University of Georgia.

Auburn, Liberty University and the University of New Orleans.

Despite strong recruiting efforts by these and several other schools, it took just a few minutes on the UGA campus to solidify my college decision. Growing up just 90 miles south of Athens, GA, I had been a life-long Bulldog fan. The feelings of joy, excitement, relief, and pride were the top few of the many emotions I felt as I finally forced my doubt aside and in mid-March of my senior season took a bold step toward my future.

One last picture before inking my deal to play at Georgia.

It was over. After four long years, a multitude of trials, tests and challenges; a giant leap had finally been taken putting me mentally and physically in much closer proximity to the plateau I was in search of. On March 20, 1993, after a game against the same team we defeated for the previous year's state championship I signed a scholarship with the University of Georgia. A host of family and friends gathered that day in the library of my high school to watch me make it official. Many who were there that day had been a part of my dream since the beginning and I think they felt almost as much satisfaction as I did witnessing the tangible result of their many years of encouragement and support. Looking back that was one of the proudest days of my life, not for receiving a piece of paper that said I could play baseball at the University of Georgia, but for knowing that all of the special people around me who had made such a concerted effort to encourage and support me over the years would not be let down. I felt as though it was as much their accomplishment as it was mine.

Mom, Dad and I just after signing my ride to UGA.

Finally, a very long sigh. The tumultuous waters of uncertainty had been navigated and it seemed I could settle back into just playing baseball and begin making my plans for the fall. But what did I say about life? Nothing can ever just be simple!

No sooner had the ink dried on my UGA scholarship than the professional baseball scouts began circling with renewed vigor. There had always been a few scouts at every game, but as if smelling a challenge, it seemed that a dozen or more would converge every time I was set to take the hill. The backstop would be two and sometimes three deep with radar guns and note pads clocking, charting and dissecting. It seemed that act two of "nervous wreck Johnny" was about to begin.

It was the end of March and the June draft was looming. I had gotten relatively familiar and even comfortable with the courtship process of the amateur suitors. It was almost friendly. The college coaches knew it was better to approach a new recruit as somewhat of a "father figure" as many kids and their parents viewed a coaching staff as playing that type of role in their kid's life over the next four years.

The pro guys on the other hand approach things a bit differently. To most professional scouts a player at any level is nothing more than a talented piece of meat, a racehorse to be ridden to the winner's circle. To say that professional baseball is an extremely competitive and lucrative game would be a gross understatement and an incorrect one at that. By the time a "game" gets to the professional level it's no longer a "game;" it's a business. Even at the age of 18 these kids, these players, these "people," are often times stripped of most of their human qualities in the eyes of their beholders.

To most pro scouts, area cross-checkers, national cross-checkers, scouting directors and the like, these wide-eyed kids living on nothing more than hopes and dreams are merely future stats in a score box. They represent potential wins at the Big League level, maybe a 40-homerun season with a .320 batting average and 130 RBIs. Who knows, maybe this kid will win 20 one day, or that one will save 40. At the end of the day it's all about one thing: produce a stat that wins a ballgame, which sells a ticket — that puts asses in the seats — to make the MONEY that makes that world go around. And if you can't do that, boy, then the pasture is THAT way; don't let the door hit you in the ass.

Unfortunately, the reality of professional sports can be harsh. It took me a few years to understand and come to terms with the "what have you done for me lately" mentality of it all. Unfortunately, during this whole process I hadn't gotten that memo and was nothing more than a naive, cock-eyed optimist who had no idea how to play this game or even realize that there was one being played.

It wasn't until a few years later after my professional career was well under way that I saw behind the curtain and began to fully understand the dance that takes place between player and organization. The most complicated of these dances is definitely the one involving the amateurs prior to the June draft. Most of these unsophisticated kids think all they have to do is stand in the corner of the gymnasium wearing a nice dress, look pretty and surely one of these Major League organizations will ask for a dance. It's hardly that simple.

Scouting, evaluating and drafting amateur players has evolved over the years into a fine science. With a six- and sometimes a seven-figure signing bonus at stake, not to mention what a key draft pick can do long term for an organization, no stone is left unturned when a club is putting its draft board together. Many people assume that scouting a player involves nothing more than evaluating an individual's talent. Can this boy hit? Can he throw? What kind of range does he have? Although that is a key first step, before a franchise will begin to seriously think about spending a draft pick on a player, especially a top 10 pick, they want to know EVERYTHING about that player.

Looking back and recalling the interrogation process I endured from dozens of scouts, scouting directors and cross checkers I often wonder if being drafted to play professional baseball shouldn't have also come with some level of national-security clearance. On an almost daily basis I was being grilled with questions like, "How willing and eager was I to sign a professional contract?"

"What were my thoughts about playing at UGA?"

"How important was it to get a college education?"

"How important was it for my family to see me get a college education?"

"What was my family life like?"

"How close was I to my parents?"

"How much influence did they have on any decision I made?"

"Did I have a girlfriend?"

"How serious was that relationship?"

"How would leaving home at this age for a prolonged period of time affect me?"

"How much influence did my high school coach have in this process?"

"How high would I have to be drafted in order to sign?"

"What kind of signing bonus would I consider?"

Question after question. Good God man, I'm 18 years old, not Nostradamus!

It seemed as if there was going to an infinite amount of prodding and probing that was going to go much deeper than simply evaluating my "talent." In addition to the almost-daily game of 20 questions I can also distinctly remember on several occasions having to meet an area scout for him to administer a "psychiatric evaluation." Even before you say it, I know what you're thinking, "Wow, someone really screwed up on that one"!

In all seriousness, though, it's quite unnerving for an 18-year-old kid who just wants to play baseball to meet an area scout for the Toronto Blue Jays at a local hotel who, upon arrival, presents a 300-question multiple choice questionnaire and says, "You've got one hour," and then stares at you while you complete it.

This "game" went on for weeks and without the wisdom of the world in my possession I was no match for my competition. Like a cheap lawn chair I folded under the cross-examination. I was completely oblivious to the need to be wily and cunning during this courtship process. Instead, I sang like a canary.

"I don't think I'm ready to play professional baseball yet."

"I've always seen myself getting a college education first."

"I think I need time to mature before I start a career like this."

"I don't think I would be comfortable being away from my family, friends and girlfriend for such long periods of time."

YOU IDIOT! I would love for 36-year-old John to go back in time and punch 18-year-old John in his face! In the dog-eat-dog world of professional sports you have to sell yourself, man. I would rarely give anyone asking for advice the recommendation to "lie through your teeth" and in fact, I won't here. I'll just say: you need to "sell yourself".

In the cutthroat world of big business (which professional sports has become) you tell people what they want to hear that ultimately puts YOU in the best possible position. If the St. Louis Cardinals scout asks, "If we draft you will you sign?" You say, "Absolutely, I've always wanted to play for the St. Louis Cardinals."

If the Los Angeles Dodgers' scout asks, "Do you think you're ready to begin a career as a professional athlete?" You say, "Absolutely! I think I've really matured during the last year and I would be thrilled with the opportunity. I've always wanted to play for the Los Angeles Dodgers."

Sell yourself! Because God knows if you don't get them; they'll sure as hell get you. I found that out the hard way.

During the weeks leading up to the draft everyone in the circles of professional baseball had me slated somewhere in the top five rounds despite being only six months' removed from a shoulder surgery. That is before I opened my big naïve mouth and was obnoxiously "honest." That blatant honesty drastically affected what was known as my "signability." In the hearts and minds of the powers that be within professional organizations these men want to feel certain that if they spend a draft pick on you, particularly a high one, you're going to sign your name on that dotted line. I've actually known of scouts getting fired for being unable to sign a player who they recommended be taken in a top round. Looking back and being very familiar now with the inner workings of these huge "corporations," especially concerning the amateur draft, I can safely say that I did myself no favors with my pre-draft posturing. As it were things eventually turned out fine for me, but many are not nearly so lucky. For the enormous majority of guys, most of prosperity that professional baseball will ever give them comes during that brief window of opportunity surrounding the amateur draft. I can remember the culmination of my brief window like it happened last week.

It's my opinion that there are only a few times in a person's life which carry such a level of significance that no matter how old you live to be, or how senile you become during the years it takes to grow that old; you will always remember exactly where you were when you heard the news. You will always remember who told you, what they were wearing, how their voice sounded, and what the first thing was that went through your mind immediately afterwards. I can remember precisely where I was and how I learned about 9/11. If asked I could put my feet in the exact spot I was standing when Jeff Cox, my Triple-A manager, told me I was going to the Big Leagues. The same is true for when I learned of my father's passing.

June 3, 1993, was the first day I ever experienced such a moment.

In my mind's eye I can still recall the exact scene as it unfolded. I was at Windsor Academy just south of Macon, Georgia working out with the American Legion team I played with. Future Major League catcher Mark Johnson, who would be drafted in the first round the following year, and I had just finished a bullpen session when I saw my father drive up in his blue, four-door company car. It was common for my Dad to ride out after work to watch us practice, but even I wasn't so oblivious to not realize that on this day he may have a different motivation for making that 30-minute drive after work. This was a day, "THE DAY" that I, my family, close friends and about half a dozen members of my Post 3 American Legion baseball team had been waiting on for several months. It was the first day of the 1993 professional baseball amateur draft.

As my father got out of his car and began walking around the outfield fence I could see the look on his face. Instantly it became very obvious that this trip was not his typical, afternoon visit. It had a purpose. He knew he had caught my attention and motioned for me to meet him over at the chain linked fence.

"I spoke to Rob English with the Braves about an hour ago!" he shouted from a distance of about 50 yards.

Rob English was a scout for the Atlanta Braves and had been making quite an effort at getting to know my family and me over the previous months. Despite my questionable opinion of most pro scouts, the same does not hold true for Rob, however. I have known Rob for nearly 20 years now. Last I heard he was still scouting the southeast for the Boston Red Sox. Every couple of years I will run into Rob, usually at some random place or event. To this day he still treats me in an almost grandfather/grandson manner. We'll ask the usual "catching up" questions. "How's your mom doing?" "When was the last time you talked to 'so and so'?"

I'll inquire about his wife or when the last time was he went out and caught a fish. He even thought enough of me to attend my father's funeral a few years ago.

Fortunately for me, as scouts go, Rob is a different sort. As I've grown to understand over the years most scouts and front office personnel are nothing more than "yes men," used car salesmen of the industry trying to manipulate kids into rolling the extremely risky dice of playing professional sports. Most of them couldn't care less about what's best for the kid or his family and their particular situation. All many of them see is what could possibly be in it for them — a possible stepping-stone to a better, more lucrative title within the organization should a kid they draft turn out to be the next Derek Jeter.

Rob, although understanding the rules of engagement, didn't see us kids as some place to hang his hat on the way up the organizational ladder to a potential scouting director's position. He fully understands that the kids he meets and talks with are actually people with real lives and very concerned mothers and fathers — and that these kids have futures. Futures that are unpredictable and worrisome at best. Now knowing what the alternatives could have been, I can say with certainty that this experience which many dream of and would ultimately change my life forever was a much better one thanks to Rob English.

Hearing my father's initial words as he continued toward me that day on the field, I knew could only mean one thing. Instantly, my thoughts began to race, for in that brief prelude a thousand questions immediately took shape. "Was my father getting ready to tell me that the Atlanta Braves, the team I had cheered for since the age of three, had just drafted me?"

"What if he was getting ready to tell me they had NOT drafted me and were NOT going to?"

"Did I get drafted in a high round?"

He's only 40 yards away!

"Was there already an offer on the table?"

"What about my scholarship to Georgia?"

"Who would help me make this decision?"

Thirty yards!

"If I decide to sign where would I go?"

"How much longer before I will have to leave?"

Twenty yards!

"What will I say to the Georgia head coach?"

"How long before I have to make a decision?"

Ten yards!

With thoughts swirling I came face to face with my Dad and one sentence that changed my life forever. While standing in foul ground down the left field line of the Windsor Academy baseball field, wearing old gym shorts and a black sleeveless T, shortly after completing a bullpen session with fellow future Big Leaguer Mark Johnson, my father, speaking through a chain-link fence, said: "Son, I just spoke with Rob English. The Braves drafted you in the 18th round today."

I remember every detail like an instant replay. I remember exactly how my extremely proud father's face looked as he delivered the news. I also remember wishing he hadn't spoken the last half of that sentence. I had been drafted by the Atlanta Braves! In the … 18th round? I suddenly felt like someone who was just told they "used to" be really attractive, or they're not "that" fat. Being drafted by the Atlanta Braves, a team that had been to the World Series the two previous seasons, a team that I had cheered for since I was three years old, through the Dale Murphy years, the Claudell Washington years, the Chris Chambliss and Bob Horner years, was the thrill of my short lifetime. Being drafted in the 18th round was downright insulting. Even though I had spent the last several weeks trying to convince myself and most everyone else that I wasn't ready to be a professional, subconsciously I still had this grand fantasy of finding myself in the enviable position of negotiating a top-round contract. I would secretly daydream about being THE guy that all the teams were fighting over and the victor presenting me with a first-round contract, which I would shrewdly negotiate into a record-signing bonus. It certainly is entertaining to reminisce about the flights of the adolescent imagination. And how far off they sometimes can be!

Instantly my father could see that I wasn't pleased. To this day I still regret my reaction. My father, like many fathers, lived somewhat vicariously through me, especially when it came to sports. On occasion I still run into old friends of his who comment on how often me and my sports were the topic of so many of his social conversations. I always joke at how annoying that must have been for them. Truth is, I wouldn't have changed that about my father for all the Cy Youngs in the world. He was one proud poppa, and this was perhaps the proudest moment of his 18 years of fatherhood. So what did I do to this special, once-in-a-lifetime moment for him, this moment that was almost as much his as it was mine? Like a typical selfish teenager I pissed all over it.

"EIGHTEENTH ROUND? SERIOUSLY? What happened to all of those top-five round predictions? What the hell? That sucks!"

It hurts me to say, but to this day I can't recall another time where I've seen a person deflate so rapidly. My father thought he was bringing me the greatest news I had ever heard. And, on one hand, it was. But I can still see the pride and excitement in his face disappear as I reacted like I had just been told my best friend died. What an asshole. And I don't think I ever apologized. It took me many years to finally realize that not every situation is always about "you" even when it seems like it certainly should be. I wish I had understood that then.

Well, after dousing my father's parade I walked to the outfield to pout for a while and mull over my new circumstance. As I sat and pondered my disappointment the feelings began growing stronger and stronger within me that maybe in fact I wasn't ready to make the jump to the professional level. After all, that's what I had been telling everyone for the last several weeks. Despite my subconscious fantasies, maybe all of these scouts in their infinite wisdom and experience were simply forcing me to accept that all of the "poor mouthing" I had been doing in regard to my own maturity and ability wasn't just lip service. As romantic as all of those fantasies were in my imagination, at least for now they would have to remain fantasies. Maybe I was just going to have to accept the fact that for my ultimate fantasy to exist there was still a lot of work left to be done.

As I continued having this conversation with myself, I slowly began putting a different spin on what had upset me so terribly just an hour earlier. Today I would call this exercise "reframing the situation" and as I alluded to earlier I have become very good at it over the years. This may have actually been my first effort at performing such a task that in years to come I would rely on almost daily. As an 18-year- newbie, however, I was simply trying to look on the bright side of things.

By the time I exited the field that day I had come to terms with my disappointment. I knew and stressed significantly at the anxiety and sleepless nights that would be created by a legitimate "College Ball vs. Pro Ball" scenario. In my mind being drafted in the 18th round didn't create a legitimate scenario. So after I absorbed the initial sting to my pride, the 18th round was no longer an insult; it was a decision maker. It looked like it was going to be the University of Georgia.

As the days went by I slowly began to accept the fact that I was not going to be the next pitching prodigy. It had been a lofty fantasy, but in my mind (and only my mind) it had been one that I was getting a bit romantically attached to. Now it was time to come back down to earth and rejoin reality, which in the overall scheme of things wasn't such a bad place. After all I did have a scholarship to the University of Georgia and though I hadn't been drafted in a place to my satisfaction I had been drafted nonetheless, and though I couldn't say I was on the fast track to fulfilling my ultimate dream at least I was still on track.

Although I wasn't able to grasp this concept until years later, in my opinion the ability to reframe goals is often vital to ultimately achieving them. We all want to put ourselves in a time warp when it comes to accomplishment. We want our dreams and everything that comes with them now! As we've all experienced, and if you haven't you will at some point, it usually doesn't work that way. I've generally found great benefit, however, in focusing on accomplishing much smaller, successive goals on the way to the ultimate one. By focusing on these smaller successes you can avoid being overwhelmed by the presumed magnitude of what you are trying to achieve, yet still monitor yourself that you are heading in the right direction. It's much easier to reframe the timing of your goal(s) than to actually reframe the goal itself, which usually results in compromising what you desire. At least that's what has worked best for me.

As the summer wore on I began eagerly planning for my September departure to Athens. The coaching staff and I were becoming fast friends and with each passing day it seemed that fate had "forced" me into what was promising to be a great situation. I hadn't even registered for classes yet and was being told that they were penciling me in as the number two starter for the following spring.

"This whole deal is turning out all right," I remember thinking to myself. I couldn't wait to get on campus — the college parties, the chicks; it's what every teenage boy fantasizes about while he's lying in his bed on a Friday night knowing there's got to be something much better out there he could be doing. And oh, yeah, baseball too!

With preparation for the beginning of college life in high gear I suddenly became aware that something I assumed had been pronounced dead and buried had resurfaced. That "something" was the lingering of a potential professional career. I thought the sideways compliment of being drafted in the 18th round along with my flippant rejection of Atlanta's initial offer was enough to put that issue to rest. What I soon began to discover, however, is evidently the men making the decisions in professional baseball organizations covet their 18th round picks a little more than one would expect.

In the short term following my rejection of Atlanta's initial offer all had been silent. They had taken "no" for an answer, or so I thought. Case closed. The horizon was calm for a week or two and then the aerial assault along with a steady ground attack began. The "aerial assault" came in the form of a barrage of phone calls from what seemed like everyone in the Atlanta Brave's front office. Calls from my scout, Rob English, as well as scouting directors, cross checkers and even the assistant GM himself, Chuck Lamar, came almost daily.

Shortly after the initial aerial deployment, the ground phase of their operation began. Most of my American Legion games, especially the ones I pitched, were attended by at least one member of the Brave's organization. Living just 90 miles south of Atlanta I was within easy striking distance for these short-term visits. With each visit came all of the usual "glad handing," and "atta boys" along with all of the other typical brown-nosing tactics one learns in Manipulation 101. And as I said earlier my level of experience and understanding was no match for these coercive mind games and strategies that were being used on me.

As if sensing I was still holding on to the disappointment of falling to the 18th round, I was inundated with a litany of reasons as to why I wasn't taken much earlier. My shoulder surgery, my signability, other needs the organization was trying to fill, all were just a few of the "excuses" I was given as to why my draft selection had fallen lower than expected. Looking back I now know what a load of #@% that was. If an organization wants you, they will go after you, and if they want you bad enough it will be at most any cost. At the time, however, all of these "logical reasons" made sense. "Oh, OK. Now I understand. That makes perfect sense," I naively told myself.

"Maybe I had made a big mistake. What if an injury prevents me from getting this opportunity again? I can go to school at any age. They really and truly 'wanted' to draft me much higher. This is one of the best organizations in baseball. The level of coaching I will get is much better than at the college level."

These were all the thoughts and rational that began going through my simple head in the weeks after the assault began. Of course, most of the ideas swirling through my mind had been put there by my "attackers."

Not exactly fair poker for a kid trying to make the biggest decision of his life.

They definitely got my attention, though. Beginning to sense that I was weakening, the big gun was brought in … money. With every few days that went by Atlanta seemed to increase its previous offer ever so ever slightly trying in attempts to hit that precise number it would take to bring me around. In most "hold-out" negotiations money is generally the dispute and adding more gold to the pot is usually the fix all.

In my case, however, it wasn't about the money. I know that's a typical cliché, but when you're negotiating 18th round money in 1993 we're not talking about "life changing" dollars by any degree. I was much more concerned about making the correct decision that would result in the best overall outcome for my life. I didn't want to end up 30 years old, uneducated, pumping gas for a living. What was the right "life decision," but just as important what was the right decision to give me the best chance of achieving my ultimate goal?

My family and I mulled over the consistent contract offers and listened to the constant hounding for what seemed like weeks. No matter how hard I tried, however, I just couldn't get comfortable with taking a leap like that. Whether it was the self-confidence I lacked, or just thought the college experience would serve me better in the long run; I just couldn't bring myself to pull the trigger.

As indecision plagued my family and me, the beginning of my college career was fast approaching. The time was coming where my ability to decide would expire and the calendar would make the decision for me. This fact became glaringly obvious when a registration letter from UGA arrived in the mail. I responded to the letter accordingly and scheduled my orientation for the week of August 15th with classes to begin September 3rd. The window of opportunity to give back my scholarship and accept my first pro contract was growing narrower by the day. Flip a coin! Do something! Make a decision already. The indecisiveness was scrambling my brain!

Sensing I was like a boxer on the ropes Atlanta stopped messing around and went for the jugular. With a class schedule in hand and school set to begin in less than two weeks, the Braves made an offer they knew I couldn't refuse, which would put them in position to play me like a piano. Late August, shortly after completing UGA orientation, they gave me the opportunity to do something that would be the highlight of nearly any teenage boy's life. I was invited to work out in the old Fulton County Stadium, pre-game, with the National League Champion Atlanta Braves!

"John, we want you to come up to the stadium and throw in the bullpen with Leo (Mazzone) before tomorrow night's game against the Giants," Chuck Lamar told me in yet another one of his weekly coaxing conversations. This time they weren't playing around. I guess they figured if the money wouldn't talk maybe the red carpet would, and for a kid who grew up just 90 miles from that stadium and had sat in the nosebleed section more times than he could remember, what a red carpet it was. No sooner than Chuck's words fell on my ears did I accept. At this point the battle between John Rocker and the Atlanta Braves was all but over. The Braves flipped their hole card, and it turned up the ace of spades.

As I sit here and write this book, I have lived something short of 14,000 days, and taking into consideration all that I've seen and everything I've done during those days I still regard that day as being one of the most special. Wow, what a day for an ambitious 18-year-old athlete! Sheepishly walking into the clubhouse during what would soon become my normal batting practice time I spotted a locker they had set up for me in the corner right next to Steve Bedrosian.

As I enter the clubhouse I began to look around and survey my surroundings.

"Oh my god, there's Dave Justice and Steve Avery"!

"Dude, it's Tom Glavine and there's Sid Bream"!

"Whoa, it's Deion Sanders"!

Little did I know as I struggled mightily to make the precise choice regarding my future that many in this clubhouse would be my teammates, friends and opponents within a few short years. In fact I'm sure a few of the guys I just mentioned will read this and give me a healthy load of crap next time I see them.

"Hey, I was an 18-year-old kid who had been a diehard Braves fan since I was three; SO GET OFF MY ASS! Especially you, Ave! Screw you!"

After I rolled my tongue back up, Leo, who I'm sure was wise to the scheme,

*Leo telling me to hold the God @#$%, *%&#ing curveball this way.*

came over to my locker as I was getting dressed to introduce himself. I can't remember exactly what his first words to me were, but knowing Leo as well as I do now, I'm sure there were a few expletives in there. After a short exchange I followed Leo down the tunnel and out into the vastness of old "Fulco." I remember being too terrified and overwhelmed to say much; I just starred, wide-eyed, trying to take it all in. Who knew if I would ever be on this or any other Big League diamond ever again?

Rob English and my father were waiting for Leo and me as we made our way down to the bullpen. The Braves weren't taking any chances with this one. The scout was there, the father was there, the National League Champion Atlanta Braves were just starting to take batting practice. As far as the Braves were concerned, today would be my signing day.

The workout was uneventful for the most part as workouts go. My surroundings were mesmerizing, but my performance itself was typical. After my session I thanked Leo and vacated the mound for Marvin Freeman to get his work in. As I headed back toward the dugout Rob and my father were walking with me. "Chuck Lamar and John Schuerholz want to see you guys in Chuck's office when you're done showering, John," Rob informed us.

"I'll come to the clubhouse and get you in about 20 minutes."

As soon as these

My first day on a big league field under the toolage of soon to be pitching coach Leo Mazzone. I would sign my first professional contract about two hours from then.

words were processed a swarm of butterflies began racing through my body. I felt like I was being called to the principal's office. To some extent I had been expecting a scenario to arise where they would take advantage of their home field advantage in an effort to get me to sign that risky first professional autograph.

"How would it go down?" I asked myself a couple of times earlier in the day. Would there be Gestapo-like tactics involved, or would it simply be a lopsided game of mind manipulation? As the day progressed and the red carpet got longer and longer, I slowly realized that whatever "signing" game or tactic they decide to use, I was probably going to lose. They had me right where they wanted me.

Walking back in that Brave's clubhouse my thoughts were spinning like a top as I tried to process all that had gone on in the previous hour and a half, and trying to predict what would happen during the next 90 minutes. As I've already said a number of times it is tough to calculate what moments in our lives will ultimately hold a personal significance and nearly impossible to anticipate exactly to what level. Although fully understanding and appreciating what a special and significant day this was, there was no way for me to know that when I got out of my shower I would face the most important 90 minutes of my life.

As promised Rob walked in looking for me exactly 20 minutes from the time I left him. He actually walked over and interrupted a conversation I was having with John Smoltz on how I thought he should hold his slider. A few years later when John and I became teammates he told me he had been using the grip I suggested during that conversation, and it had been working great for him ever since ... OK! I totally just made all that up ... that never really happened! Truth is I was much too nervous/worried to even look at, much less speak, to anyone.

The understanding that an extremely important decision affecting my entire future would have to be made in a matter of minutes was becoming more apparent every second.

I got Rob's attention and he made his way over to my temporary corner locker.

"You about ready?" he asked. "They're upstairs waiting on you."

Being completely out of my comfort zone I felt as if Rob was the jailer sent here to escort me to the gallows.

"Yea, sure," I responded as I finished buttoning up my shirt.

Rob stood there making idle chit chat with me for the next few minutes, I'm assuming to calm my nerves. Through this whole process, as I've said, Rob had a very firm grasp on just what a huge deal this was for my family and me. He had become somewhat of a father figure to not only me, but also to my mother and father as this was a huge decision affecting their lives as well. It was to the point, however, where he had done about all he could do. He had held my (our) hand(s) and done his best to empathize with all the issues we as a family were struggling to become comfortable with.

His job on this day, however, would be to lead me into the lion's den and wish me luck. The Braves front office had politely taken no for an answer up 'til now as we all danced around the "strawberry patch." I was quite sure the word "no" would be received with a very different attitude today.

"I'm ready, Rob. You lead the way," I said with a fake confident air.

With that we walked out on my first Big League clubhouse experience and into the tunnel underneath the stadium. My parents, along with my uncle, were waiting on me, as we had all been invited up for this little "conference." I think the boys in the front office wanted all of the dissenters present so everyone's concerns could simultaneously be manipulated and massaged until at the end the only right answers would be theirs.

We slowly but deliberately made our way through the tunnel and up the elevators to the office of assistant GM Chuck Lamar. As we walked into Chuck's office I noticed my unsigned contract sitting front and center on his desk. Now I'm not sure if Chuck is a betting man, but I think he would have placed pretty high odds on getting me to touch that contract with a pen in my hand sometime before the evening was over. The second thing I noticed when I walked in was John Schuerholz sitting to his right, and the third thing I noticed was that this was a suit and tie day. All of the other times I had met with Chuck (and I had never met with John) he was dressed more "come as you are." It had usually been after a high school or American Legion ballgame in golf shorts and a collared shirt or at my family's house in jeans and a button down. Tonight was suit night and we weren't here to discuss baseball; we were here to discuss business.

To the best of my recollection, if this meeting was a heavyweight fight it would have only gone about five rounds. After the initial pleasantries were over I can distinctly remember Chuck wasting no time. His first words after the brief glad-handing had subsided were: "Let's get a deal done. What are ya'll's concerns?"

Like the captain of a Harvard debate team every question or concern I or my parents raised was surgically dissected and disemboweled of all merit or anxiety we had ascribed to it. He enchanted us into feeling completely educated and at ease. By the end of round four my family and I were running out of excuses, fears, and worries to further prolong the inevitable beginning of my professional career. Looking back I fully understand what created all of the worry and apprehension, but I still find it a bit humorous at how hard I fought AGAINST someone trying to give me a relatively large sum of money and a contract to play professional baseball.

If you gave me a contract and a pair of spikes today, I would be on the 6 A.M. flight to wherever it was you told me I could play. To have one more day: what would I do to have just one more day? One more day to have the smell of the ballpark in my nose. One more day to feel my spikes dig into the freshly cut outfield grass. One more day to have the bright sun on my face and the mound under my feet. One more day to feel one last fastball snap from my fingertips and explode in a cloud of dust into the catcher's mitt. What I would I give for just one more day?

As it turned out, August 23, 1993, became the first day of which I would give almost anything for just one more.

I lost and won, I guess you could say, by TKO in the fifth round that night in Chuck Lamar's office shortly before the Braves took the field against the San Francisco Giants. Now all that was left to do was bridge that small distance from the office I was sitting in to the field down below. In actuality it was but just a few short feet, but in reality it was still many, many moons away.

CHAPTER FOUR

Just Another Salmon

Be careful what you wish for because you might actually get it. We've all heard that old statement, which was one of the first thoughts that went through my head when my eyes opened the morning after signing my first professional contract. What in the hell do I do now? It seems I had grabbed the proverbial "tiger by the tail," and now I had to figure out how to hop on and ride.

Although part of me was absolutely terrified at the vast number of unknown aspects regarding the journey I was about to embark on, the other half of me had a goofy grin stuck on my face that a punch to the gut couldn't get rid of. As I stated earlier, in my opinion, there's no better feeling I can think of than to establish a goal; map out a plan for achievement; stick to that plan and then eventually hold the fruits of your labor in the palm of your hand. Though my situation didn't necessarily play out as it had in my daydreams I could now say that one goal that was born five years earlier to an underdeveloped punk kid was in the books. All of the doubts, fears, anxiety, and frustration had been conquered, persevered through and overcome, answering my own relentless self-criticism, questioning if I was good enough to someday be a professional. Well, "someday" had arrived.

It didn't take long, however, for the magnitude of my reality to set in and begin to wipe that silly smile of success off my face. It was as if my mind had crawled inside a time warp and turned back the clock to my freshmen year. Gradually the same thoughts of inadequacy and doubt began to play pepper with my confidence just as they had done years earlier while observing all those "cool ass" seniors who seemed so impressive. Now, however, it wasn't some modestly talented private school "athlete" I was running my self-comparisons against. It was the best in the world that became my basis for critique. Slowly, I began to realize that not only was an obvious physical transformation going to have to take place if I was ever going to return to Fulton County Stadium, but a mental conversion would be necessary once again as well.

Within a few days of making my status as a professional athlete official, Rob English called to inform me that the actual "on field" beginning to my career would start a lot sooner than he or I expected. I was instructed to report to the organization's training facility in West Palm Beach, Florida, on September 15 which was just over two weeks away for the start of the Fall Instructional League.

His words sent an initial wave of anxiety through me. I anticipated having the entire fall and winter to do some bulking up and fortification of my still somewhat flimsy body. I had been combating my recently instigated angst concerning my new career path by convincing myself that I would work harder than ever during the next several months and by the time Spring Training arrived I'd be fortified and ready to hit the ground running with all barrels loaded to begin my career on as solid a foundation as I could create.

No such luck, however. There would be no time for "fortification." There would be no time for mental preparation. In just two short weeks I would be thrown into the rapidly flowing river of professional baseball along with thousands of other fledgling salmon to begin fighting that down stream current towards the golden pond of Major League Baseball. The process had begun and I was terrified. The train had already left the station and there was nothing stopping it. I had but two options; become one of the three percent of drafted players who actually end up putting on a Big League uniform or fail and watch the fulfillment of a childhood passion vanish forever. There was no in between and the rubber was going to meet the road very soon.

By September 14, 1993, all my "goodbyes" had been said, all preparations had been made, the car was packed and aimed south from Macon, Georgia, down I-75 toward Palm Beach. In just 24 short hours my career and my

My 19th birthday during my first instructional league with Atlanta at the team hotel in Palm Beach.

first definitive step towards what once seemed like the most unattainable of goals would commence. The following day would begin the process of a bunch of hot headed kids with way too much lead in their pencils, and no idea what to do with it, sizing one another up in an attempt to establish a sort of pecking order that we all felt may ultimately dictate who would eventually receive the grand prize we all pursued. Dozens of kids from all over the world would be required to brag about themselves and lie about themselves in an effort to convince those within earshot that they in fact would be the one to beat the odds and win a Cy Young, Gold Glove or batting title one day. This would be the day that I would begin playing with and against not just all-star caliber players, but the MVP's of those all-star teams and realize that for the most part only a small fraction separated our talent levels. Tomorrow would also be the day that, without even realizing, lifelong friendships would begin to form that in many ways became the most cherished possession I have from the 12 years I spent wearing a professional uniform. I couldn't wait until tomorrow!

I finally arrived at the team hotel in West Palm Beach, late in the afternoon on the 14th to find an eighteen-year-old Kevin Millwood sitting on the bed in our room watching TV while applying ointment to his newly inked Marvin Martian tattoo.

"Hey man, I'm Kevin Millwood," he said as he walked across the room to shake my hand for the first time.

"I'm from Bessemer City, North Carolina. Where you from?"

"How ya doin'? John Rocker. I'm from Macon, Georgia," I answered as I returned his handshake.

The balance of my first of many evenings in a team hotel was spent meeting and exchanging initial greetings with wide eyed, hope-filled kids just like me who were all optimistic but equally doubtful as to what their futures held. It was somehow comforting to know that my boat which was getting ready to set sail was filled with hundreds of others just like me who were embarking on the same journey. Some tried to present an over the top air of confidence, but even in these initial encounters I could see they were just as scared and nervous as I was. We all knew the statistics and the odds and understood that the overwhelming majority of us would not see a happy, successful end to this voyage. With the exception of death not being the feared result, we were like the soldiers before the invasion of Normandy. All of us were departing on the same trip, and we knew that very few of us would ever make it through to the other side. At times, however, cock-eyed optimism like that can be beautiful. Mediocrity never comes with risk. Anything that's truly great is worth risking it all to achieve and failure in the face of such risk is nothing to be ashamed or afraid of. After all, what can fear actually do for you anyway?

The next day my career as a professional athlete officially began. Little did I know at the time that I would eventually emerge as one of the fortunate few and successfully traverse the land-mine-laden battlefield of minor league baseball, and that this day would be the first of nearly 5,000 that I would spend as a professional baseball player. Obviously, not being privy to such knowledge, I was like a spotted fawn in the headlights as I walked into the clubhouse of the Atlanta Braves training facility for my first day of workouts. These players, the coaching staff, this organization would basically become my family over the next many years and would be responsible for my transformation from adolescence to manhood. I wouldn't necessarily describe this environment as the best place for a naive teenager to receive his final life lessons before becoming an adult, but such is reality in a world where maturity must come quickly.

As I took my first steps into the clubhouse that day I immediately looked for some of the familiar faces I had met at the hotel the night before. Within a few seconds I was called over to a corner by two of my fellow pitching brethren, Wes Culp and Damian Moss, who invite me to set up shop in a locker near theirs.

A fact I would soon discover is the significant importance of getting a good locker spot, particularly in minor league spring training and instructional league. Let's face it, in professional baseball a substantially greater amount of time is spent lounging in the clubhouse rather than actually playing or working out. I quickly realized that in a setting where approximately 60 to more than 200 ball players are stuffed into a single clubhouse, having a locker near your buddies is crucial to passing those hours in an entertaining fashion.

Excited to see I was making friends, I began to unpack my things and set up my first locker in preparation for my two-month trial in the instructional league. After my knew home was arranged there was still a full hour before my first official workout would begin; so with the extra time I decided to mingle a bit and meet a few of my new teammates. As I made my way around the clubhouse I became acquainted for the first time with what would turn out to be some of the closest friends I have even to this day. I think there is always a special bond formed amongst the people of any group who are lumped into a particular situation where success will be difficult, struggles will be similar and at some point in time each person will have to depend on another for their own personal as well as the overall group's achievement. I would not realize this dynamic until many years later but to some degree or another this bond still exists with everyone I had the pleasure of playing with during my career. Without having the ability to understand what was taking place at the time those connections began as I mingled my way through the clubhouse that first day, shaking hands and introducing myself to all those kids who were wearing the same shoes I was.

I met Brad Clontz for the first time, and Glenn Williams. I saw a chiseled sixteen-year-old Andruw Jones, shirt off, strutting through the clubhouse wearing that signature goofy grin of his. My initial reaction was "who the @#%& is this guy?" I would soon find out: "That's Andruw Jones. He'll be hitting home runs in the World Series in about two years." The rest of us did our best to exude confidence with the hopes of backing it up; Andruw ate, slept and drank confidence and backing it up was just a formality.

I also met Travis Cain and John LeRoy (RIP), Pascual Matos, Del Mathews, and Eric Olshewski. During that one brief hour I met guys who became brothers and would assist me in my transition to maturity and would depend on me for their own transition. I only stay in touch with a few of the guys I met in my initial hours in professional baseball, but the trials we endured both on and off the field during the coming years while chasing our elusive dream will forever link us at our core. (If any of the guys I'm talking about, and you know who you are, are reading this book, I miss you guys. Not many days go by where I don't think about the times we had together. They were the best.)

Well, as things have a way of doing, even during the most difficult of transitions, I finally settled into a routine and became comfortable with my surroundings and new place in life. As with the pursuit of any goal, especially ones of the monumental variety, plateaus are reached where you have the ability to look back at all that has been accomplished while standing in front of another mountain that must be overcome to reach the next plateau. My initial introduction into professional baseball provided a somewhat elevated plateau from which to look back down the mountain and see just how far I had come since my early teenage years. It also provided a place from which to view the long difficult climb that was ahead of me to reach my final destination.

It was initially overwhelming to say the least as I stood at the lowliest place in professional baseball as a newborn 18-year-old rookie, and became aware of the vast divide between my current talent level and that of seasoned Big League veterans. I confronted on a daily basis all of the inadequacies that existed and had to be improved upon if I would ever visit Fulton County Stadium again wearing that red, white and blue uniform of the Atlanta Braves. For the first several weeks of my new career I often became disheartened as I pondered all of the areas that needed focus and vast improvement until one day I stumbled upon what should have been an obvious realization. Despite the seemingly insurmountable reality of it all, in actuality there was but one simply thing that must be done if I desired to see the attainment of my ultimate goal. I had to face the fact that there was A LOT of work to be done, and simply get started.

Every marathon begins with one step; every life has a first day; every book starts with a single word. No matter what goal or achievement is sought it all has to start somewhere. Everything in life no matter how monumental it may seem must have a beginning. I had to forget the knowledge that the minuscule amount of minor league ball players who actually get a shot in the Majors will spend 300 plus days a year for four to six years doing something "baseball" before their dream ever becomes a reality. There would be no holidays; there would be no vacations; it would be a requirement every day of my life.

The trip through minor league baseball on the way to the pinnacle of the sport is not a marathon; it's a triathlon and an Iron Man at that. It's every day; day in and day out in some of the most thankless almost degrading scenarios you can think of. It's spending twelve hours on a bus traveling from one small town to another with a broken air conditioner. It's eating meal after meal at truck stops and Waffle Houses on twenty dollars a day. It's showing up at the ballpark for a Sunday day game in Charleston, South Carolina, only to discover the clubhouse flooded the night before because of a heavy rain and most of the clothes and equipment you need for the game that day are soaking wet. But such is reality on any level where grand achievement is pursued. The difficulties will always be there. Hard, sometimes painstaking work will be an absolute requirement and the only strategy will be to confront the difficulties, confront the struggles, confront the required effort and simply insist on overcoming them.

I felt fortunate I made this realization very early in my career and also made the conscious decision to try and ignore all of the thoughts that were overwhelming me and just get started with the process of accomplishing. Without even realizing it at the time I reverted back to a tactic that had worked several years earlier when the thought of one day becoming a professional athlete had seemed overwhelming as well. I began to establish and focus on many smaller, more short-term goals that I felt would create a path which would ultimately lead me where I wanted to go. There was a goal for today; there was also one for tomorrow that in conjunction would hopefully create a path to success for a single week which in turn would give way to a prosperous month, and so on. I would have to learn to focus on success in very small increments on the shortest of terms because as I've said before the attainment of any goal is generally not the result of a single grand victory but instead a collection of many much smaller triumphs. Learning to strictly focus on being successful today and only today must become an absolute. Win today, period!

By the end of my initial baptism into professional baseball I had acquired an incredible amount of knowledge, most of it pertaining to the realization of my many flaws and deficiencies. As the winter approached the effort to fill all the voids I possessed began. A workout program was implemented by the Atlanta training staff that required three and sometimes four-hour workouts six days a week, and in an effort to fill the deficit that existed with my still-underdeveloped physique, this program was followed to a T. I also understood that my mental focus, preparation and overall toughness were another area of notable concern. With renewed inspiration I began scouring the book stores for any literature that through its study would improve my mental edge.

What many people don't understand and rarely realize is that Major League athletes, while possessing razor sharp physical skills, are about as mentally tough as you get. While other sports such as golf and tennis require precise timing, skill and coordination, the atmosphere in which these sports exist is extremely controlled. Officials stand on the edge of the fairway or court and call for silence as the players' strain for concentration while competing. Anyone who has ever been to a professional baseball game, particularly one in places like Yankee Stadium, Fenway Park or Wrigley Field, knows that the environment is anything but controlled. Retaining mental focus with the surrounding circus atmosphere can be difficult in and of itself before one even gets to the task of trying to paint an 0-2 fastball down and away with the winning run on third; two outs in the bottom of the ninth with Derek Jeter at the plate looking to line one back up the middle off your face. Possessing the ability to keep your head together in such situations must begin many years before such scenarios arise and it takes a great deal of effort and experience to finally master.

With winter coming to an end and the reporting date for my first spring training drawing near I felt as though I had made great strides since my departure from the Fall Instructional League, and was eagerly anticipating the beginning of camp.

The initial days of spring training are always the best. You've been home all winter, usually freezing and working your butt off preparing and preparing and preparing for the beginning of spring, and ultimately the start of a new hope-filled season; so by the time that first faithful day arrives it means the close of a long boring chapter. It means the end of all those long mundane hours inside a gym pushing yourself through a four-hour leg and cardio workout. It means no more throwing in dreary indoor facilities off turf mounds because it's thirty-five degrees outside and raining. It's the end of chiropractors and massage therapists constantly poking, prodding and twisting a sore, achy body that's continuously wearing itself out in preparation for the upcoming 200-game season.

The first few days of spring training are truly magical. They're a time for the six-year-old in every player to be reborn and come out to play once again. They're a time for him to pick up his ball and glove and join his pals, who haven't been seen for months, in a freshly cut outfield for a simple game of catch. Early in spring the "adult" is there to work; he's there to get his arm in shape, he's there to find the release point on his breaking ball, and get his "baseball" legs under him again. The other half of that "adult" is still just a kid re-experiencing all of the excitement that once existed the first time he ever stepped onto a diamond. The surroundings have drastically changed since those early days, but the same aspects that created his love for the game remain. The sun is on his face as he steps across the chalk line for the first time since September. The sights, sounds, and smells of the ballpark are dominating his senses and make him fall in love with the game all over again. The beginning of spring training is like the rebirth of his soul.

Spring training is one of the greatest times of the year for all players. It's a fresh time; a time where all statistics both good and bad are cleaned from the slate of this knew season and replaced with high hopes and promise. It's a time to reunite with your idiot buddies to rekindle all of the stupid jokes, make up a few new ones, and just play some good ole' fashion "grab ass." Those first few days of spring training every year were perhaps my favorite time of the season, but as things generally do, the newness always wears off, the initial excitement subsides and a normal routine is fallen in to.

My first spring was no different. After the "new" had worn off I settled into my routine and quickly became very aware of one glaring fact concerning my reality. This was actually a JOB! I'm a "professional" now, a working man. This isn't jacking around, high school, American Legion BS anymore; you have been "hired" and are being paid for your services to do a JOB. During my short stint in the Fall Instructional League I had tried to make myself comprehend this

Me and one of my dearest friends, Glenn Williams, posing with my hometown friends, Lynn and Paul Durden at minor league spring training in Palm Beach.

fact, but with everything so new and different this reality didn't really take hold. Early on in spring, however, as I began to understand exactly what obligations this career entailed I began having some serious conversations with myself. It was going to be a long time before I was going to see mommy and daddy again; it was going to be a long time before I was going to see my girlfriend again and a long time before I was going to see my own bed again. I would, on the other hand, be getting very familiar with two-star hotels/motels, run-down clubhouses, buses and greasy spoon restaurants during the next eight months and the coming years for that matter.

"Boy, I hope I made the right decision" was the statement made during many of those internal dialogues. After several weeks of going rounds with my perception concerning the reality of my current situation, I finally had to throw in the proverbial towel regarding my own neurotic obsession and face the facts: This was going to be a long journey as well as a difficult one. There were going to be many times when you're just going to feel like walking away, but this was your reality, this was your life, this was the decision you made and these were the only two choices you have, given the path you've chosen: Put your head down and with every bit of strength and endurance you can muster push that metaphorical boulder to the top of the mountain for as long as it may take until the pinnacle you seek is reached, or possibly fail. But failure will only be accepted after every drop of blood has been bled, after every ounce of energy has been used, and after every breath has been exhausted; I will adamantly persevere through every difficulty that is awaiting me on this path I've chosen because anything that is truly worth having is worth suffering for. It was with this understanding late in the spring of 1994 that my career formally began.

With the newly acknowledged perspective that there would be no turning back and I was in a proverbial "fight to the death" scenario with the fulfillment of my childhood obsession; I stopped stressing over all the unknowns and sold out to the dream. I would not be the "what if" guy ten years from now wondering what happened to the one chance I had been given: What if I had just spent more time? What if I had just worked a little harder? What if I had just been more coachable? What if I had not let the fear control me? What if? During my entire career the only thing I feared was one day looking back and being forced to say "what if." I decided at nineteen years old I would never be that guy. In my opinion, the only way we achieve to the level that so many of us desire is to sell out for those desires. Holding back because of fear, doubt, uncertainty, whatever it may be, only increases our odds of failure. I know it's a worn out cliché but "life IS short." Fifteen minutes ago I was a wide-eyed naive 19-year-old minor-league kid who knew nothing about nothing. Ten minutes ago I was closing games every night on national TV and loving my place in life. Five minutes ago I destroyed my shoulder and my career ended. Currently, I'm writing this book. It all truly goes by in the blink of an eye. Don't ever risk being the person that looks back over it all and says "what if." Sell out for whatever it is you truly desire. It's your life; you only get one chance at it and it will pass you by if you let it.

With stubborn mentality firmly in hand the ship that was my career set sail on the sea of minor league baseball. Just as I had done in high school I kept secret fantasies of being the "out of nowhere" pitching prodigy that rocketed up through the ranks and joined the big league club in record time (yea.... not so much). Similar to the delusions of grandeur leading up to the amateur draft, my minor league career would have mimicked anything but a rocket. For the first three years I seemed to be firmly secured in the "two steps forward and one step back" routine, always managing to find a job on some roster without ever consistently "wowing" anyone. I did have my good moments, and even a few great ones. I actually threw a no hitter in A ball, but of course followed that up with an outing that lasted just two and a third innings while giving up eight.

The best I can figure the main reason I stayed around was because of my "potential." It's hard for me to even say that word without getting sick to my stomach. Potential? Potential is a word used by losers during their explanation as to why they lost. I got so obnoxiously tired during those early years of being told how much @#&*ing "potential" I had I wanted to put my head in a vice. In my opinion when someone tells you that you have a lot of potential; all they're actually saying is that you could be good, but right now you stink. Potential is possessed by those who will spend the rest of their lives saying "what if." Life is about production. Give me something I can use. As it were, however, for those first three years I was pretty much all potential with only slight, brief glimpses of production.

Many years removed from the experiences of minor league baseball and with a lot of living done in between, I can accurately say that traversing the minefields of the minor leagues was the toughest thing I had ever attempted and thankfully accomplished. My first full season as a young minor league pup was spent in the fine town of Danville, Virginia, as a Danville Brave. All in all I had a respectable season there with respectable numbers. As I said before, not good enough to "wow" anyone, but did earn a promotion to Class A Macon the following spring.

Andruw Jones, myself and Glenn Williams act like teenage idiots at my parents house in Macon one afternoon before our Macon Braves game.

Now Macon was my hometown and I had been looking forward to this "homecoming" and the opportunity to play in a Macon Braves uniform from nearly the initial moment I signed my first professional contract. But with the same mindset as I began this chapter, concerning the caution one needs to use when wishing for a particular something, the reality of playing in my home town fell far short of my grand expectations. Sure, it was nice being close to family and friends, but all of those family, friends, and numerous third party acquaintances that considered themselves friends expected to see "John Rocker" the high school pitcher from years past who averaged two strike outs per inning and gave up barely two hits a game. Fortunately and unfortunately, the competition had gotten "slightly" better since the last time many of these folks had seen me throw.

In my mind there seemed to be a dark cloud of insurmountable expectations ominously and constantly following me. Fully realizing what was expected of me, the pressure I put on myself to live up to these outside expectations began to pointedly affect my performance. As I've always said, the only pressure that exists is that which we create. Pressure doesn't actually exist in the real world; it is created purely and simply from our own doubts concerning our ability to succeed. Not understanding this realization as the young "newbie" I was; I allowed these expectations, which soon became my expectations to unravel every process I was working toward. By midseason I wasn't bad; I was horse @#%$, which finally earned me a one-way demotion to the organization's short season team in Eugene, Oregon, of the Northern League.

This would be the first of many setbacks which I knew were awaiting me along my path to The Show, but even still, being knocked off my feet and receiving a demotion in front of the home town crowd was certainly a blow to the ego. When I had arrived in Macon, the local community had expected so much and in turn I expected to not disappoint. A demotion to a lower level was downright embarrassing. After arriving in Eugene, it took me a few days to gain my composure and come to terms with what, for the most part, was the first real failure I had ever experienced. During those initial days in the Northern League I did my best to look for the positives, without much success. Amidst my search, however, I recalled the realization I had just a year and a half earlier and the promise I made to myself. This was just one of the presumably many difficulties I will face on this journey. Don't try to rationalize or analyze it; just stand firmly behind that boulder and keep pushing. Perseverance will always trump failure.

Imaginably so, I never became overly excited about my existence as a Eugene Emerald of the Northern League, but I did manage to finish the season in moderately respectable fashion, giving me hope that with a strong spring I would be able to skip Class A Macon and catch back up to my draft class at high A Durham. Just as in the prior season, however, disappointment struck again and I was reassigned for my second season as a Macon Brave, forcing me once again to remind myself of the commitment I had made despite the fact that my pet boulder seemed to be getting heavier by the day.

Gradually my perseverance, stubbornness and hard work began to pay off, and I actually found myself pitching pretty well during my second tour through the

South Atlantic League. In my opinion, unwavering determination is a must when seeking the accomplishment of any goal, but it is always nice and certainly helpful when a little positive reinforcement is received. By the middle of the season I had been able to fight through the demons of expectation and was promoted to the high A Durham Bulls to rejoin my draft class.

Naturally this promotion and the confidence that was created in conjunction had me tuned up and swearing I could see the Big Leagues right around the corner. I became pretty high on myself; thought I was going pretty good. Maybe I would be the next "pitching prodigy" after all. It seemed for a brief few moments at least that my boulder had suddenly gotten considerably lighter.

As the season wound down I looked back and realized I had put up some pretty respectable numbers and rebounded nicely from the prior year's disappointment. I had led the Braves minor league system in strikeouts, and was in the top five in wins and ERA. To me it seemed like a formality to waltz into spring training, keep the train clipping along the track; make the Double A team out of camp and then head on to ATLANTA! I certainly had high expectations and lofty plans for myself heading into that 1997 season. Little did I know as spring training began the next six months were going to give me the education of a lifetime and provide most of the mental armor I would need as a Major League player. The next few months would leave me scarred, but definitely smarter.

As life so often does it rarely consults with us concerning the scheduling of events in our lives or their timing. According to my own personal schedule I was set to arrive in Atlanta sometime during the later part of the summer and certainly by September. As things would have it, however, I should have asked life's advice before mentally creating such grand plans for the upcoming season. When camp broke I found myself back in Durham, which in and of itself wouldn't have been the worst thing in the world, but I had been stripped of my duties as a starting pitcher and in my opinion "demoted" to the bullpen to serve as a long reliever.

For those of you who aren't privy to the pecking order of pitching staffs, the arrangement goes something like this: The "top dog" on any staff is the number one starter. It's a big deal. You're number one guy is the best pitcher on the staff and as starters go it digresses down from there to number five. Where the bullpen is concerned you're closer is the king of that club. Then comes your left handed and right handed set up guys, followed by your left and right-handed specialists. Bringing up the rear is what's known as the "mop up guy" or long reliever. When this guy sees action it's generally because one of your five starters has had "one of those days" and needs to be relieved in the 4th inning. Needless to say, when your "mop up guy" is in there you're most likely not going to put one in the win column.

When I went back to Durham in the spring of '97 after coming off what I surmised to have been a moderately impressive year and mentally already had my locker picked out in Atlanta I showed up as the bullpen's "mop up guy". WTF! Somehow I had managed to go from leading the entire organization in strikeouts the prior season to mopping up in a league I had succeeded in quite comfortably just a few months prior. It's a drastic understatement to say that this sent my fragile confidence into a full on tailspin.

Not only was I frustrated and extremely disappointed, but the mental wrestling match going on inside my head began causing me to break one of the cardinal rules of achievement. I began holding on too tight; I began becoming to acquainted with "fear" and was allowing the fear to infiltrate every aspect of my process to accomplish. With the success I had experienced the previous season my senses could almost smell the sweet aroma of the Majors. In light of my most recent set back, however, coupled with my fragile and inexperienced psyche, I flipped a mental U-turn from where I had been just a few weeks prior. All of a sudden I wasn't mapping out the last leg of my trip to the Majors, I was incessantly wondering if I wasn't on the short list to being released and having my dream possibly derailed forever. It's amazing how unseasoned "mental toughness" can quickly spin out of control when faced with adversity.

What had I done? I thought I had pitched pretty well last year. Was there something I was missing? Daily, nightly, on holidays and weekends I constantly obsessed about this new direction my career had taken. Every outing, every inning, every pitch was analyzed and reanalyzed post and sometimes intra game. I was slowly becoming a mental mess of paranoia and fear and in doing so was breaking one of the absolutes of achievement. You can never succeed when you're afraid to fail.

With my twenty-one year old naive mentality, however, I had not yet come to realize this fact. All I knew was I had come into spring training with what I presumed to be the end of my journey in sight only to find myself seemingly heading back down the figurative mountain I had just climbed, which in my mind may result in becoming an out-of-work ball player much sooner than I wanted or expected. I was letting the fear control me, dominate me and manipulate me. With that kind of mental approach to any task failure is inevitable. As fate would have it I would learn this lesson just a few short months later and gain some monumental perspective on fear and how to deal with self-doubt and the unknown. For the time being, though, I was struggling mightily.

Then it happened. I don't know why it happened as I certainly wasn't pitching well enough to warrant such an event. Maybe the baseball gods thought I had suffered enough because "divine" intervention is the only logical explanation I can create to explain why a petrified "mop up guy" with a 5.00 ERA would be promoted to Double A and handed a job in the starting rotation again. Nevertheless, after a meaningless game one night in late May, my manager, Paul Runge, called me into his office. For a brief moment a terrible panic came over me as I initially anticipated the possibility of some unfavorable news. To my great relief and surprise, however, Paul called me in to inform me I would need to be in uniform tomorrow night in Greenville. I stood there in disbelief and waited for the punch line. After some mild questioning he convinced me he was serious and I wasn't about to stand around and argue with him. I don't even think I showered that night. I packed my bag as fast as my sweaty hands could function, said a few goodbyes and sped home to get the rest of my things together.

I was up well before my alarm went off the next morning to retake my hypothetical place back on the train heading for the Majors. It seems interesting to me at times when I become consciously aware of my own self perception and how it has changed based on a particular circumstance, whether that circumstance be good or bad. Remove the event and I'm still the same person with the same attributes as well as flaws, but somehow a specific event has caused the perception I have about myself to change. At the end of the day our success or failure in pursuit of achievement largely depends on the opinions we carry regarding ourselves. In my view, the definition of mental weakness is when outside circumstances have the ability to consistently affect the perception we have concerning ourselves personally and our ability to succeed; therefore mental toughness would be the exact opposite. There is nothing good or bad, but our thoughts will make it so.

As I arrived in Greenville I was filled with positive anticipation at what the next several months may hold, yet despite my renewed confidence that was based on nothing more than an outside event of which I had no control, there was still a significant hurdle of doubt to overcome that I had brought with me from Durham. The disappointments from the past several months had shaken my psyche and it was going to take more than a single positive event to heal those scars of doubt. I knew there was only one way to legitimately restore belief in myself. I would have to perform. But what "reason(s)" could I focus on in the meantime that would convince me I should believe in myself again? After the unsettling experiences of the last two and a half months I had nothing to lean on to bolster my ego and persuade myself that success was possible. (Do you see what invaluable lesson I'm about to learn?) I had nothing, and furthermore knew I had done nothing in the immediate past to warrant my promotion to Double A.

Around the corner I would soon understand that confidence; carrying yourself with confidence, thinking with confidence, speaking with confidence in every situation where the possibility of success and failure exists is a must if you desire to experience the former. In all situations the level to which we succeed is in large part proportionate to the level with which we believe we can. In addition this assurance should never be tied to events that please us and therefore justify us to believe we can succeed, because where there are good situations there will also be bad. Confidence in yourself must be constant; it must be unwavering despite the reality of our surroundings. After all, what can doubt actually do for you? What benefit does it serve? In the opposite direction, what harm can be had from unwavering faith in oneself? In my opinion, someone performs a degree of suicide when they stubbornly doubt, while the ability to have confidence always exists. At times it literally comes down to a conscious choice. Choose to be confident in yourself.

As the days stretched into weeks with the Greenville Braves I stumbled along looking for some solidifying factor that I could grasp and put an end to my mental roller coaster ride. With each good outing I would find myself mapping out my Big League future once again, contrasted by thoughts of "life after baseball" following each bad appearance. No matter what profession one finds oneself in, constant highs and lows dependent strictly upon performance is not an enjoyable existence. After a short while you begin to dread the possibility of failure as you know the mental devastation that must be dealt with until an opportunity to redeem yourself arises. It's no way to live, but such was my daily grind for nearly three months as I struggled to find the mental "middle."

I don't think anyone will argue the fact that there are many factors that must be present for one to succeed. There must be talent, drive, determination, willingness to sacrifice, and perseverance. There's one key factor, in my opinion, which may sound a bit "hoakie" but I feel to some degree or another is integral in the fulfillment of most of our desires. In my opinion there are times when it simply comes down to just good ole fashion "fate." Chance, being in the right place at the right time, falling bass akwards into a situation and coming out clean on the other side.

To this point in my career I possessed and practiced the absolutes of success to a neurotic level yet still was barely getting by and certainly was not having much fun in the process. I was teetering on all-out schizophrenia as my entire mood was strictly dependent on my last performance. I was well aware that something needed to change, but really wasn't sure exactly what, and most importantly how. Luckily "fate" was one step ahead of me.

As the season started to wind down I began reflecting back over it all, particularly the past three months, in an effort to impose some rigid self-criticism on how my season had unfolded and hopefully gain some level of satisfaction with it all. Annually, I would aim a significant amount of scrutiny at myself, but that year I was being especially critical. Despite the drastic number of highs, lows and various disappointments that had labeled my young career as inconsistent at best, I had some how managed to traverse enough of the pitfalls to find myself as a Double A player at a fairly young age. Not that this is a lofty accomplishment by any means, but over the last several years I had witnessed the derailment of a number of my colleagues' careers and had left many others behind to continue their struggles in the lower minor leagues. Although not entirely happy with the way things had unfolded during these first four years, I evidently had been doing something at least partially right. The level to which I criticized myself as the end of the season approached had much more bearing than in prior years, however, as two very important milestones lay shortly ahead that would give a very strong indication as to what track I was on in this long winding journey.

After a minor league player has been in a particular system for four years the organization has to choose whether or not to protect that player on what's known as the 40-man roster. This elite group consists of 25 guys at the Big League level with the balance being rounded out by the organization's top prospects at generally the Double A and Triple A levels. Need less to say, being placed on the "40-man" is quite significant to a young player for a number of reasons. First and foremost it makes a clear statement as to what the organization thinks about your talents, as well as their plans regarding your future. Secondly, it's an extremely encouraging and foreshadowing event, as most clubs ordinarily call up the remaining members of the 40-man when rosters expand each September. Therefore, being put on this list makes an appearance in The Show the following September somewhat of a formality. You can basically start counting down the days to the fulfillment of this lifelong fantasy, which many have sought but few will ever realize. As long as you stay healthy, don't have a miserable season and don't die, you will most likely find yourself rubbing elbows with the gods of baseball in the very near future. As my season with the Greenville Braves came to a close this monumental possibility was in my thoughts every hour of every day, perched right along side my harsh critical opinion as to whether or not I had done enough to deserve such an honor.

In addition to the obsessive desire to be a participant on the 40-man, another foretelling possibility was looming large in my mind and waiting on the horizon to create additional assurance that in fact "Major League Baseball Player" may soon appear on my resume. With the culmination of each season, organizations begin making their selections as to which players will be sent to participate in what's known as the Arizona Fall League. To be selected to play in the Fall League is perhaps the next best thing to being placed on the 40-man roster, and one usually goes hand-in-hand with the other. It's an extremely big deal.

At the end of each minor league season, approximately four to six of an organization's top prospects, at usually the Double A and Triple A levels, are invited to participate in this special league, which consists of eight teams that play a sixty game schedule in the Phoenix, Arizona, area during September, October, and November. Each team is basically a minor league all-star team and to be selected by your organization is a vote of extreme confidence that you in fact are firmly on their radar screen. Statistics show that 70% of all Arizona Fall League players will be in the Big Leagues sometime during the following season. That's what the numbers say and every minor league player and Arizona Fall League hopeful is fully aware.

Daily, my mind obsessed concerning these two possibilities that lay in front of me and what they would mean for my career then as well as moving forward. Still easily manipulated by outside circumstances regarding my mood and self opinion, I felt with almost panicked desire that if I could just get invited to the Fall League or nominated to the 40-man roster all of the confidence and belief I would need to perform with the self assured attitude I had been desiring would be created. Needless to say, the cart was being placed well before the horse, but this ass backwards, failure-conducive mentality unfortunately was the mindset I was working with. Luckily for me and my Major League career that unknowingly was looming on the horizon, I was about to get a mental makeover.

As things would have it, Arizona Fall League selections were finally announced and I found myself as one of five nominees from the Braves organization. After weeks and weeks of constant fixation, the initial news, which was received during batting practice one afternoon from my manager, Randy Ingle, sent 50 different emotions racing through my body, all of them overwhelmingly good. From unbridled excitement, to relief, to anticipation and every feeling in between, this opportunity was undoubtedly the best thing that had happened thus far in my short-lived career.

Over the next few days my initial thrill began to subside and I slowly became aware of a feeling of substantial confidence that I had never experienced before. This was not the pride one feels when a solitary "good job" is done creating a momentary feeling of self worth. This feeling had roots; it had depth. Other than the initial event of being drafted, this was the most significant step which had been taken that produced a significant level of assurance that in fact the end of this very long road I had been traveling may actually be reached. I saw this gesture by the organization as a proof positive sign that maybe I was actually becoming the player I had always hoped I would become; even if through my own self-appointed criticism I couldn't realize it.

Although this manufactured level of belief was much better than my alternative thoughts of past months it was in fact manufactured. I basically had confidence in myself because I felt others did. There again, even though the outside source created a positive result; it was still an outside source that was manipulating my thoughts. True faith in one's abilities, the kind that must exist for substantial achievement to exist, has to come from within. It has to be a part of you like your blood type. It has to be absolute. Something needed to take place to allow that all-important self-assurance to come from within and not consistently from extracurricular circumstances.

As I stated earlier, during the initial years of my career I practiced every tangible aspect necessary to achieve my goal with obnoxious consistency. Not a day went by where I was not making every effort I deemed essential to reaching my goal, yet inconsistency especially on the mental front constantly plagued me and was ultimately holding and would continue to hold me back unless I found some way to create a new mentality. But how? I already went to relentless lengths for the sake of my goal. What else could be done?

Sometimes it's not up to us, however. To this day it's still my firm belief, as I've said before, that despite every painstaking effort that we can mustered in the pursuit of achievement, every now and then it's simply "fate" that ultimately brings us the final pieces to our puzzle. More times than not we don't recognize it when it comes calling, but looking back years later we can definitely see the effects of its hand as it altered the course of our lives.

Although still brimming with confidence from my Fall League assignment, deep down I knew it wouldn't last. I knew the first negative experience I had would start the cycle all over again. In my mind I was doing everything I thought I should do and everything I thought was required to get where I wanted to go, but something was still missing. A solidifying aspect to bring it all together was still necessary. Physically I had all the tools, but a link in the chain was still missing as it related to the all-important mentality, which must exist to play the game of baseball at its highest level.

It was about this time where manufactured confidence was high, but so was my awareness that a missing piece still existed when "fate" decided to show up. To this day I credit two games played in early September for the initial creation of the much-needed mental approach, which would ultimately mature and become the final piece to the collective framework that would propel me to a career in the Majors. Two simple games; one of which, to everyone but me, meant nothing and the other, for all intents and purposes, I should have never pitched in at all, but as it were "fate" picked these moments to begin laying the foundation to establish the final missing piece which would ultimately send me on my way to the realization of my childhood dream.

It was the last weekend of the season in September 1997. The Greenville Braves were playing the Jacksonville Suns in a three-game set for the final spot in the Double A playoffs. Whoever won the series was in while the loser got an early vacation. As the rotation was set, I was in line to throw what could be the "do or die" third game on Sunday afternoon, depending on the outcome of Friday's and Saturday's competition. If the first two games of the series were split, Sunday would be for the season.

Each year there are two specific games no one wants to play in: the last game of Spring Training and the last game of the season where no implications exist regarding its outcome. The atmosphere of these two games is in the realm of "I've had enough. Let's just get this thing over with." Jokes are made in the clubhouse prior to the first pitch that fines will be levied if a hitter sees more than three pitches and if a pitcher dares to walk anyone. Either the season is over and guys are eager to get home to their families or spring is over and everyone is chomping at the bit to get the new season started. Which ever one it is, as a pitcher, those two games are not the ones you want to be handed the ball for. It's simply tough to get motivated.

Well, as what I thought to be my unfortunate luck would have it, we clinched Saturday night in extra innings, which meant I had the unenviable duty of throwing Sunday afternoon in what amounted to a meaningless game. Good for me! So while the rest of my teammates went out in Jacksonville that night to celebrate our playoff berth I stayed back at the team hotel to rest up for the next day's outing because even when a particular game is technically pointless, most players at the professional level have a degree of pride and no matter what significance or lack thereof a game may hold, they have no interest in going out there and embarrassing themselves. With that in mind I basically had no choice but to go through the same pre-game preparation I would for any start.

As I lay in my hotel bed that night missing the festivities, I'm not even going to lie: I was pissed!

"Why couldn't I have started tonight, or Thursday or hell even Friday for that matter, any day but tomorrow? How typical is it that I would get stuck throwing this useless game? This sucks!"

Little did I know "fate" was working behind the scenes and already had things all mapped out. This seemingly "meaningless" game would prove to be a turning point in my career and serve as the catalyst to the mental rearrangement that was necessary if any kind of future in Major League Baseball was to be had.

I think we can all relate to experiences in our lives where our thoughts, realizations, understandings (whatever you want to call it) fly out of nowhere and hit us like a ton of bricks. Some call it an epiphany; others refer to it as an "awakening."

No matter what term you use; I think we have all been a part to such events where one day you're simply sitting around having a totally "normal" moment and then suddenly are blind sided with a notion that should have seemed so obvious which either transforms your life or more likely becomes the beginning of a significant transformation. As I lay in my hotel bed that Saturday night while the rest of my idiot buddies were out having a good time, with no warning whatsoever I had one of those moments.

In the midst of the internal conversation I was having, which had an overtly irritable tone, SLAP!! It was as if my subconscious without notice released what should have been an obvious notion to my conscious mind and set into motion the wheels of a mental transformation.

"Wait a minute! Tomorrow's game is MEANINGLESS (without even realizing, this was one of my first real efforts at "reframing" my situation)!! And not only is tomorrow's game meaningless, everything about my individual season is for all intents and purposes finalized. I've already had a pretty good year; I'm moderately satisfied overall. The five or six innings I will pitch tomorrow won't weigh very heavily on the numbers I've accumulated over the past 6 months. My numbers are what they are and tomorrow's game will basically have no effect on them. Not only is tomorrow's game technically pointless, but also so are the innings I will pitch. I've already been named to the Arizona Fall League, which starts in a few weeks; that can't be taken away from me. Oh my god! I can go out there tomorrow and just PLAY! For the first time in as long as I can remember I can play a baseball game that has no "consequences"! When was the last time I had an opportunity like this? Oh my god, I can just PLAY!"

"Remember those days? Remember when I used to put on my uniform because it simply brought me joy to do so? Remember when I used to be so excited by lunch about that afternoon's game I could barely hold a thought in my head? Remember when I played with passion and intensity instead of fear, anxiety and obligation? Remember? What has happened to me? What happened to the kid that once took the mound with a smile on his face as big as all center field? What happened to the kid that didn't calculate his earned run average DURING the game? Where has that kid gone? What the hell have I become? I don't enjoy playing this game anymore. I basically haven't enjoyed it since I became a professional. It's been all about goals and self-criticisms and making sure the powers that be are satisfied with me. This game HAS become a job. For the first time in a very long time tomorrow doesn't have to be about the "stats." It doesn't have to be about what the manager will say in his report to the front office after my outing," I thought to myself.

"Tomorrow I can just play. For the first time in a very long time I can strip away this neurotic obsession that has plagued me these many years and in some ways has come to define me as I relentlessly pursue the one and only thing I think life is about. Tomorrow I can once again play with the same passion, intensity, fire, and love that I had long ago when the game was just a game. Before it was a job; before I saw each outing as nothing more than a line in a box score; with a collection of stats representing the supposed means to some greater obsessive end. If only for one day, I don't have to hold on so tight. It doesn't have to be about my stats, or the write up that will be turned in to the front office about how many first pitch strikes I threw, or how the command of my breaking ball was. Hell, tomorrow doesn't even have to be about winning. Tomorrow can simply be about "playing."

As I lay in bed that night and all of these realizations began flooding into my conscious mind an overall excitement came over me that I had not experienced in a very long time. I went from dreading the "meaningless" game of tomorrow to anticipating it as if it were Christmas morning. It was at this point I basically made a conscious decision that if only for tomorrow, consequences be damned. For at least this one day I would not care about the outcome. For once I would not obsess about how this one single outing could/would/may affect the realization of my ultimate prize. I would not focus on what thoughts and opinions the coaching staff may or may not have. I would not naively obsess at how this one single outing could possibly impact me ultimately becoming or not becoming a Major Leaguer as I had done so many times before.

"Tomorrow I will say &@#$ it to every possible consequence and play because I simply love to play. Tomorrow I will actually enjoy myself for the first time in a very long time. I will attack every hitter. I will attack every pitch with no worry of the possible outcomes. Remember, "Fastballs and upper cuts," just like it used to be when things were simpler. I will carry myself with the confidence of someone who doesn't care what the results may be. Tomorrow I will compete my ass off and enjoy the competition for the sheer pleasure one gets from simply competing against another for no other reason than to find out who's better. It will be nothing more than that."

Unknowingly, with this internal conversation and the drastically amended "game plan" that had been decided upon, my mental transformation had begun. As I've said for many years, success cannot exist along side fear. Since the beginning of my career I had played/pitched every game with fear and anxiety as to what possible yet unknown consequences may result and without ever realizing, it was this mentality that was ultimately holding me back and perpetuating the inconsistency I loathed. On this day I made the conscious decision that even if only for the immediate moment "fear and anxiety" would have the day off.

When the next morning arrived the conversation I had with myself the evening before was the first thing on my mind as my eyes popped open. The normal angst that ordinarily occupied my mindset during the day of most starts was not present as the attitude I had consciously chosen to adopt was filling me with some much missed excitement and positive anticipation regarding that day's game. I couldn't wait to get out there and compete with largely the same demeanor and confidence I once had as a much younger man before an unwholesome ideology had tainted me. I had no plans for thought processes or mental strategies after today; all I knew was that this one game would be about playing without the fear and anxiety which had been robbing me of the enjoyment and passion I once had. Today, I would allow everything to hang out and the consequences could sort themselves out. Today I would simply say, "%$#@ it!"

Who would have "thunk" it? Who would have thought that formulating a mental strategy centered around two simple words which create such an overtly simplistic ideology have the ability to produce results so amazingly different on so many levels. "#$%@ it!" I certainly know that my traditional 21- year-old logic would have never dreamed of adopting such a radical approach under normal circumstances. Had that Sunday's game been for all the marbles as could have been the situation; I have no doubt that I would have shown up as my usual fearful, "oh my God what if …" self with an ass so tight it could have turned a Louisville Slugger into sawdust. On this day, however, "fate" gave me the opportunity to try something a little different and what an eye opening and literally career altering experience it turned out to be.

That Sunday afternoon in late August 1997 in what to everyone else was a pointless game I turned in what was perhaps my best outing of the season and got my first brief glimpse at what possessing internally induced confidence of an unwavering variety can produce. Not only did I actually enjoy the game that day and wasn't constantly wrestling with the demons of doubt, but the results on the field more than satisfied everything my critical nature would expect.

On the bus ride back to Greenville that night I relentlessly contemplated the outing of that afternoon. Not for my line in the box score or how many strike outs I had, but for the different feelings my consciously adjusted mental approach created before, during and after the game. It was a great feeling to play devoid of the fear and anxiety I had gotten so used to and for all intents and purposes assumed was just a part of my nature. It was a great feeling to not obsess intra game regarding what impact to my career a good versus bad outing may have. It was great to play with a conscious realization that no matter what happens I will have unwavering confidence and will display such. As I rode through the dark on that G Braves team bus, I subtly began to realize I might be on to something.

Yogi Berra has a funny quote affectionately called a "Yogism" which wisely quips that "90 percent of the game is half mental." That may come across as a bit hoakie or confusing to some; so for those of you who don't speak "Berra" it basically sums up the fact that the majority of the game is played on that five inch field which exists between your ears. Over the next few days as I continued to dissect what had transpired during Saturday evening and Sunday's game I began to become aware of a reality regarding me personally. I had spent countless hours over many years working out, throwing, watching film, running, etc., in a tireless effort to physically enable myself to perform at the highest level possible. Despite my obnoxiously diligent efforts, however, I had always seemed to just barely break even and only on rare occasions slightly excel. For the past several years I had obsessed as to the precise link that seemed to be missing which through its discovery would transform me into the player I had long desired to become. What was that link? What was the correct adjustment that needed to be made to make me a complete player and therefore Big League bound?

As more and more thought was given to the previous weekend I began understanding that the approach which had supposedly been adopted for just one day had to become my on field "personality." The fear could be no more. The anxiety regarding the possible ramifications around each and every start, each and every inning, each and every hitter had to end. On the one hand, living like that was just plain tiring, and on the other I finally began to realize it was overwhelmingly detrimental to the overall process of what I was trying to accomplish. In my opinion I think many of us often get the notion in our heads that by squeezing what we desire as tight as our fists will clinch we can strangle success from beneath our grip. In my experience this approach produces nothing more than returns that consistently diminish. The tighter our grip becomes the more our desires escape us. We actually become hindrances to our own success. Once we are able to let go and trust fate, trust preparation and most importantly trust ourselves, we then become ready to receive. During seven short innings of a meaningless Double A baseball game I was shown the tremendous benefit of simply "letting go." Sometimes that's all it takes for that missing link to begin to form.

Most roads to ultimate success are generally paved with repetition. Figure out how to succeed and then repeat the process, and when you're done repeating the process; repeat it some more, and then just when you think you have it down; repeat it again. Consistent repetition of a successful process is what ultimately leads to realizing the goals we desire. Additionally, as we climb the ladder to achievement we must learn to overcome our failures by making adjustments to ensure that those same failures are not repeated. Along the path we travel towards accomplishment the adjustments, which are made to avoid our past failures, must transform themselves from one-time modifications into simply becoming the normal way of doing things.

As I've already said, I had somewhat of an epiphany, an awakening in relation to this situation by which a much better way of doing things was revealed. All I had to do now was repeat the process enough times until it became my nature and the transformation would eventually complete itself.

Unfortunately, by the time this revelation took place the regular season was at an end and only eight possible playoff games remained, of which just two were guaranteed. I may not get a chance to repeat my process for success again for several weeks, when the Fall League begins. If the theory that repetition of successful process is a must to ultimate achievement, then the timing of my realization couldn't have been worse. I may not pitch again in live game competition for weeks and who knows what events may take place in the meantime. I needed to keep the process of this transformation moving forward, not sitting idly by, and possibly allowing my revelation to be tampered with by a weak mentality. Luckily, "fate" once again was preparing to take control of the situation and my overall destiny.

As the playoffs lined up and the pitching rotation was set, I found myself nowhere in the mix. Fortunately for the Greenville Braves that year we had a tremendous staff; unfortunately for John Rocker during the playoffs that year we had a tremendous staff. Everyone in the starting rotation that season and three members of the bullpen made it to the Majors and had careers of varying success. To say the least we were stacked from one through eleven and even though I managed to finish up with a pretty nice season there were still a few guys ahead of me as far as seniority and overall numbers were concerned.

When the pitching staff had its meeting on the off day prior to the first game in order to lay out everyone's expectations I was basically a non-factor in the overall scheme. We would be going with a four-man rotation which bumped the fifth guy (me) to the bullpen. Ordinarily this would not be a huge deal and the likelihood of seeing some action would still have been high, except for the fact that three members of our bullpen staff had sub 2.00 ERA's and would undoubtedly be worked and over worked during the short series that were forthcoming. I had basically come full circle, back to my early season "mop up" days as a Durham Bull and could already see the handwriting on the wall regarding my participation in the upcoming playoff games. Seeing the mound the next two to possibly eight games was unlikely at best. I just needed to find myself a comfy seat on the bench, enjoy the show and wait for the Fall League.

Fate, however, was preparing a far different outcome from what seemed to be so initially obvious. As I reflect back a decade and a half later I still have no rational explanation as to why certain events unfolded, other than to say it was just simply my time. I have no logical reason as to why I was the beneficiary of such an extremely bizarre and thankfully fortunate scenario, which created the opportunity for some much-needed solidification to take place regarding the transformation of my overall mental approach. It's safe to say that the biggest game of my minor league career and one which had a tremendous impact on fortifying the ideology that would eventually allow my Major League future to materialize and ultimately sustain me through some of the biggest moments on the grandest stages baseball can create should have never seen my participation. As I look back on how the whole situation unfolded the only way I can explain the circumstances as they happened is to say it was simply the hand of fate.

As the playoffs began we opened up the first series in Knoxville, Tennessee, to play the Toronto Blue Jays' affiliate in a best-of-three series. According to my memory we swept the first two games, propelling ourselves to the championship round against the winners of the other division, the Huntsville Stars, who were the affiliate of the Oakland A's. Now the Huntsville club had a strong team with a stacked lineup boasting names such as Ben Grieve, Miguel Tejada, and Ryan Christensen, all of whom went on to have great Major League careers. With our pitching versus their hitting this Double A championship series was poised to be quite a matchup and from all "on paper" indications was going to be a battle for all twenty-seven outs each night of this best of five set.

As the series began my own personal expectations concerning any on field participation was exactly what I had expected. I never even came close to touching fair territory during the first two games in Tennessee and from what I can remember didn't so much as even climbed on top of a mound. For all intents and purposes I was a glorified cheerleader wearing number 19 on his back. It was kind of pathetic and highly frustrating. These were the playoffs and I desperately wanted to help my team in any manner possible other than handing out "atta boys" at the top step of the dugout between innings. My role was sealed though. I wasn't in the rotation and our bullpen was so strong it was very doubtful I would see any action in relief. I guess I would just sit and deal with it. As I've consistently said, however, fate was well ahead of my short-sided expectations.

We opened the series in Greenville and left town with a split, heading to Huntsville for a crucial game three that would obviously put the winner firmly in the driver's seat regarding the outcome of this championship series. Jamie Arnold, who had been Atlanta's overall number one pick just a few years prior and had quite a year himself, was slated as our starter for this pivotal third game.

As game time approached it was your typical muggy late summer Southern afternoon. Jaime was getting loose and I was stretching my vocal cords for another night leading the cheers. Little did I know, my role as head cheerleader was about to be drastically adjusted.

Jaime had a great season in 1997 and was one of the organizations top prospects. On this night, however, Jaime had "one of those nights." By the third inning it was 6-0 Stars and it appeared the game and maybe the series would be lost. That is until fate showed up and decided to change the course of destiny for the 1997 Greenville Braves as a whole and me more specifically.

Now if anyone has ever spent any portion of time in the South during the summer you can relate from experience as to the frequency and sometimes-violent nature of the very common afternoon thunderstorm. It's usually not a matter of when it will happen but where and everyone, particularly in the baseball community of such areas, is always prepared. No one, however, was prepared for the kind of storm that hit during the third inning of what was setting up to be a drubbing by the Huntsville Stars.

With limited warning and insufficient time for reaction the skies opened up and began dumping buckets of rain to the earth. As quickly as could be managed the grounds crew at Municipal Stadium that night rushed into action and began unrolling the infield tarp in an effort to cover the diamond and hopefully preserve the game and the Stars' six-run lead. The men on the crew, however, proved to be no match for the torrents of rain pelting the field. It was raining so hard that by the time the tarp was stretched barely to second base so much water was weighing down upon it the cover wouldn't budge another inch leaving two thirds of the infield exposed to be relentlessly soaked by the heavy downpour. To this day I still have a picture in my minds eye of a half a dozen ground crew guys along with the entire Huntsville Stars team under pouring down rain tugging with every ounce of strength they could collectively muster trying to drag that tarp across the remainder of the infield. To our luck and their misfortune no such possibility was going to exist. Guys were sliding in the fresh mud and being soaked by the unrelenting sheets of rain as they desperately tried to preserve their game. All the while we were in the dugout screaming for more rain, and much more rain is exactly what we got!

After a moderate time of desperate effort all who were involved in trying to salvage the game that evening finally gave up and succumbed to the downpour. The game was lost and there was nothing anyone could do about it. It was just one of those things that for us (and especially me) came along at precisely the right time and in exactly the right place. If that storm had hit an hour earlier the game would have been called before it even began and postponed to the next day with nothing more being lost than a solitary evening. Had the storm hit an hour later, it would be very likely that five innings would have been completed thus being ruled an official game. By the storm showing up precisely in the third inning as it did, producing such a large amount of rain in such a short period of time and leaving the field totally unplayable there was no choice but to erase all records of the game and start over the next day in the top of the first. The Stars six run lead was lost and tomorrow would be a fresh day with nothing but zeros on the board.

The G Braves had certainly dodged a bullet. After being down six runs in the "rubber" game of a best of five series we had new life. A general sense of relief was the main theme in the clubhouse that night as we all showered and prepared to head back to the hotel. It was somewhat of a celebratory atmosphere as each of us knew how lucky we had just gotten. In my estimation and from the "bird's eye" perspective from which I'm able to view things at this point in my life, luck had nothing to do with it. I'm convinced and always will be that fate showed up at that exact moment to alter the path we were on. The timing and nature of this one event played a significant role in shifting my course and made a tremendous difference in dictating the direction I would ultimately take.

Relieved to have sidestepped a devastating upper cut that night; I was enjoying the lighthearted clubhouse environment with the rest of my teammates when our pitching coach, Bruce Del Canton, approached me in the training room.

"Hey Rock," he barked, "Jaime threw too many pitches tonight; you're gonna go for us tomorrow."

"Uhh, sure Bruce," I managed to stutter. "I'll be ready. Had plenty of rest."

An accurate adjustment made but merely one time doth not make a changed man. As I've already iterated numerous times, perhaps the most key component in achieving to the level we desire is discovering that which is keeping us from success, making the correct adjustment and then repeating that adjustment until it becomes a part of us at our core. At this fledgling stage of my career I had for the most part been dominated by fear, doubt, anxiety, and worry. The game was not an enjoyable experience for me as it once had been. I had, however, been given a unique opportunity on the last day of my Double A season to pitch a game which had no consequences and allowed me to "safely" adjust my mindset accordingly.

It had only been one game, though: one game to experience an altered mental mind set amidst years and years of an unhealthy and somewhat masochistic perspective. When Bruce delivered the news of my selection as the next night's starting pitcher my redundant detrimental mentality immediately took over. I had not had the opportunity to repeat the adjusted process, which had proven to be a very successful modification. Therefore, when faced with a familiar situation I responded in my usual familiar way. I panicked. I obsessed. I immediately began running every negative scenario I could possibly think of through my head as to what horrible outcomes may befall me the next evening … (Nice mentality! How or why I even used to get out of bed back then I will never know. What an idiot!)

Once again I found myself in an old familiar place. Tomorrow night's game was by far the biggest of the season thus far and the biggest in my young career; consequently for the next several hours I obsessed over the task I had been given. Then, just as a marathon runner who can't take another step, I became exhausted with my whole usual neurotic process.

"I'm tired of living like this," I thought to myself.

"I don't care how big this game is tomorrow; I am going to approach it with the same mentality I applied during my last start in Jacksonville just a few days ago. I don't care if tomorrow's game is basically for the Southern League Championship and the biggest start of my short professional career. I'm tired of doubting myself all the time. I'm tired of being afraid. I'm tired of worry and anxiety controlling me. I'm just tired. It doesn't have to be like this. I can choose my thoughts. I can choose my emotional state. I can choose to have unwavering internally derived confidence in myself. I can choose to carry myself with the demeanor of someone who doesn't care what consequences may exist around the corner. I'm exhausted living this way. This adjusted approach worked once. #$@% it! I'll try it again!"

That was basically the gist of the conversation I had with myself in Huntsville, Alabama, the night before the biggest start of my career. The logic behind the determination to modify my mental approach was a bit different but the philosophy was the same. Big game or not, important game or not; I would carry myself outwardly and inwardly with unwavering confidence possibly bordering on arrogance. I will not be manipulated by the fear of consequence. I will attack each hitter and every pitch with the staunch belief that I will ultimately prevail. I will not be controlled by fear; I will create fear.

I had long known that an adjustment somewhere in my game was needed to create the consistently different outcomes I had desired for the past several years. Fate had presented a scenario on the last day of the regular season and almost by accident I discovered an adjusted mentality that had made me seriously rethink my entire approach. Now again it seemed that fate had stepped in to create another situation by which my new mental perspective could begin taking hold within my overall psyche.

The longer I sat in my second rate hotel room that night and dissected what lay before me; the more it became apparent that adjusting my perception concerning myself and my reality was the missing link I had to seize. I was slowly beginning to understand the fact that the perception we hold concerning everything in our lives is what our reality eventually becomes. What we believe ourselves to be will ultimately come to pass. If I desired to see a successful end to my journey the choice to unconsciously believe in myself had to become a fact of my existence.

As game time approached the next day I had spent nearly 24 hours becoming committed to the idea that this "adjusted mindset thing" was not just a one time gimmick to be adopted for a single meaningless game, but rather had to become a part of my foundation. I had to believe with all my heart and soul that I was not the one who had the unenviable task of facing a stacked Huntsville Stars line up, but instead they had the unenviable task of facing me. This had to be my perception, thus creating my reality therefore making the probability of my success that much more likely.

I spent the next seven innings displaying both internally and externally a level of confidence I hadn't held since my high school years. The internal conversations I had during that game inspired me to feel as if I was the badest man on the planet, which in turn came through in my on-field persona. Watching from the grandstand that night one might have wondered, "Who in the hell is this arrogant SOB?" Moving forward, however, such views from extracurricular sources would be of no concern. From that day on I had but one opinion to satisfy and that opinion was mine.

From my own personal experience, more times than not, I feel the response we receive from others is based largely on the demeanor, which we exhibit. If you want to be respected, have respect for yourself and make sure you carry yourself as such. Finally realizing this to be true, I spent the majority of my career intentionally emitting an air of rigid confidence to a level most would call obnoxious. It was always my intent to convince a hitter through my mannerisms that I thoroughly believed I was going to stick it squarely up his ass and strongly intended to do just that. If a glimpse of such thinking ever entered a batter's head then for all intents and purposes, the battle was over before it even began. The belief I held concerning my success had to be greater than the belief he held concerning his.

The first step to the creation of this mentality, which in my opinion became profoundly integral to my success at the Major League level, began during this single game of which I should have never participated except for the timely arrival of a torrential downpour and a tarp that wouldn't budge.

As it were, this game turned out to be as equally a dominating performance as had been turned in the week before in Jacksonville, Florida, but with much more on the line. I went seven strong innings while striking out ten against a line up of future Major League all-stars. By the third time through the order I could visibly see the beaten/frustrated looks on the faces of the opposing hitters, which was the final straw needed to convince me that my adjusted mentality and demeanor was in fact the missing link which was needed to begin bringing things all together. The final and perhaps most important piece of the blueprint for success in the Majors had finally been implemented. Now all I had to do was repeat the process until it merged into the fabric of my being.

Throughout my minor league career I always had the physical tools for success, but as I've repeatedly discussed, my weak mental state had consistently held me back. In my opinion, we only succeed to the degree our beliefs will permit us. After fate did its part by allowing me the opportunities to make what was possibly the single most important adjustment of my entire 12-year career, it was all pretty much downhill from there.

The 1997 Greenville Braves went on to win the Southern League Championship a few days later and shortly thereafter I set off to Phoenix, Arizona, to begin the much-anticipated Fall League season. During the days leading up to my departure I spent many hours contemplating the mental discovery I had stumbled upon during the past several weeks. The more I thought about how drastically different everything appeared to me regarding all aspects of my career on account of my altered perceptions the more excited I got about the possibilities that lay ahead. At one point, although being very excited to have been invited to participate in an elite league like the AFL, I was also extremely timid and doubtful. After the awakening I experienced, however, my only thoughts were of eager anticipation and a burning desire to make my mark in the coming days. I was becoming a transformed man with every passing day and now I finally had the culmination of a decade-long journey firmly in sight.

Armed with unwavering confidence that was becoming more solidified at a steadying pace and a heart that was set on conquering doubt and fear I breezed through the Fall League schedule with greater ease than even my most arrogant predictions would have ever anticipated. Despite the level of competition I faced being far greater than anything I had ever consistently experienced, I soon found myself to be the proud owner of stats to which I hadn't been privy to since I was seventeen. By the end of Fall League competition my mental transformation had translated to on field success in such a degree I became the fortunate recipient of a much coveted spot on the 40-man roster and was asked to continue my travels down to the Puerto Rican winter league in Mayaguez, Puerto Rico.

With these new developments providing further assurance that I had in fact been making the correct adjustments along my path, I once and for all understood that this mentality and the persona which it created had to become my "religion." I had finally identified myself and knew who I had to permanently become. The "John Rocker" of old could be no more.

Upon arriving for the first time in a foreign place I wasn't sure what to expect. For the first time in my life though I had "me" and as far as I was concerned that was enough. Shortly after my initial arrival at the stadium in Mayaguez I was called in to meet my new manager, Tom Gamboa, and new pitching coach, Guy Hansen, who informed me straight away of my specific purpose.

"John, the Braves have sent you down here because there will likely be an opening in the bullpen when the upcoming season begins and they think you can fill it."

As you can imagine, news of this sort sent my 22-year-old state of mind into orbit! I had never had anyone verbalize to me specifically anything regarding the actual realization of the ultimate reality I had been in pursuit of for as long as I could remember. Hearing those words for the first time took the fantasy out of the dream and gave it an almost tangible actuality. I could see, taste, and feel those golden gates of "heaven." They were right there... Can you see them? With a tear in my eye I still can... I would do anything to walk inside of them again.

Now the only other relief experience I possessed to this point had been during a much different scenario and a somewhat unpleasant one at that. This time, however, I would be honing myself for a spot in the Major Leagues. Relief role or not I was at the short end of a very long road that had been more than ten years in the making. I would have sold my soul to the devil to taste what I desired and finally strap that red, white and blue jersey of the Atlanta Braves across my back.

"Just let me know what you guys need me to do," I replied.

A few days went by as the coaching staff allowed me to settle into my surroundings before I was activated for my first action. Now the Fall League had presented some talented competition, which even somewhat to my own surprise I had excelled quite nicely against. The Puerto Rican Winter League, however, was a bit of a different animal and proved to be an outstanding league all the way around. Each team fielded a majority of its roster with current mainstay Major Leaguers as well as numerous ex-Big League guys who were only slightly past their prime. Names like Javy Lopez, Ricky Ledee, Bernie Williams, Pudge Rodriguez, Jose Valentine, Carlos Beltran and Wil Cordero peppered the lineups each night. From 1 to 25, teams in this league are not quite up to the caliber of a Major League roster, but they're not far off. They really play a great brand of ball down there.

As I sat back and watched during the first few nights and saw the class of player as well as some of the very recognizable names that were being run out there I began to slowly realize exactly what was going on. I was being set up for my final test. I had managed to put together a moderately impressive year, particularly near the end of my Double A campaign. I had passed the challenges presented by the Fall League in somewhat impressive fashion. As I sat and studied the games those first few nights I began to notice the writing on the wall. Only part of this trip was for the intent of acclimating me to the duties of relief pitching. The foremost objective seemed to be for the Atlanta Braves to find out here and now whether I was going to make a player or not. It's time to sink or swim, boy. Can you float?

When this realization first crawled inside my head I was struck by an initial wave of surrealness as to the magnitude of my reality. More than ten long years had been spent on a steep, rocky, winding road trudging through knee-deep quicksand at times. All of a sudden I came to understand that the next ten innings created the most significant crossroad I had ever faced. Of the thousands of times I had climbed on top of a mound since the spawning of this monumental dream and the tens of thousands of throws that had been made in the pursuit of its fulfillment, it all came down to approximately the next two hundred pitches. Two hundred pitches to determine the rest of my life. Create success with those two hundred pitches and become one of the microscopic few who ever walk behind the curtain of Major League Baseball; create failure and possibly fade forever into the abyss of anonymity. What's it gonna be?

Six months earlier such awareness would have left me paralyzed with fear of every negative hypothetical "what if" I could imagine. With my mental transformation on firm footing and growing stronger by the day, however, I was like a starving animal with teeth bared greedily waiting to attack what appeared to be my final challenge.

Poised and intently determined to seize the destiny that I intended my life to be I competed with an intensity that bordered on ferocious during my internment as a Mayaguez Indio. This would be my initial baptism into the realm of competing with and against legitimate Major League competition, and I didn't want to leave any doubt in the minds of the governing powers that this kid's coming-of-age had finally arrived.

With an almost rabid mentality I sought to dominate anyone who in my mind had the guts to step in against me. Without even fully grasping the level to which my intensity had grown, the first time I was called upon to begin finding out just what kind of man I was going to become, a side of me was released from the depths of my psyche of which I never knew existed. Without contemplation or prior forethought a signature characteristic would soon emerge and create a simple straightforward definition summing up my on field personality.

I hadn't pitched since the Fall League and as my first game available for "live duty" went along I did my best to try and acclimate myself to my new bullpen surroundings. I was originally told upon my arrival that I would most likely be used in seventh- and eighth-inning set-up situations, so with that in mind I allowed the innings to pass and did what I thought I needed to do to have myself ready should such a situation arise.

It was early in the seventh inning and having no access to a bullpen phone my pitching coach, Guy Hansen, made a walk down from the dugout to talk with me in person.

"Hey Rock, Ivan Rodriguez is due up fourth next inning. If we get to him you've got him. Start getting loose."

Now many years later Pudge and I would become friends and battery mates while with the Texas Rangers. On this day, however, Pudge represented the most significant litmus test I had faced thus far during any point of my baseball life. To this point in my career I naturally had faced some very talented hitters. This scenario, however, went far beyond simply facing a "talented" hitter. This was one of the game's most prolific offensive weapons and proving to the baseball world I was capable of handling such threatening hitters was precisely why I was there. It's an understatement to say that Ivan signified the biggest out of my life and that "at bat" even to this day stands as one of if not the single most important hitter I ever faced.

I had come to realize over the past several days what my main purpose in Puerto Rico was. It was for the Atlanta Braves, along with myself, to find out if I could get guys like Ivan "Pudge" Rodriguez out or not. In a scenario such as this there are no C+ grades given. Either you pass or you fail. Not a big deal though; it's just your life. It's just the culmination of a decade-long journey that has now been confined to a finite number of situations that can ultimately determine if it was all worth it or not.

Following Guy's instructions I began getting a sweat going in preparation to meet the first legitimate Major League hitter I had ever faced. And what a task to pop your cherry. This wasn't some run-of-the-mill chump who had been sucking up Big League time as a journeyman utility guy. This was five-time All-Star (at the time), Gold Glove winner, future Hall-of-Famer, perennial .300 hitter, and local hero, Pudge Rodriguez.

"Well, I guess there'll be no "easing" in to this thing," I thought.

Now technically there was a condition to this pending showdown. Pudge was due up fourth in the top of the eighth; so a one, two, three inning would mean my "swimming lessons" would have to begin another night. I had become all too familiar over the last several months, however, with the various situations fate was consistently laying in front of me. Despite the possibilities, I knew my trial by fire would begin very shortly.

Sure enough, with the opening of the eighth the lead-off hitter reached right away. Now only a double play could divert the initial discovery of what my future may hold. At this point I could waste no time. My first significant test against a Big League stud was just two hitters and about two minutes away. The last decade of my life had been spent preparing and obsessively desiring to succeed in a situation such as this, thereby proving to the powers-that-be, as well as to myself, that I was worthy of realizing my dream. Succeed, and I could possibly spend the next decade living my fantasy. Fail, and …

As the final seconds ticked off the clock counting down towards this moment of truth the demons of the past decade began to come loose. The demons from the seemingly endless years of desire, of struggle, of sleepless nights in the back of buses with only redundant thoughts of Major League fantasy flowing through your mind, all of the pain, the sacrifice and physical exhaustion; it was all for a moment such as this that lay only seconds away, a moment which had more potential than any I had yet faced to propel me to the realization of what my entire life had come to revolve. The demons of a decade-long struggle came loose within me during the final minutes leading up to what I saw as the most significant doorway yet to my Big League future.

I was as loose as I was going to get. There was nothing further that could be done. The time was now. Was I good enough? Had I prepared enough during these long grueling years? Did I have what it took? Steadily pacing back and forth on top of the mound in that dimly lit bullpen of Mayaguez Stadium I was being held back by a dozen metaphorical chains, all waiting to snap as soon as the image of my manager, Tom Gamboa, was seen heading out to the mound to make the switch. The intensity within me continued to build at a surging pace. The demons were churning for freedom and seething to dominate this first challenge that had been placed before them.

Suddenly, when no more patience could be mustered, Tom emerged from the dugout and while heading for the mound raised a left arm to the bullpen. This was it. My first taste of the Big Leagues was just on the other side of that foul line. All at once the chains that hemmed me in and suppressed me to the lowly Minor Leagues were ripped away and I took off head long to seize my future. With no forethought or even conscious understanding as to why; I tore out for the center of that diamond fueled by the demons from ten years of unwavering desire and aspiration; scowl draped firmly across my face, eyes narrowed with the intention of throwing my fastball clean through Ivan's Louisville Slugger. And thus the signature charge from the bullpen was born and the final finishing touches to the on-field mentality were created.

Now Ivan is one of the best hitters I've ever had the pleasure of playing with or against. (On a quick side note, if you ever find yourself facing Pudge and your fortunate enough to work him into a two strike count DO NOT try and paint a fastball down and away. He WILL lace it to right field for you.) It was certainly special to have had the opportunity to play with him. As for the first night I met Ivan, however, I would not have wanted to be at the other end of what he was facing. I was absolutely slinging it that night and to this day when I close my eyes and reflect back I can still visualize with vivid clarity my 1-2 slider as it took a hard right turn six inches under Ivan's bat.

The first test had been passed with flying colors. At least for the time being it seemed I could float. Four pitches for the rest of your life, kid.

It has long been my belief that our perceptions, especially those that concern us specifically, will ultimately become our reality. With that principle in mind I began to perceive myself as Big League bound in the days following my successful encounter with Pudge, and as this belief began to grow and infiltrate my mentality I began to pitch in a way I never thought possible. As I sit back many years later with a much deeper understanding I still find it amazing what we can accomplish when we are able to overcome our own mental shortcomings about our presumed physical abilities or lack thereof. When the mind is unequivocally committed the body can accomplish anything.

With confidence birthing additional confidence the balance of my stay in Puerto Rico mimicked my initial outing against Ivan. At this point I saw myself as a Major Leaguer; I perceived my abilities to be that of a Major Leaguer; I carried myself as a Major Leaguer and held the firm belief that the actuality of finally becoming a Major Leaguer was just a simple formality. From that point forward I merely had to just "be" until the day which I was certain lay ahead finally arrived.

Despite being scarcely ten months removed from my mop-up days as a Durham Bull, when my first Major League spring training began I had every intention of making the club. Although putting up good numbers, I guess the all-knowing baseball gods deemed I was not quite ready to be a part of their show just yet and my talents were sent a bit farther up the road to the Triple A club in Richmond, Virginia.

Now, in past years a let down/set back such as this would have sent me into an all-out tail spin of mental doubt and anguish. I would have obsessed for days while whining, complaining and just plain irritating anyone within earshot about my struggle and the presumed unfairness of it all. This unanticipated scenario was received much differently this time, however. Instead of the neurotic fixation of my prior mentality I was barely fazed by this undesired development. I already knew I was physically prepared for Major League competition, and my reaction to what should have been an extremely disappointing situation finally convinced me that I was capable of handling the crucially important mental side the profession as well. At last, after enduring a maturation process that was nearly a decade in the making and included a roller coaster of highs and lows, I finally knew I was ready in all areas to step into my dream. It was now up to the decision makers to make that realization as well.

No matter how fulfilling a life one leads there will only be a handful of days where each and every detail will always be remembered with infinite clarity. Anyone who has children will never forget a single aspect of the day their child was born. All of us will remember exactly what we were doing when we learned a loved one had passed on. Anyone who has been married can likely recall every minute characteristic of how his or her engagement came to be. In situations such as these most of us can easily recollect what we were wearing, where we were standing, words that were said and by whom they were spoken.

At 36 years old I have only experienced a few of these days in my life. I've already referenced June 3, 1993 as being the first day I ever experienced such a phenomenon; May 3, 1998 became the second. One such day was May 3, 1998. For those of you who don't remember, May 3rd was a Sunday. It was for most a typical spring Sunday with weather still continuing to warm from the winter, which had only passed a few weeks before. For me, however, it was the day my life would change forever. It became the day I had been waiting on, preparing for and dreaming of since long before puberty. It was a day I had been chasing nearly my entire life with no guarantee of its arrival. I didn't know what May 3rd was going to mean to me when my eyes opened that morning, but by the time they closed that night it had become the greatest day of my life.

On this day I found myself in Charlotte, North Carolina, on the final day of a six game road trip, finishing out a series against the Florida Marlins' affiliate, the Charlotte Knights. So far during this new season the transformation that had taken place during the past six months was still in full effect. All the same principles and adjustments that had been made were still producing the same success I had enjoyed during the Fall League and Puerto Rico. Despite the fact that I was trying to break in with a perennial contender with a loaded staff, I still held firm to my mental surety that my time was very near.

As I arrived at the ballpark the haze with which the day had begun was burning away and a warm spring sun was peaking through the clouds. Batting practice had not been schedule for this Sunday day game; so I took my time getting ready and then lazily made my way down to the field to play some catch with Rudy Seanez and prepare for the one o'clock start as we listened to Marilyn Manson's "The Beautiful People" on the stadium sound system. On the way off the field I can recall having a brief conversation with my parents and two of their friends who had made the four-hour trip up from Macon to catch the game. Other than that I can't recall much detail to the early part of the day.

As the game started and rolled along it was typical of the thousands of other games I had been a part of. Guys got hits, guys got out, a pitcher walked someone followed by a strike out. It was blatantly ordinary and offered nothing I hadn't already seen hundreds upon hundreds of times. Other than pitching a scoreless ninth to earn a save and preserve a 4-1 Richmond victory there was not much that was even moderately special about the game itself. Just a few short minutes after recording that final out, however, this mundane, game number 28 of the 1998 Triple A season was going to take on a significance like no other I had ever been a part of or would ever be again.

After the on-field congratulating was over for a job well done it was up to the clubhouse to shower, eat a little dinner and then climb on the bus back to the hotel. Little did I know the final minutes of my dream were being lived. Ten years had been reduced to a final ten minutes.

Post game, the clubhouse was functioning according to the normal order of things. Guys were packing up, getting undressed, eating their dinner, engaging in various forms of mindless conversation and just as I had done after hundreds of other games I was going through my normal routine. I walked to my locker, took off my jersey and spikes, put on my flip-flops and headed to the kitchen to get rid of my appetite. Then out of nowhere my life turned on a dime.

On May 3, 1998, after a 4-1 victory over the Charlotte Knights of the International League, while striding through the clubhouse in my gray road pants, flip flops and black undershirt carrying a plate of post-game dinner, my manager, Jeff Cox, met me in the center of the room. With a smile spread across his face that would only be slightly overshadowed by the one that was about to appear on mine Coxy uttered the words that to this day mark the greatest sounds I have ever heard. After 10 long years of trials, sacrifice, anguish, blood, sweat and seemingly endless hours of grueling work and effort it instantly became all worth it. Standing in the middle of the visitor's clubhouse in Charlotte, North Carolina wearing gray road pants and white flip flops holding a plate of food in my hand in the blink of an eye with a single breath it all ended. The dreaming was over.

"Hey Rock, the big club had to put Wholers on the DL after the game today. They need you in Atlanta for tomorrow night's game against the Dodgers. Congratulations, John; you're going to the Big Leagues."

And just like that, it was all over. The dream which had spawned from a simple love of the game that originated on little league fields, sandlots, and playgrounds was now a reality. That metaphorical boulder which had pushed heavily against me for all those years was finally at the top of the imaginary yet all-too-real mountain with me finally standing right beside it.

I have always considered myself to be somewhat handy with words. This book you've been reading was crafted almost entirely from my own personal hand. Yet that event, those thirty seconds of life, that contained a brief simple phrase which held the information that the journey which had lasted over half of my lifetime was now over; I do not have the words to describe all of the thoughts, feelings and emotions that consumed me during that instant yet those indescribable sensations will forever be burned into my soul. It is a moment I will reflect upon even in my dying hour. There are no words that can be used to accurately express an event that has the ability to stay with you like that and it's probably best not to even try.

Finally the circle had been completed. The fear, doubt and anxiety which plagued me those many years had all been for nothing, while the monumental dream that had once seemed light-years away had proven to be well worth dreaming. It had been four-and-a-half long years and a lifetime of experiences since I stepped off the field in old Fulton County Stadium with no way of knowing if I would ever find myself with a Major League diamond under my feet again. I guess the gods of baseball had chosen to smile on me and finally bring me into their flock, of which I will be eternally grateful.

A split second before delivering my first pitch in the major leagues. It was a fastball strike down and away to Todd Hollingsworth.

A split second after delivering my first pitch in the major leagues.

I will forever be indebt to baseball's supernatural beings for allowing me to become one of the miniscule fortunate few who have the ability to say "I fulfilled my ultimate childhood dream." As I've said before, many dream and some dream big, but very few ever wake up to discover their dream has become a reality. I will always feel privileged that I woke up to such a discovery and will always be at ease knowing that the satisfaction of that fulfillment will live inside of me until the day I die. Despite all of the hardships, stresses and battles, the juice was definitely worth the squeeze.

I'm sure there are many out there who have imagined what it must be like to live the life of a Major League ball player. Let me be the first to tell you that whatever thoughts you may have; multiply them by a thousand. As it was tough for me to describe my initial feelings upon learning that in fact I was going to be a part of that life, it is similarly difficult to convey the actuality of what that existence is truly like. I feel the best description I can offer is summed up neatly and succinctly in an extremely uncomplicated monologue from the movie Bull Durham by the character known as Crash Davis when he states, "Yeah, I was in the show. I was in the show for 21 days once; the greatest 21 days of my life. You know, you never handle your own luggage in the Show. Someone else carries your bags. It was great. You hit white balls for batting practice; the ballparks are like cathedrals; the hotels all have room service and the women all have long legs and brains." At a glance this narrative may seem much too crude and simple to adequately describe the pageantry that must encompass a life of Major League fantasy. Just as this quote, however, contains a kind of "elegant" simplicity, it so too is the elementary and pure aspects of the game of baseball that grasp the Major League player at his core, as most of us fell in love with this game while we were just mere children, and as the love grew the game gradually became a part of us and to some degree or another always will be.

It's the love of the game's purity that lives inside the Major League athlete and unless you've been there I wouldn't even know where to begin trying to pass along such an internal dynamic. It's what he's been through to get where he is that makes the game so special to him. It's the unconscious knowledge that he is the best of the best of the best at what he does. All the while he loves the game like a father loves a son yet in this bizarre world has found a scenario by which he actually gets paid to do something he would gladly do for free. Playing the game is like a physical characteristic to him just the same as having brown hair or blue eyes. Playing the game is not what he does; it is who he is and will be so until the day he is no longer on this earth.

Sure, the fanfare is great, the private planes and five-star hotels are nice as well, but if none of that existed the Major League player still would. He would play in the lowliest, most thankless of places if that was the only option made available to him and for most of his life that's exactly what he's done. He plays because the game is in his soul and always will be. He enjoys the perks, but at the end of the day he's a guy with sweat on his brow, chalk and dirt under his finger nails and on his uniform, pine tar on his palms, the smell of leather in his nose and rosin on his hat and at that moment is as happy as he will ever be. I will leave this earth one day, and on the day I do I will still be a Major League ball player. It's truly a beautiful life.

I was allowed to live my ultimate fantasy for six years and will always feel unbelievably blessed for having had the opportunity to do so. I have talked many times about having the "dream" to become a Major League ball player, but when my "dream" finally became a reality it all still seemed like a dream.

I was fortunate enough for the gods to allow me to be a part of some incredible things during my time among them. Being part of a World Series in Yankee Stadium along side the ghosts of Ruth, Mantle and DiMaggio, as a baseball purist, is the pinnacle of anything that could ever be desired for someone like me. In the "coming of age" years I would have never imagined being a part of something so amazing. I also will always greatly appreciate the opportunity I was given during my first four seasons to play for teams that perennially won 100-plus games. I fully comprehend what a blessing it was to be a part of so many truly great teams, and why the gods allowed me that good fortune I will never know, but will always be grateful.

To me, the experiences in and around the game which I was lucky enough to enjoy have done a great deal to shape the person I will be for the rest of my life. I will be forever thankful to have had the opportunity to play in the postseason for four years of my career and to be a part of so many unforgettable events that took place, many of which will live forever within the eye of my mind and the soul of my heart. I will reflect until I am too old to hold a thought in my head on my first at-bat in the Major Leagues, which took place in game five of the 1998 National League Championship Series. I walked on four pitches and then scored

A somewhat pieced together bullpen that managed to have the 3rd best ERA in the league that year. (That's Adam Butler 3rd from right)

the tying run from first on a one-out double by Tony Graffanino while running over the catcher.

As I sit here now, I can still picture the scene through my own eyes as third base coach, Bobby Dews, waves me around third in front of 70,000 raucous San Diego fans who were begging me to lose the foot race with the incoming throw from deep left-center field. Upon arriving home just ahead of the relay I can still feel the physical sensation as I barrel into Carlos Hernandez to plate the games tying run. What a way to cap off your first Major League AB!

I was fortunate enough to be a part of many other great moments, like the night I notched my first Major League save, in an effort which preserved a victory for my good friend Dennis Martinez, whereby making him the winningest Latin pitcher of all time. I still have high hopes that one day that victory will someday propel Dennis into the Hall of Fame and I feel so thankful to have been a part of Denny's historic night.

I will always have a fond recollection of a game I was lucky enough to get a victory in when I was with the Cleveland Indians, which marked the largest come back in baseball history. Down by twelve runs in the seventh inning our hard-hitting lineup, with names like Thome, Burks, Gonzalez and Fryman, mounted a rally in the final two innings against the Seattle Mariners (who won 114 games that

The end result of my first major league at bat which came during game 2 of the NCLS against San Diego. Don't stand on the track when the train is coming through.

Pop the corks! Team mob at home plate after the last out of the 99' National League Championship Series

All fired up!

year) to send us into extras. We walked off the field that night with a 15-14 victory in 11, marking the biggest comeback of all time. It was one of the greatest games I've ever been involved in.

I will also relive over and over again in my aging years what I consider to be the best performance of my career and perhaps my favorite game of which I was ever a participant. I would qualify it as my greatest baseball memory of all time and have had numerous people stop me on the street and tell me it was theirs as well. I've already briefly mentioned game three of the 1999 National League Division Series in the Houston Astrodome. With the series tied at one a piece, game three was knotted at 3 all in the bottom of the tenth. Russ Springer, who had a tremendous season that year, didn't have his best stuff that day and loaded the bases with nobody out. As I've had a bit of a tough time in this chapter conveying specific emotions, it would take a writer much more talented than I to describe what I was feeling and thinking while getting loose to come into the game that afternoon. With each passing second the crowd inside that dome grew louder and louder as the Astros inched ever closer to pushing the winning run across home plate and taking a 2-1 series lead.

I would love to have seen the look on my face as my charge from the bullpen came to an end on top of that mound and I was handed the game ball by Bobby. Well, two ground balls (one of which is in my top-five greatest plays of all time) and a punch-out later I erupted into a primal scream toward the heavens and 50,000 now-dejected Houston fans on my way off the field. It was undoubtedly the most intense moment of my career, and as I've mentioned we won in 12 and took the series the next day. Perhaps my greatest baseball memory and thoughts of that game can still put me in a daze of daydreams when I stop and think back.

I could go on and on with fond recollections of my days inside the golden gates because even a bad day in the Big Leagues is better than a good day doing anything else. Besides having had many great experiences that have created invaluable lifetime memories, the baseball gods also bestowed upon me the opportunity to play with some tremendous players. I will always consider myself unbelievably fortunate to have spent significant time in the presence of three of the game's greatest pitchers of all time, Greg Maddux, Tom Glavine, and John Smoltz. Do you have any idea what it means to a baseball purist to have front row seats night after night to watch those three line up and toe the rubber? It was truly a blessing to have spent four seasons as a part of one of the greatest pitching staffs ever assembled. I will always consider that as one of the most special aspects of my career.

I also hold a high degree of appreciation for having had the pleasure of playing with many other outstanding players. Being able to say I played along side such legends as Jim Thome, Ellis Burks, Robbie Alomar, Ivan Rodriguez, Juan Gonzalez, Alex Rodriguez, Rafael Palmeiro, Chipper Jones, Omar Vizquel and Michael Young, just to name a few, truly holds a special place within the memories of my career. Of course by the shear simple fact we were Big Leaguers means all the guys I played with were extremely talented, but playing along side guys that you know are Hall-of-Fame bound is really a treat and I will always consider myself very fortunate to have shared a diamond with them.

All in all, the memories I possess along with the experiences I had and the relationships I forged are my most valued possessions in this life. For more than two decades I dedicated everything I had and everything I was to the fulfillment and sustainment of this dream. If I could create a perfect world I would still have a jersey on my back and a mound under my feet, but as we all know, however, the baseball gods giveth, and they also taketh away.

A group bullpen photo with the shirts the guys made to feed my ego.

CHAPTER FIVE

The Gods Giveth and The Gods Taketh Away

I died on a Sunday evening. While dining at a restaurant in Melbourne, Florida, on December 19, 1999, I came face to face with the grim reaper, who appeared before me in the form of media's biased scrutiny and rabid lust for the sensational, and watched as my soul was put to death right before my very eyes. There was no discretion taken, there was no objectivity considered, there was no truth sought: A mafia-style murder with a proverbial bullet to the back of the head to appease the godfather of sensationalism for the sake of ratings and drama. Exploitation at its finest.

Now of course I didn't die in a literal sense that day, but I might as well have. Technically, I'm still breathing and the soulless shell that is my body continues to walk around upright appearing to be intact. Make no mistake about it, however, everything inside of me that day, everything I worked a lifetime to become, who I was at the core of my being which took more than a decade to create was laid to waste in one fell blow all for the sake of selling a few fucking magazines. The death to my one chance in life, the death of my hopes and dreams, which will never be again. The death of my family's name. All for $3.95. At this point all that's left is a flesh-covered shell inhabited by a beating heart right next to where a soul once existed. I hope it was worth it.

In the ten years since my assassination a steady barrage of the media's venom has continued to poison the still-living, breathing person known as John Rocker.

For what reason I can not tell; to serve what purpose I am not sure, and most likely will never have a full understanding as to why thousands of vilifying articles have been penned in my "honor" and many more commentaries spoken as if in some way I personally harmed the journalists who now spew their vitriol consistently in my direction. Maybe degrading me in some way makes the degrader feel a sense of politically correct superiority. As if to say to his/her audience; "I would never think, feel, or dare speak such politically incorrect foulness as came forth from John Rocker's mouth, and just to show you how pious I am; I will now chastise him..."

In my opinion, it should take much more than a solitary article to indefinitely brand a man with the type of polarizing labels created by a four-page transcript in a sporting magazine. Yet to this day, the cover piece in the December 1999 issue of Sports Illustrated contains the only ideas, accusations and claims that have ever existed in such a realm, and despite the media's relentless attempts to support their theology, no other proof has ever been discovered. Even after months and months of persistent searching in attempts to find a collaborating party, no such person was discovered to give the media the secondary confirmation for which they were so desperately looking. No one from the 21 years I resided in Macon, Georgia. No one from the nearly 10 years I spent with the Atlanta Braves organization. None of the dozens of people from all walks of life and from all parts of my past ever agreed with the accusations the media in their witch hunt for the sensational were and to this day continue to make. Despite the unrelenting attempts, the media's foot soldiers only received consistent accounts speaking to the contrary of their vicious claims and as such were largely unreported.

With this dynamic in mind is it not an understatement to assume that with the public's appetite for the ever-precious fifteen minutes of fame someone would have emerged, solicited or otherwise, longing to have their face appear on TV or be quoted in the New York Post confirming everything that media so desperately wants to be true about me. Recent history has unequivocally proven that after the first "domino" falls it's generally an all out land rush to the head of the line, seeking to voice a supporting claim or accusation and enjoy those fifteen glorious minutes. In most recent history, how long did it take the mistresses of Tiger Woods to come forward after number one was first discovered? You wouldn't see women move that fast if Tiffany announced they were giving away free diamonds. (A joke — lighten up!)

With me specifically, however, the only ones who ever came forward adamantly insisted the media's claims to be incorrect. Yet anyone with a media credential in hand will hold as belief to his dying day an opinion regarding me that was derived from a lone writer/assassin, Jeff Pearlman, who possesses an extremely long and rich history of vilifying, defaming, degrading, damning and chastising nearly every subject he encounters. A writer who's nearly 20-year career in journalism mimics a postwar battle field littered with mangled bodies that were once the focus of his ambush style of defamatory "journalism."

Taking the accolades of those with talent far beyond that of merely pushing a pencil, Pearlman seems to gain his sustenance from trying to destroy and demean the character and accomplishments of those who in some cases have succeeded to legendary heights. From individuals such as David Wells, Roger Clemens, Barry Bonds and Brian Cashman to entire teams like the 1986 Mets and even dynasties like the 1990's Dallas Cowboys, Pearlman's "M.O." for nearly two decades has been that of nothing more than a beauty-parlor gossip whore cattily airing presumed and most times irrelevant dirty laundry about "Susie Johnson" supposedly having an affair with "Mr. Smith the banker" or making sure that everyone in town knows "Alice Butler" has a drinking problem. It is truly pathetic and abhorable the tone and angle Pearlman seems to take with obnoxious consistency. I guess if you can't be one of them, you might as well exploit them.

Whether it's supposed drug abuse, a racial angle or attacks on something as straightforward and irrelevant as someone's physical appearance, this bottom feeder of "sports" journalism always seems to have, or create, or invent, or embellish, or … or … or … anything he can to make sure he stays squarely in the vein of "Jerry Springer" journalism. Shit sells and Jeff certainly can sling it. I have been personally approached on several occasions by people who are/were involved in the athletic programs at the University of Delaware who say Pearlman has been running this gig since his early college years there and was finally ostracized from a number of the athletic facilities and programs as a result.

In article after article, book after book, the hateful, degrading "shtick" seems to be the same. In a piece about David Wells which should have focused on Wells' upcoming start in the 2000 All-Star Game, and the fact that David was leading the AL in strikeouts, ERA and wins and was poised to win the AL Cy Young, Pearlman instead spent nearly three pages of Sports Illustrated magazine space sarcastically focusing on David's physical stature, physique, somewhat unkempt facial hair and off-field lifestyle. After the interview and subsequent article, Wells responded, "All it talks about is me being fat and what I did when I was in New York basically. Read it. It's stupid. The guy screwed John Rocker and all of a sudden I'm victim number two."

Well unfortunately for the American public, who must be infiltrated by the writings of this no-talent clown, David was by no means "victim number two." Nearly everyone who has the distasteful pleasure of coming within any remote version of contact with Pearlman is worse for the experience. In the grotesque work "The

Rocket That Fell to Earth" Pearlman uses quite a holier-than-thou approach in his chastisement of perhaps the games greatest and most decorated pitcher of all time, Roger Clemens. To which Clemens responded, "He's a low life wanna-be. By his looks he could star on 'The Addams Family.'"

Additionally, in the same cesspool of literary garbage the GM of the New York Yankees, Brian Cashman was also dragged into the mix of Pearlman's typical efforts at demonizing. Cashman, who has never personally met the author, was quoted in the book when Pearlman cites a comment that was supposedly made by Cashman in which the GM was reportedly watching Jason Giambi on television and yelled at the screen for Giambi to "get back on whatever you were taking in Oakland." After being contacted by reporters from the New York Times, Cashman adamantly denied the authenticity of the comment and said he was never contacted by Pearlman to discuss the quote, saying, "You would think he would have done some fact-checking." But Brian, with all due respect, if Jeff checks his facts and is actually held to the truth and some form of ethics, he would be unable to sling the kind of filth and pointless degrading blather he is so lovingly endeared to. Pearlman allowed the phantom quote to run in the hardback version, but removed it in the paper back; so at least there would only be lying, fabricated BS in half the copies in circulation. But hey, that's how Jeffy gets those delicious little rumors started that sell his books! The truth is overrated anyway.

I obviously can relate on a very personal level to Pearlman's hit-and-run style of trash journalism through my own experience and from those of my fellow baseball brethren. Many of us within the baseball fraternity have fallen victim to his irrelevant damnation so much so that Sports Illustrated no longer employs his "talents." Sort of hard to work for a sporting magazine as their baseball writer when any athlete you're attempting to interview had rather sit down with a guy wearing a bomb than talk to you. It wasn't too many years after the articles concerning me and Wells that Pearlman was basically blackballed throughout the league.

Don't think, however, that such a minor setback would deter Jeff from pushing forward in his commitment to spread irrelevant filth and dirty laundry the world over. In his most recent endeavor Pearlman actually has the guts or gutlessness (however you want to look at it) to attack the character and name of one of America's greatest sports icons, Walter Payton. In typical fashion Pearlman runs the same redundant scathing play where by taking the untarnished name of a revered legend and pissing all over it. With what many feel are undocumented accounts, Pearlman irreverently drones on regarding Payton's supposed addiction to painkillers, thoughts of suicide and as every juicy gossip-laden book needs, the report of a long-time mistress.

"I'd spit on the author of the Walter Payton book," snapped former legendary

Chicago Bear coach and long time Payton friend Mike Ditka. "(The book is) Pathetic. Despicable. It serves no purpose. What's the point? What's the point? The point is one thing only — to sell books. It's a bunch of crap, first of all."

It's well known among the athletes of the sporting community who are privy to the private, behind-the-scenes lives and personalities of Pearlman's targets to a degree which the lay fan is not that the author is nothing more than an elementary schoolyard brat stirring the pot with false assumptions and misplaced defamation with the pen he holds in his little hand in an effort to peddle his useless works of literature. Maybe the degradation of others in some way gives Jeff the ability to tolerate his own short-comings and self-loathing.

Whatever the justification may be the mystery that resides within me will always be the same as to why media for more than 10 long years has emphatically insisted I am the man who Jeff Pearlman painted me to be. Even after literally dozens of people who have been close to me for decades in some cases have tried to straighten the record it still seems to be hell bent in a biased direction. Even after my dearest friend since childhood, Ched Smaha and his family, who are third generation Lebanese immigrants, conducted numerous interviews in my defense; the labels still remain. Even after very publicly dating an African American woman for nearly three years, the media, who insisted it was a publicity stunt, (I moved her to Atlanta, Georgia from New York City, of all places. Quite a THREE-YEAR "PR" stunt, huh?) still adamantly claim I am a racist. And even despite the dozens of teammates such as Javy Lopez, Otis Nixon, Andruw Jones, Chan Ho Park, Rudy Seanez, Ellis Burks, C.C. Sabathia, many of whom are still good friends insisting contrarily to what one "man" with a consistent propensity for trash journalism who spent one day with me wrote; to the media I am and always will be a monster.

In the coming pages, I plan to revisit some of the issues that were raised in that damning Sports Illustrated article which have given leave for some to define me as a racist, homophobic Neanderthal. In the midst of lengthy discussion I did say, "one of the things I don't like about New York City are the foreigners." As well as "I'm not a very big fan of foreigners…" The "meat" and context around such a crude comment leaves a much different impression to most, however.

It is my strong feeling that if a person has immigrated to this country legally and has the desire to become a productive member of our American society then I wish them all the success they can possibly achieve. In no way am I oblivious to the fact that in some form or fashion we are all products of the successful migration of our ancestors and should feel very blessed to be a part of that lucky sperm club. On the other hand, there have been, are, and will continue to be that segment of immigrant who simply doesn't think the rules of our ancestors apply to them. Many of these people have no respect for our immigration policies as our great-grandparents once did. They have no respect for our American heritage and, in my opinion, the main thought within some of their minds when they illegally penetrate our borders is to see just how thoroughly they can exploit all that this great country has to offer.

If you are that type of immigrant, then Sports Illustrated got it right. I sure as hell don't like you, and have high hopes that at some point you will be forced to drag your freeloading, parasitic ass back to wherever it is that you came from. If that belief system bothers you then I guess you do have a problem with me and for that I apologize. I apologize for feeling that everyone should play by the same set of rules. I apologize for feeling that you have to put something in before you can take something out. I apologize for feeling that while you're in Rome you should do as the Romans.

I will always have great respect and admiration for all the immigrants of yesterday, today and tomorrow who have come and hopefully will continue to come to this country in a legitimate manner; do things the right way and work hard to build a better life for themselves and their families. America would not be a glimmer of the nation it is without people such as that. To those immigrants I say "thank you" and will always welcome you with open arms. To those of you who don't have the moral conviction and ethical fortitude to do things the right way you should be ashamed of yourselves. It is a pathetic life you lead embezzling your satisfaction and security from the hard work and effort of so many who have chosen to do things the way they should be done. To those with desires of exploitation I hope America is a cold place for you and have faith that one day our government will have the ability to not only give you a one-way ticket back to wherever it was you defected from, but also to keep you there until the time comes when are ready to come back and join America on OUR terms, not yours. We would love to have you, but according the set of rules all prior generations have followed. (By the way, that was basically the same conversation I had with Jeff Pearlman, who simply decided to crudely state that I "don't like foreigners.")

In the next several chapters I will add some much needed "meat" to the "bones" of specific comments, which were not just sentence fragments, but were fragments of fragments creating the desired outcome, which Pearlman, based on his proven track record, most likely intended from the start. For over a decade the media has emphatically insisted that Jeff Pearlman has given a much more accurate depiction of me than that of my closest friends and colleagues who have spoken on my behalf over the past several years. The media have insisted that the crudely disgusting sentence fragments with which Pearlman used to create his image of me are as accurate as testimony given under oath while seeming to never take into consideration the extremely consistent tone of Pearlman's writings or the numerous contrary accounts of those who actually know me best. In the upcoming chapters my voice and my voice alone will speak concerning the issues for which labels such as bigot, racists, intolerant, homophobic, etc., have followed me these many years. After reading the coming dialogue you may still think I am a bigoted intolerant racist and if so that's fine, but maybe to some degree at least the label of "idiot" may be removed.

CHAPTER SIX

The Myth of Free Speech

It seems to me the term "free speech" has become more of an oxymoron than an absolute.

Ideally, we are all given the undeniable right to speak freely, according to our Constitution. I technically have the right to speak just as you supposedly do. In a perfect world my rights should be no different than yours. I don't think given the stage of the world's social climate, however, that anyone is kidding themselves any longer with the ridiculous notion that our world is perfect. Our "perfect" world was replaced many moons ago by the grossly imperfect reality in which we all currently reside, and one of the blatant imperfections with which we all must deal is the censorship that undoubtedly exists for some while never darkening the door of others.

I can already hear the screams of the Media for using the "c" word, but that's exactly what it is. Oh, it may not be the same censorship that exists in the Chinas and North Koreas of the world, but rest assured it is censorship nonetheless. One may not have their toe nails pulled out or be thrown into a Red Chinese prison for speaking inappropriately, but rest assured if you say something that media in their infinite, self-proclaimed wisdom deem to be unsuitable; you WILL be sternly rebuked. You WILL be publically scrutinized. You WILL be verbally assaulted. And you WILL be made an example of for all others to witness which blares at 120 decibels: "YOU SEE WHAT HAPPENED TO THIS GUY? YOU'VE BEEN

WARNED!" The good Lord knows I'm living proof.

What gives any of us the right to judge another's commentary that may express opinions that differ from our own? Shouldn't free speech give us all the right to say what's on our minds and have the media cover it without bias? Why is it that media determine which comments and which philosophies are correct and which ones are not even supposed to slip past our lips?

I admittedly made comments during an interview for Sports Illustrate in the winter of 1999 that when presented as they were would make even the most foul-mouthed racist blush. Upon reading that article for the first time and seeing those comments in the context in which they were used it even made me squeamish. There is no other way to react. They came across cold, heartless and as they were presented just downright mean.

I consider myself very fortunate, however, to have the opportunity to write this book and put some much needed "meat" around the "bones" of those glaringly cruel statements. Entire chapters have been penned discussing such things as the state of immigration in our country, and the lack of desire held by many immigrants to assimilate to our culture in simple yet integral ways, like speaking our native English language. These chapters in large part contain much of the same conversation which was had that faithful day in 1999 in which all that was taken away and placed into an extremely scathing article was, "John Rocker hates all foreigners" and "John Rocker hates you if you can't speak English". What a ridiculously obnoxious notion, but people bought it and the media loved selling it.

At the end of the day my opinion is irrelevant, but the right I have to freely voice my opinion certainly is not. English biographer Evelyn Beatrice Hall paraphrased French writer Voltaire when she wrote, in 1906, "I disapprove of what you say, but will defend to the death your right to say it." Something tells me the media never got that memo; they certainly don't behave as such.

Now I absolutely don't expect my words to be defended no matter how irresponsibly they were reported, but I do expect my ability to speak freely without the fear of being publicly prosecuted by media. In my opinion it is this fear of unrestricted persecution with which the media in their subverted way ultimately censors us all. Media, in large part, does not exist without the provisions which are laid out in our First Amendment, yet voice one statement in which they do not agree and you'll quickly learn just how limited your presumed rights actually are.

Fortunately or unfortunately, however you want to look at it, these limitations do not apply equally to all. In our society there is a clear double standard in relation to free speech on a host of issues which generally stems from the media — or their sponsors' — definition of what is acceptable and what is not, what should be considered inappropriate or what is fair comment with the ultimate determinative factor existing within the answer to one simple question, "From whose mouth did these words come?"

The media have declared themselves judge, jury and executioner in the world of free speech and political correctness, and if you offer up an opinion they don't agree with rest assured they are going to put the crosshairs right on you.

I have often wondered why I have been such an intriguing character of negativity with the liberal media of this country. This question further puzzled me about a year after the Sports Illustrated article was published when Allen Iverson, an African American basketball player for the Philadelphia 76ers, wrote and produced a rap album where he "sang" about raping women, killing police officers, and murdering homosexuals. Now it would seem logical to me that, if media, supposedly being fair and unbiased, actually wanted to live up to the expectation of being impartial on issues of political correctness, wouldn't it make sense that Mr. Iverson should have been attacked as vigorously, if not more so, by media than I was? Shouldn't 4,000 articles have been written about him over a ten-year period of time reciting his lyrics and then offering up opinions of what the NBA and society should do with him and/or to him?

I watched intently as this whole episode unfolded as I saw the obvious similarities and as I recall, Iverson made a half-hearted apology on ESPN, received a small fine by the NBA and the whole thing blew over in about a week and basically has never been spoken of again. He wrote, sang and recorded lyrics about raping women and killing cops, whereas I made some objectionable and ill-advised statements and quips in a magazine article, none of which were violent in nature that were handpicked out of nearly ten hours of very long winded commentary and more than a decade later I am still identified with them more than I am my accomplishments as a Major League pitcher.

Why do you think these two situations while moderately similar in nature were handled so drastically different by media? I have my theories but would be more interested in hearing yours. Whatever the correct logic may be, one thing is for certain, as far as the media of the United States of America is concerned: I do not have the same rights to speak freely as Mr. Iverson possesses. With that in mind I would like to take this opportunity now to inform Mr. Iverson in case for some odd reason he doesn't already know that he has hereby been given the right to speak freely. I can't help but wonder when that same right will be granted to me.

I've been told by some that I didn't stand a chance and probably still don't as I am a successful, conservative white male from the South. The liberal New York media, at least, is never going to cut me a break. It's almost as if it doesn't really matter what has been said but much more importantly who the speaker is.

One story I can recall absolutely blew my mind. I was in Cleveland a few years back giving a live radio interview to two hosts of a sports talk show; one host was white while the other was black.

The commentary began something like this, "Now John, five years ago you made some comments in a Sports Illustrated article that have many people labeling you a racist," is basically how the show started.

"Are you a racist?"

My response was, "Absolutely not." (I mean, if I were, it sure would have come as a shock to my black girlfriend of 3 years)

Upon my response, the black host of the show identified himself to the audience as a black man and said, "Well John, I actually am a racist."

After this comment all parties present pretty much seemed unfazed. There was no Jesse Jackson-esque activist calling in with threats of picketing the station and the show's producer did not threaten the man with his job.

Instead, the show simply continued with the next question. Now, for the black host of a radio show interviewing me to admit he is a racist would suggest several things to me: First of all, he hates me; secondly, he hates his white co-host along with a great number of his listeners. And to this comment no one seemed to be bothered. Imagine for a second that a different scenario had taken place. Suppose that when the host of this show had asked the question, "[John] Are you a racist?" I had responded in the affirmative. Can you imagine the excrement filled storm that would have been ensued! I cannot even fathom the fallout from my teammates at the time, Major League Baseball, the Cleveland Indians organization, as well as the backlash from the "Rainbow Push Coalitions" of the world. It would have been an absolute disaster, yet when this black host openly admitted during a live radio interview to in fact being a racist no one skipped a beat. Tu' comprende, "double standard?"

My personal experiences make a point, but there are certainly other situations that blatantly reveal the double standard created by the media in choosing who to persecute and whom not to. Bethany Hamilton was a 13-year-old white girl who lost her arm to a shark in a tragic surfing accident in Hawaii. Tom Joyner was at the time was a nationally syndicated black radio host. Shortly after Miss Hamilton was attacked, Joyner and his black co-host morbidly teased the young girl about her tragic accident. They made specific references to the fact that she is white, and they sang a version of 'Mack the Knife' with words including;

"When that shark bites / He bites only Whites /

Stay out de water, White people / Shark's gonna bite you /

That's why he keeps on bitin' White."

Followed by mocking laughter.

This radio personality was nationally syndicated by ABC at the time and as far as

I know was never reprimanded, fined, suspended etc. and the story largely got very little attention. Once again, reverse the roles and imagine the outcome.

I like to call it the "haves" and the "have-nots" of free speech.

Imagine Rush Limbaugh trying to get away with that — not that I think it would ever occur to him to make fun of someone's tragic accident no matter what race or creed they are. But a similar occurrence did take place involving Rush when he spent a brief (very brief) stint as a host on a Sunday morning NFL countdown show. Limbaugh's tenure was so short lived due to his infringement upon a cardinal media rule that basically must be followed by any cracker. Limbaugh engaged in a discussion in which he criticized Donovan McNabb, who was the quarterback for the Philadelphia Eagles and is an African American man, not that it should make any difference. But Rush said he believed McNabb was getting undeserved attention and credit for the team's performances than was warranted because of his race. Now this comment is in no way, shape or form a malicious or racially charged comment. Limbaugh simply stated his OPINION that he felt the media gave Donovan McNabb more credit than he deserved because he is African American. Needless to say, the media took yet another opportunity to show conservatives — especially white males — that comments made about minorities are strictly off limits. Rush Limbaugh was fired the very next day after criticism from the black community along with unbridled media support for that criticism.

Why in Limbaugh's case was he fired and then publicly ridiculed by the media for making a comment much less inflammatory than the black radio host I sat in front of? If the answer is not obvious to you then maybe this scenario will help create some thought. James Brown was also a co-host of Limbaugh's on the same NFL morning show who happens to be a black man. Let's create a hypothetical situation by which Mr. Brown had made the exact same comment about Donovan McNabb instead of Rush Limbaugh. Do you think there is a snowball's chance in hell that Brown would have been fired or even moderately chastised by anyone including the media? Don't kid yourself. In this situation and in so many others it is becoming glaringly obvious that the comments themselves don't matter to the media or even the general public for that matter who in large part are merely spoon fed their opinions by media — but who says them certainly does.

Now on a lighter note, but an equally thought provoking one I think. I am a big fan of Chris Rock. I think his standup comedy routines are some of the funniest I've ever seen. His routines which have brought me to tears on a number of occasions also create another surface for discussion regarding the discrepancy between the "haves" and "have nots" of free speech. Chris Rock regularly jokes about everything from race to sex and pretty much all that's in between during his act. One night I was watching an HBO special of his when he began making light of certain racial scenarios. Chris started giving his opinion of whom black people did and did not hate in the realm of race and ethnicity. His comments were as follows: "Let's get one thing straight. Black people don't hate Chinese people; black people don't hate Latin people. Black people hate white people ..."

I fully understand that Chris Rock is a comedian and was merely trying — and succeeded, in getting a rise out of his crowd. But imagine instead in a hypothetical scenario that it had been Robin Williams on stage in front of 5,000 people and being televised to millions more saying "Let's get one thing straight — white people hate black people!"

Can you even comprehend such a situation? The NAACP, Jesse Jackson, Rev. Al Sharpton and a host of activists carrying lit torches would set up a gallows pole and demanded the man's head before sundown. It would be the END of Robin Williams' career just as Michael Richards and Mel Gibson will probably never make it back to Hollywood's Big Table again. And who, may I ask, would give the NAACP and the Rainbow PUSH Coalition their soapbox to stand on? America's print, radio and television media of course. And just whose side do you suppose they would take? Would members of the journalistic community defend with even one breath Williams' right to free speech in this imaginary scenario? Would anyone paraphrase Voltaire and disagree with what has been said, but defend to the death Mr. Williams' right to say it? I think the mere idea of presenting such hypothetical questions is absurd. We all know and have witnessed time and time again the treatment delivered to those who sit on the wrong side of the proverbial free speech fence by media and the self-proclaimed "PC Police."

It's no secret that the media has taken its obsession with racism and diversity and tried to force feed their ideas into American culture. The media loves diversity. It loves diversity in the workplace. It loves diversity in our schools and universities. And the media certainly loves diversity in their newsrooms. They love diversity of race, religion, and sexual orientation — just about anything that can make one person different from another; they're in to it. It's almost as if the majority of media is engaged in some grand race to moral superiority based on who can display the greatest appearance of accepting diversity through rhetoric, work surroundings, lifestyle, etc.

What I can't quite comprehend, however, is why it seems media is so against diversity of thoughts and opinions.

I think it's pretty difficult to argue that mass media in North America is very left leaning. My co-writer, J. Marshall Craig, was a radio, television and newspaper writer and editor for roughly 20 years. He IS a liberal, and an immigrant at that. Through the beauty of the exchange of unimpeded ideas in our friendship, we have had great conversations where by his life experiences have made me reconsider some of my previously held opinions and he has told me I have, with my life's experiences, helped him become more clearly and widely informed about certain issues.

He has told me that he has always experienced a left bias in media — with the exception of occasional right-wing columnists or commentators who, he himself claims, have a far harder road to traverse than a columnist or commentator who is as equally extreme with liberal views, unless that journalist is working for a decidedly right-leaning publication or broadcaster.

"Why," Jeff told me once," do you think the traditional media ignored the Internet for so long ... they hoped it would just go away like a faddish videogame. At every newspaper I wrote for or worked at as an editor, we had a meeting once or twice a day in which a bunch of people sat around a boardroom and, like dictators, decided what we would and would not put in the paper the next morning, how big we'd make the headlines to attract your attention (or not). Here's a good example: If the paper had endorsed a certain political candidate, and once elected he or she got a DUI; we'd report the story but would bury it as much as possible unless it was impossible to do otherwise. In the other direction, I can think of one or two papers I worked for who would go to the other extreme to distance themselves from the candidate and would go on the attack and destroy the politician, all the while somehow neglecting to mention the paper's previous endorsement of that candidate."

"Because of television and the Internet particularly, newspapers have lost much of their power. Before television and the Internet, newspaper editors played god every night. And believe me, they HATE it that, especially because of the Internet, they can't do that anymore. Television's not the same threat it once was as well because all the major news outlets are basically just "bottom-line driven" corporations that try to squeeze every advertising dollar they can out of every minute of programming and the news hole on most of the majors is getting smaller and smaller by the day – so you hardly get a great deal of insight from television anymore."

That's part of Jeff's view from inside the newsrooms but I still challenge him and everyone currently in media with the question: Why is media against, or at least appears to be against diversity of thought and opinion? Approximately how many media outlets employ journalists who do not see eye to eye with a majority of the American populace on many critical social issues this country faces such as abortion, affirmative action, immigration reform, or gay marriage? How many members of the media do you think would identify themselves as Republican or at least socially conservative? I strongly doubt the percentages of political persuasion exist equally amongst members of the journalistic community. In fact, one poll taken shortly after the 2008 presidential election cited that over 80% of those in the field of journalism voted along Democratic lines. With that in mind it's idiotic to think that biased thoughts don't resonate throughout our airwaves and printing presses with the overwhelming majority of those creating these thoughts thinking in the same direction.

Isn't diversity of thought just as important as diversity of every other sort? The Constitution of the United States seems to think so. The First Amendment is not just centered on the right to speak, but the right for a free marketplace of ideas to exist.

I believe, and I believe I've shown, that in our racially diverse society, the liberal media have established a sort of unwritten code which grants passage to certain groups of people to say things that other groups may not, at least not without the risk of harsh retribution.

As I have cited earlier with examples such as Rush Limbaugh and Allen Iverson, the media seems to place more emphasis on who makes certain comments rather than focusing on the comments themselves and engaging in any debate on whether those comments have validity or warrant further intelligent discussion.

To me, it seems media sees minorities (generally speaking) as oppressed by majorities, and it's as if the media are attempting in some way to cure this grand presumed injustice within our society by giving certain minorities a looser rein regarding free speech and the resulting criticism that often times ensues when particular opinions are voiced.

Like anything, there are exceptions, however. Not only do the media take exception with who can and cannot make certain comments, they also take exception to whom the comments are directed. The media were definitely uncomfortable when comedian and (and doctor of education) Bill Cosby took the stage in Washington in 2005 to mark the anniversary of the landmark Brown v. Board of Education of Topeka Supreme Court decision, that declared state laws establishing separate public schools for black and white students unconstitutional. Generally it was seen as a ruling that helped pave the way for integration and the civil rights movement.

In his speech. Cosby came out swinging and said what was on a lot of people's minds at the time, and still continues to be. He made a case that in his OPINION the ruling had little positive effect on blacks and that American black people are – in a wide generalization – not benefiting from all of the advantages America has to offer.

Needless to say, Bill Cosby in one fell swoop angered the NAACP, NAACP Legal Defense and Education Fund, along with Howard University and irreparably disrupted a gala celebration of the anniversary of the desegregation decision.

In his talk Mr. Cosby let it fly. He obviously has a passion for his community and seeing the members of his community succeed. Unfortunately, it was a bit too heavy a dose of reality for the community to which he spoke and the journalistic community as well. It's becoming increasingly frustrating to see how hard it truly is to get people to accept reality. Bill Cosby portrayed reality as he sees it, and if we were all honest we know exactly what he's talking about which doesn't make the man a racist; it makes him a realist. But admitting that a man who is simply exercising his right to speak freely actually has a point invokes many in our society to cast convenient yet harsh labels such as "racist," "homophobe" or some other neat and tidy word that will allow one to excuse certain comments and continue to ignore reality while the person who has spoken must defend such allegations and warn others to keep their mouths shut lest they receive the same fate.

To understand this point here is an excerpt from Dr. Cosby's speech:

"Ladies and gentlemen," he started, "these people set, they opened the doors, they gave us the right, and today, ladies and gentlemen, in our cities and public schools we have a 50 percent drop out. In our own neighborhood, we have men in prison ..."

" Ladies and gentlemen, the lower economic and lower middle economic people are not holding their end in this deal. In the neighborhood that most of us grew up in, parenting is not going on ... I'm talking about these people who cry when their son is standing there in an orange suit. Where were you when he was two? Where were you when he was 12? Where were you when he was 18, and how come you don't know he had a pistol? And where is his father, and why don't you know where he is? And why doesn't the father show up to talk to this boy?

"We cannot blame white people. White people ... white people don't live over there.

"Fifty percent dropout rate, I'm telling you, and people in jail, and women having children by five, six different men ... Looking at the incarcerated, these are not political criminals. These are people going around stealing Coca Cola. People getting shot in the back of the head over a piece of pound cake! Then we all run out and are outraged, 'The cops shouldn't have shot him.' What the hell was he doing with the pound cake in his hand?

"Are you not paying attention, people with their hat on backwards, pants down around their crack. Isn't that a sign of something, or are you waiting for Jesus to pull his pants up? What part of Africa did this come from? We are not Africans. Those people are not Africans, they don't know a damned thing about Africa. With names like Shaniqua, Shaligua, Mohammed and all that crap and all of them are in jail.

"Brown versus the Board of Education is no longer the white person's problem.

We've got to take the neighborhood back. We've got to go in there. Just forget telling your child to go to the Peace Corps. It's right around the corner. It's standing on the corner. It can't speak English. It doesn't want to speak English. I can't even talk the way these people talk. "Why you ain't where you is go, be," I don't know who these people are. And I blamed the kid until I heard the mother talk. Then I heard the father talk. This is all in the house. You used to talk a certain way on the corner and you got into the house and switched to English. Everybody knows it's important to speak English except these knuckleheads. You can't land a plane with "why you ain't …" You can't be a doctor with that kind of crap coming out of your mouth …"

"Now look, I'm telling you. It's not what they're doing to us. It's what we're not doing. Fifty percent drop out. Look, we're raising our own ingrown immigrants. These people are fighting hard to be ignorant. There's no English being spoken, and they're walking and they're angry. Oh God, they're angry and they have pistols and they shoot and they do stupid things. And after they kill somebody, they don't have a plan. Just murder somebody. Boom. Over what? A pizza?

"It's time for you to not accept the language that these people are speaking, which will take them nowhere. What the hell good is Brown V. Board of Education if nobody wants it?

"Who are these sick black people and where did they come from and why haven't they been parented to shut up? … And then they stand there in an orange suit and you drop to your knees, '(crying sound) He didn't do anything, he didn't do anything.' Yes, he did do it. And you need to have an orange suit on too."

"Brown vs. Board of Education, these people who marched and were hit in the face with rocks and punched in the face to get an education and we got these knuckleheads walking around who don't want to learn English.

"I know that you all know it. I just want to get you as angry as you ought to be. When you walk around the neighborhood and you see this stuff, that stuff's not funny. These people are not funny anymore. And that's not my brother. And that's not my sister. They're faking and they're dragging me way down because the state, the city and all these people have to pick up the tab on them because they don't want to accept that they have to study to get an education."

"Basketball players, multimillionaires can't write a paragraph. Football players, multimillionaires, can't read. Yes. Multimillionaires. Well, Brown v. Board of Education, where are we today? It's there. They paved the way. What did we do with it? The white man, he's laughing, got to be laughing. Fifty percent drop out, rest of them in prison."

Damn Bill, you sounded like Dirty Harry just then.

While there was some applause and the occasional nervous laughter during Cosby's speech, the media did not react well to his obvious anger at the black community and call to embrace the opportunities every American is afforded. In fact, a number of media outlets and commentators came out with basically a "how dare you" reaction to Cosby's obviously impassioned speech.

Whether you agree with the content of Mr. Cosby's speech is not the issue here. Mr. Cosby was simply using a public forum, to which he was invited, to speak frankly and candidly about a topic he has strong convictions for. He was exercising his right to free speech and should not be subjected to post-comment fall out based on the media's judgment of his opinions and the presumed differences regarding those opinions.

Yet, he was.

"His extended outburst, presented without the evident benefit of even the most rudimentary preparation, was a gross violation of professional and personal discipline ..." one commentator wrote. "He played elderly "shock jock" frothing and flailing away, spewing a sewer of abuse."

This quote displays my argument precisely. So if I'm understanding the journalist in the prior sentence correctly; when a man expresses opinions that you in your opinion don't agree with, it is "OK" to describe that man using negative connotations such as "frothing," "flailing," and "spewing," in an attempt to encourage others to take up your dislike for the comments as well as the man himself. Is that what I'm to understand? I think it's pretty obvious at this time in our society that I'm absolutely correct in my assumptions. Such efforts have become about as original as a Fog Hat concert.

This inflammatory criticism (which was just one example of many) was incited simply from Bill Cosby having an opinion different from the article's author. When will journalists realize that having conflicting opinions is not a license to verbally attack someone just because you have an open forum? What gives you the right to judge anybody, Mr. Journalist? What gives you the right to tell someone their opinion is wrong — to chastise someone publicly in an effort to turn public perception against their opinions as well as against them personally? What possibly makes your opinion any more important or any more "right" than someone else's, just because you have a TV show, a radio show or newspaper column? Freedom of speech is what gives you the right to have a job and it's what gives everyone in this great country the right to not only say what is on his or her mind, but should ideally give each of us the ability to do so without fear of being personally attacked by someone who just happens to be in front of a TV camera and doesn't agree. Evidently the founders of the Constitution thought that free speech was pretty important (after all, they made it the First Amendment).

In Cosby's case, I believe the media's role should have been to report the story

— and perhaps asked one of the serving Supreme Court Justices for a current opinion on the landmark case, or perhaps have black civil rights leaders render their opinion — which is of equal value to Dr. Cosby's in my estimation — whether or not they're in agreement. And if they're not, there should be dialogue. Not name-calling.

Now, I can see it already — people will say, "well, John, in your one chapter you attacked the characters of several people in the public forum of this book and now you're saying media shouldn't have the same right to attack people in their various forums?"

To defend any such accusation that may arise, in the chapter that may raise a question I was not speaking as a passive observer rendering judgment on specific comments made by someone whom I've never met and probably never will. I simply have a problem on a personal level with the character of a specific individual and how in my opinion those character flaws have affected me. There is a vast divide in delivering criticism to someone you know personally and whom you feel has harmed you in a personal way as opposed to possessing a differing opinion from that of another individual and using your forum for purposes of public degradation. To the many who do such things on a daily basis I would like to pose the question, "What makes you think you have the right to pass judgment and ridicule another man because of his words (and don't say, "Because I'm on TV")? Why are your thoughts and opinions superior to those of someone else"?

What's sad is that after my whole experience with Sports Illustrated and being so vilified — still — is that I almost feel like I'm a walking (still talking!) example of free speech and just how tenuous it is. Now I will admit and repeat once again that comments which were made by me presented ideas that were cruel, heartless and inappropriate as reported. The key phrase in that sentence, however, is "as reported." Unfortunately, for the American public who listen to, read and observe media commentaries, the media has become increasingly astute over the years at the art of the sound bite and sentence fragment while leaving much of the context around such fragments to the imagination which they themselves fill in for the reader or viewer at their own discretion. In my opinion this phenomenon serves the necessity to create the sensational and dramatic which it seems our society has grown to depend on while thwarting legitimate functional dialogue. In today's modern media culture it's rare to see a politician, athlete, prominent business leader or anyone else of public relevance actually have a full thought or conversation reported in its entirety. Instead the "high points" are usually covered which may only make up one tenth of the overall commentary with the rest being generally filled in by the reporting journalist who can attempt to steer the public's opinion in any way he or she wishes through a variety of coercive tactics such as tone, voice inflection, body language, unflattering pictures or just outright biased dialogue leaving the reader or viewer with nothing more than a spoon fed mimicked opinion of the reporting journalist.

I found that out the hard way which is in part why I'm writing this book. As I've stated previously, much of this book contains the full commentary and conversations around the sound bites and sentence fragments which existed in that SI article which were then surrounded by the scathing profile/opinion of the author in order to create his desired perception of me. Here's a news flash: IT WORKED. As most of you are probably aware, I've been the poster child of racism and intolerance for over a decade now despite the glaring fact that not a single person from my past has ever come forward supporting the claims made by one lone article. The opinions discussed in this book you may not agree with and that is completely fine, but as an American I have a right to these opinions and I have a right to voice these opinions just as you have a right to disagree with them. Hopefully, with full conversation replacing sound bites and sentence fragments full reasonable dialogue will be possible where only sensational demonizing once existed.

I guess the lesson I've learned over the last decade when it comes to media and their ability to manipulate the public's perception is in line with the old cliché which states, "Don't ever pick a fight with a guy who buys ink by the truck load."

Well, I finally decided to buy my own truck.

CHAPTER SEVEN

My Country 'Tisn't Free

ou know what? We lost (technically). The terrorists have won. My nation is no longer free. And many young men and a few young women have lost their lives fighting unwinnable wars in the mountains, caves, and streets of Afghanistan, Iraq, Libya, Darfur, Sudan, Somalia, along with a number of other troubled places around the globe.

Meanwhile, here in the good ole' US of A we now have the Patriot Act, TSA and a whole host of other measures that are currently in place to help "protect" us from ourselves. Police officers are starting to randomly check people's handbags on subways and buses. And if you've been on a flight in the past few years you know what an effort in obnoxious brain damage that's become. It's only a matter of time before cavity searches become mandatory for us all (which may actually excite some, but not this kid). Law enforcement officers can search a home or business without the owner's or the occupant's consent or knowledge; the FBI now has the ability to search telephone, e-mail, and financial records without a court order, while all law enforcement agencies have unimpeded access to business records, including library and financial records. You will also recall, I mentioned in a previous chapter the very dangerous idea of the government being able to shut down our Internet with a "kill switch." In fact since its passage, several legal challenges have been brought against this Patriot Act, and Federal courts have ruled that a number of these provisions are actually unconstitutional.

Our phones, Internet, and e-mail can now be tapped without court permission, many cities have surveillance cameras on street corners, we've got body scanners at airports and some cities have established enforceable curfews — and believe me, I don't care if you're black, white, Latino, Asian, or a damn Martian if you're walking down the streets of some cities past a reasonable time of night there's a good chance you'll be stopped by authorities, and they WILL ask you:

"What are you doing?" (Bright light in your face.)

"Where are you going?"

"Why are you out here?"

"Can I see some ID?"

And here's some advice: you had better be polite; you had better be honest; and you had better not be up to anything.

Unfortunately it doesn't stop there, however. Texas is likely to be the first state whose police will routinely fly lightweight, unarmed drones up to 400 feet above the ground, "high enough for them to be largely invisible eyes in the sky. Such technology could allow police to record the activities of the public below with high-resolution, infrared and thermal-imaging cameras," according to one news report I've read.

A number of law enforcement communities have wanted drones for covert urban surveillance, such as tracking legal, peaceful protests. Others, more legitimately, I believe, could be a boon to patrolling our borders, searching for missing persons in difficult terrains and even, as one commentator suggested, safely tracking the spread of forest fires.

But should the feds or other any law enforcement agency have the right, in what's supposed to be a free country, to covertly spy on the activities of its citizens right in their own backyards without cause of suspicion? No way!

Now I can't speak for you, but that is not the country I was born into. The country I was born in you had EVERY right to say, if stopped by a peace officer without cause and questioned … "that's none of your business, sir;" because if you were doing nothing wrong, he or she didn't have the right to stop you in the first place.

The rules, regulations and protocols I just recited are horrible, moderately oppressive and infringe upon many innocent people's lives every day. What I've told you is not even the worst part of it, however. Unfortunately, the most horrific part of the Patriot Act is that in many more ways than not, it's actually very needed. We have lost. The terrorists have won. Were it not for 9/11 there would be no Patriot Act. Were it not for a well-funded radical Muslim terrorist organization that did a tragically brilliant job of infiltrating this country, there would be no need for a Patriot Act, and if other persons with similar intentions and desires weren't legally and illegally living among us as we speak there would be no "Act". Our America will never again be as we once knew it. Unfortunately, there is and probably always will be a need to protect us from ourselves.

As far as I know, with the exception of Timothy McVeigh, Eric Rudolf, Ted Kaczynski, Andre Breivik and perhaps a few others in recent history, every act of terrorism over the last 40 years has been committed by a radical Muslim from (roughly) the ages of 17 to 45, male AND female. If you are a Muslim from 17 to 45 and you don't want to commit or facilitate an act of terror … great! If you feel that people unfairly profile you, however; don't be angry with the "profilers;" get angry with the ones who have caused you and people like you to be profiled. Take it up with them. Don't take it up with the ones who are doing nothing more than trying to prevent themselves from becoming a statistic. Remember, I've always said, stereotypes are there for a reason. They don't just create themselves. You think people just randomly started making up stories about pit bull dogs being naturally – or unnaturally, as the case may be – aggressive? No, those dogs have a reputation. I'm not foolishly suggesting they're all bad – yet I'm not about to stick my hand in a pit bull's face until I have good reason to trust it.

And so it goes with racial profiling, I believe.

Take some southern bubba in overalls and a ball cap "headin' out on "uh huntin' trip" — should he REALLY have to go through a radioactive full-body scanner and take his boots off to get on a damn plane? Should grandma have to surrender her shampoo because the bottle is too big? Hell no!

But I believe, given indisputable recent history along with current events and facts, if you walk through the security line at an airport and your passport tags you as coming from a terrorist nation or a nation even suspected of sponsoring terrorism and your last name sounds more like someone clearing phlegm from their throat, well, you head into a different security area, dude, and we're going to stick you in the microwave and make damn sure there's nothing hiding in your shoes, underwear, moustache or any other clever places of concealment. I repeat: don't get mad at me or the profilers — we aren't the reason you're being profiled; the actions of your own people are. I admit, of the one billion Muslims under the age of 45, it may only be one in 100,000 or maybe even one in a million who poses a threat to the citizens of this country. The overwhelming majority are law-abiding, God-loving (or fearing, whatever your belief), fine human beings. But it wasn't an American-born who helped fly jets into the World Trade Center or the Pentagon or who sent a plane down with the loss of all hands in a Pennsylvanian field; or hid bombs in their underwear with the intent to detonate them on a plane in Detroit on Christmas Day back in 2009, or attempted to bring down a jet over the Atlantic with a shoe bomb; it was an individual or group of radical Muslims. It's not an

Italian grocer, a French pastry chef, Brazilian soccer player, Japanese fisherman, a Polish businessman, or Chinese tailor walking into a busy street market in Syria with a vest made out of dynamite and blowing up dozens of innocent people in a hellish act of random violence: It's a radical Muslim.

It's obvious to me that it's only a matter of time before an equally horrific event strikes us in one of our own back yards. Maybe it will happen in Houston. Maybe it will be in Charlotte, North Carolina, or Denver, Colorado. Maybe one of your loved ones will be there, or maybe you will. To many of you that sounds morbid and to others it may sound just plain crazy. If it was September 10, 2001, I might have to agree, but I've seen it with my own eyes. Fool me once shame on you; fool me twice shame on me. I may be a bit crazy, but I'm no fool. I'll take racial profiling over a "rising death toll" any day, and with our grossly porous borders and logical immigration laws which are trying to be implemented which ultimately protect us all constantly being challenged over hypothetical "worst case" scenarios it's only a matter of time.

Yes, we need to be vigilant against domestic terrorism, too and put up every road block we can to prevent those with ill intentions from crossing our borders, and if that means inconveniencing some for a brief period of time because they were "profiled" then so be it. Eliminating their inconvenience is not worth my death. Like the oath every member of the American military takes: "I, (NAME), do solemnly swear that I will support and defend the Constitution of the United States against all enemies, foreign and domestic."

Still, an airport scanner wouldn't have stopped McVeigh and his rental truck full of fertilizer and diesel, and having the feds tap some 13-year-old girl's cell phone and e-mail wouldn't have stopped Kaczynski from mailing out elaborate bombs.

As Anne Applebaum, a columnist for the Washington Post and Slate, stated in one of her pieces criticizing the Patriot Act and how America is not the free country it once was: "The events of 9/11 did not prove that the United States needs to spend more on local police forces and fire brigades; they proved that Americans need to learn how to make better use of the information they have and apply it with speed and efficiency.

"As for the TSA, I am not aware of a single bomber or bomb plot stopped by its time-wasting procedures. In fact, TSA screeners consistently fail to spot the majority of fake "bombs" and bomb parts the agency periodically plants to test their skills. In Los Angeles, whose airport was targeted by the "millennium plot" on New Year's 2000, screeners failed some 75 percent of these tests.

"Terrorists have been stopped since 2001 and plots prevented, but always by other means. After the Nigerian "underwear bomber" of Christmas Day 2009 was foiled, Department of Homeland Security Secretary Janet Napolitano claimed "the system worked" — but the bomber was caught by a passenger, not the feds. Richard Reid, the 2001 shoe bomber, was undone by an alert stewardess who smelled something funny. The 2006 Heathrow Airport plot was uncovered by an intelligence tip. Al Qaeda's attempt to explode cargo planes was caught by a human intelligence source, not an X-ray machine. Yet the TSA responds to these events by placing restrictions on shoes, liquids, and now perhaps printer cartridges."

She also wrote the very poignant opinion that "... Wouldn't we be safer if the vast budgets of TSA and its partners around the world were diverted away from confiscating nail scissors and toward creating better information systems and better intelligence? Imagine if security officers in Amsterdam had been made aware of the warnings the underwear bomber's father gave to the U.S. Embassy in Abuja. Or, for that matter, if consular officers had prevented him from receiving a visa in the first place."

We've had a history of violence, of riots, of assassinations — like every country — and it's not going to stop, sorry to tell you. But by tossing our rights out the window — rights that many, many men died for in two world wars, Korea, Vietnam, the Middle East, Kosovo — and the list goes on — we're surrendering. Terrorists have won. I no longer live in a free country where I'm assumed innocent until proven guilty. I have to PROVE I'm not a terrorist before I can get on a plane in Atlanta to fly to New York.

There are some libraries in the country now that destroy records as to what books patrons sign out once the books are returned since the Patriot Act would require the library to turn over reports of who borrowed certain books if ordered to by federal authorities — again, without an impartial due process of a court order. As far as I'm concerned that is NOT the act of a free nation. At least not the free nation I was born in.

Here are a few alarming examples of what kinds of behaviors our government now conducts:

On February 15, 2003, peace and justice organizations held a demonstration in Sacramento to protest the then-impending war in Iraq. Approximately 10,000 people attended the peaceful demonstration. The Sacramento Police Department actually confirmed that their videotaping of the event and its participants was at least partially intended to modify the protesters' behavior.

How's this for wise use of our law enforcement: On November 10, 2004, six undercover sheriffs deputies were among 60 people attending a lecture on the benefits of vegetarianism on a university campus in Fresno, California, because the speaker was formerly employed by People for the Ethical Treatment of Animals (PETA).

In my home state of Georgia, the School of the America's student protests outside Fort Benning became classified by the FBI as "Priority" for "Counterterrorism" monitoring.

A woman named Caitlin Childs was arrested after a peaceful protest about vegetarianism on public property outside the Honey Baked Ham store on Buford Highway in Georgia's DeKalb County for writing down the license plate number of the car belonging to the DHS agent who had been photographing the protestors all day.

Here's a topper: An FBI intelligence analyst wrote a 2005 memo "identifying future targets of the animal rights and environmental rights movements and/or those committing crimes on behalf of the movement in the Georgia area" and went on to list the Green Party as a terrorist group.

I mean, really, what the &@#$ is going on in this country? Again, the terrorists have won, and reduced many of us to mere prisoners in our own country. It doesn't have to be this way in my opinion. With the use of a little common sense and the understanding that the sensitivities of some may have to be compromised a bit for the ultimate protection of all; we could go back to living the safe, peaceful unintruded upon lives we once took for granted.

Yet many measures will most likely continue by U.S. law enforcement that would have been illegal prior to the Patriot Act and 9/11. And while I am a firm believer that if you're not doing anything illegal then what possibly do you have to worry about when it comes to law enforcement, the principle remains that this country is not the same country I was born in 36 years ago and doesn't operate the way it was founded to operate.

We were a COUNTRY again immediately after 9/11, but as commentator Glenn Beck points out, Americans rather quickly lost the spirit of unity that filled the nation after those terrorist attacks as our economy has crumbled, our rights have been eroded and there's seemingly endless arguing with no solutions and very little leadership direction on issues ranging from gun control to immigration.

I don't know who wrote this, but someone sent me a breakdown of the rights true Americans have lost over the past decades, broken down by Amendments in the Bill of Rights. Now, please don't assume I agree with each and every one of these decisions or the points being made: For instance, and before I get bashed too badly, I am, personally, a believer in a woman's right to choose with regard to the early termination of a pregnancy. I'm in no position to tell a woman I don't know and will never meet what decision she has to make regarding something as serious as child birth. Every woman has a different story and I believe it should be left up to the individual when it comes to something so personal. A decisions as life altering as that should be left to the individual to make and ultimately live with the consequences. With that said this incomplete list of how some of our constitutional amendments have been eroded is certainly worth a look for its overall unsettling trend.

First Amendment — Religious Expression:

If I'm a graduating high school student speaking at the graduation ceremony, I can't say a prayer to give thanks to God for my success.

The phrase "In God We Trust" is being taken off some forms of money and on some government buildings is being removed. I'm not much of a religious man, but make no mistake about it; America was founded on Judeo-Christian values and morals. Terms like "In God We Trust" are as American as the bald eagle. It is part of our heritage that has been ingrained within this country for hundreds of years. If this phrase troubles you; don't read it. Although those words don't bother me, I have just as much of a right to see that on my money as you think you have to remove it.

Fourth Amendment:

The federal government is making noise that it will be tracking Americans through GPS and private cell phones, all without a warrant.

State governments can set up roadblocks and search my vehicle to see if I have what could be called "contraband" (i.e., cigarettes bought in another state) in my vehicle, without a warrant or reasonable suspicion.

Fifth Amendment:

The Kelo decision allows the government to take my property and give it to another private party, as a result of the Supreme Court's bastardization of the Public Purpose Clause.

At this point, Obamacare allows the government to force me to give my money to a private health insurance provider.

Howard Zinn's book "A People's History of the United States," is a fascinating look at the ways by which Americans are now manipulated and controlled. "The American system is the most ingenious system of control in world history," he writes.

"There is none that disperses its controls more complexly through the voting system, the work situation, the church, the family, the school, the mass media— none more successful in mollifying opposition with reforms, isolating people from one another, creating patriotic loyalty. One percent of the nation owns a third of the wealth. The rest of the wealth is distributed in such a way as to turn those in the 99 percent against one another; small property owners against the property less, black against white, native-born against foreign-born, intellectuals and professionals against the uneducated and unskilled. These groups have resented one another and warred against one another with such vehemence and violence as to obscure their common position as sharers of leftovers in a very wealthy country."

If there's one thing that President Barack Obama has said that I agree with it's a statement he made during a speech in Missouri in which he said many Americans have lost faith in their government and that American suspicion of government was deepening.

"People have lost faith in government — they had lost faith in government before I ran (for president), and it has been getting worse," Obama said at a rally in St. Louis.

He quoted his political hero, U.S. Civil War-era president Abraham Lincoln, as saying that the role of government was to do what needed to be done but could not be done by citizens themselves without help. (

Well, when it comes to national security and particularly the control of our own borders, immigration, freedom of speech and, well, all the rights the founding fathers saw fit to give us, he's right.

My Nation 'Tisn't Free, and at the end of the day it is up to you, me and us to take it back. For this country is the inheritance we all have received from our fathers and grandfathers who have gone before us, and in my opinion we are squandering it like the prodigal son.

CHAPTER EIGHT

Stealing Home

Some time ago I discovered a formula to preserve our American heritage by envisioning a way in which immigrants would actually assimilate themselves into our society. In my opinion, this formula is more than just a clever rant of comic satire or a flippant opinion crafted by some cranky patriot. Instead, this plan has actually been put together with much study, research and creativity by one of America's most well-known political talk show hosts. Rush Limbaugh, who has been in the public ears and eyes for nearly 30 years, revealed a set of rules that I believe if instituted would preserve our great American tradition.

This well-crafted and thoughtfully articulate strategy to conform American immigration has been dubbed, "The Limbaugh Laws," and they read as follows:

"First, if you immigrate to the United States of America, you must speak the native language. You have to be a professional or an investor. (America is) not going to take unskilled workers ... There will be no special bilingual programs in the schools, no special ballots for elections, no government business will be conducted in your native language. Foreigners will not have the right to vote ... nor will they ever be allowed to hold political office. According to the Limbaugh Laws, if you're in our country, you cannot be a burden to taxpayers. You are not entitled, ever, to welfare, to food stamps, or other government goodies. You can come if you invest here, but it must be an amount equal to 40,000 times the daily minimum wage. If you don't have that amount of money, you can't come and you can't invest. We don't want you; it's best if you just stay home. If you do come and you want to buy land, okay, but we're going to restrict your options. You will not be allowed to buy waterfront property in the United States. That will be reserved for citizens naturally born in this country.

"In fact, as a foreigner, you must relinquish individual rights to property … And another thing. You don't have the right to protest when you come here. You're allowed no demonstrations, you cannot wave a foreign flag, no political organizing, no bad-mouthing our president or his policies, or you get sent home. You're a foreigner. You shut your mouth or you get out, and if you come here illegally, you go straight to jail and we're going to hunt you down 'til we find you."

Think the "Limbaugh Laws" are a bit harsh?

He asked the same question just before revealing, in 2006, to his audience that they weren't "Limbaugh Laws" at all. "I just read you Mexican immigration law."

Indeed, what Rush read over the air waves are the official immigration laws of Mexico.

That's how the Mexican government handles those who immigrate to its country. So while illegal immigrants protest in our streets about racial profiling, or the proposal of tough, new and very needed immigration laws; while hundreds of thousands exploit our entitlement programs and place undue burdens on the American taxpayer; the very country they came from wears a disgusted frown toward the very things many of its citizens do when they illegally cross our borders. We are at a crucial period in our nation's history, regarding our economy, our security, our national identity and most importantly our future.

I'm not so naive as to not understand that many people think some of my opinions are a bit obnoxious, and maybe rightfully so. I will admit that at one point in time I was quoted as saying "… I don't like foreigners." Let's see, however, what actually exists behind this comment which has gone untold for so many years. Now, the statement quoted above is an absolute, and if I've said it once I've said it a hundred times I hate absolutes. In fact I think they rarely exist and in even rarer cases will I use one. There are very few instances where things are entirely one way or another, and simply making an absolute statement regarding a dislike of all foreigners, period, is asinine. Immigrants who come to this country with the simple yet integral desire to make a better life for themselves and their family with all intentions and desire to immerse on all levels into the fabric that is America: I gladly welcome you with open arms. After all, this great country has thrived for generations on the backs of men and women who have possessed the desire to enjoy all that is American and in doing so have perpetuated that opportunity for future generations. At the end of the day each us owes a debt of gratitude to those who have given us the ability to proudly call ourselves Americans. It's my strong opinion that it is this meshing, this assimilation of many generations of many different cultures which has created our unique American heritage that makes this country so great. The key word, however, is "assimilation." Immigration should be about unity rather than diversity.

One of the things I loved about all the teams I played on is that these teams were a group of guys from various racial, ethnic, and socio-economic backgrounds, who all banded together for a common cause. When the umpire said, "play ball" all of those things that marked us and identify us as different essentially disappeared. During our social time I enjoyed hearing the different aspects of how my friend Pascual Matos grew up in the Dominican Republic as well as listening to the adolescent stories told by John LeRoy from Seattle, Washington, and teasing Andruw Jones about that "rock" he grew up on in the middle of the Caribbean. It was learning about and appreciating each other's differences that brought us together as a team; when the uniforms went on, however and we crossed those white lines; we weren't from the DR; we weren't from Seattle, Washington, or Macon, Georgia, or Maracaibo, Venezuela; we were a unit, and that's how America should be.

Let me state the obvious: Everyone in this country is an immigrant or is the descendent of immigrants. I myself am a fourth-generation descendent of German immigrants. My ancestors came to this country during the mid 1800s and eventually settled in coastal Georgia. America was built with the sweat and calloused hands of its immigrants. Over the history of this great country, most have understood that to truly benefit from all that America has to offer, assimilation is a must; they wanted (and needed) to learn the language, the customs and the traditions of the country they have chosen as their new home if they expect to enjoy everything America has to offer. Although some hang onto a few aspects of their homelands (which is one characteristic that makes the American culture so appealing), the goal is to become "Americanized". As a native-born American who is very proud of the country I live in, nothing flatters me more than to see someone who has come here with the desire to be an American, and to one day be filled with the same pride in this country that I and so many others possess.

Unfortunately, in my opinion the assimilated immigrant who is a tremendous benefit to our society is becoming more of an exception rather than the norm. More and more, this country is seeing its cities and towns filled with a segment of the populace that have no desire to take part in anything that is American, with the exception of government/tax payer funded social programs. In many larger cities entire communities are being carved out which look more like the inhabitants' country of origin than the United States.

America can no longer be the life raft for the world's charity cases. While many immigrants arrive in this country eager to work and build a better life, thousands of foreigners cross our borders each day with intentions to exploit the many taxpayer-funded government social programs such as medical care, social security, welfare, and free housing. Allowing my tax dollars to pay for these programs to be used by American citizens is my civic responsibility. Even though many social programs largely do nothing more than perpetuate the need for more social programs, I would rather have my hard-earned tax dollars go to support a native-born American who has several generations of history in this country and who may have an ancestor that I could thank for my freedom — as opposed to a foreign-born person who comes here to take merely advantage of these excessive social programs our moronic government has put into place.

It's quite possible that many of you have never given much thought to the disturbing reality that is allowed to exist in this country. Unfortunately for we the taxpayer our grossly flawed system of government social programs allows many immigrants who have never paid one dime to support any of these various programs to greatly subsidize if not totally support their livelihoods. As I've said so often in this book, I will very rarely use an absolute and here I'm certainly not suggesting that all immigrants behave like this, but there are definitely enough who are more than willing to suckle at the government tit which ultimately comes at your expense and mine.

To illustrate my point I would like to share a story of a close friend who some years ago opened my eyes to this disgusting reality. My friend's younger sister suffered from Cerebral Palsy, and at the time of this story she was approximately 12 or 13 years old. As you can imagine, the cost of caring for a girl in her condition was quite expensive. Her parents made a comfortable middle-class living but still had a tough time meeting the financial obligation of caring for their daughter. One day my friend's stepfather, who served this country in Vietnam, along with her mother, took the little girl to the Health Department of the town in which they lived to apply for medical aid to help offset the financial burden created by their daughter's illness. Their request was denied. How appalling!

The story doesn't end here, however. It actually gets much more nauseating. As my friend's family was being denied benefits, at the next window a woman who had recently emigrated from the Philippines was at the counter with her elderly mother. The elderly woman, who had been in America for only a few short months, had obviously never contributed any monies to social security, Medicare, Medicaid etc. Now the Filipino immigrant was at the Health Department making application for financial aid for her aging mother. What do you think happened? The elderly woman who had been in this country for only a brief period; had never contributed one dime was granted social security benefits, along with full dental and medical. A YOUNG HANDICAPED GIRL WHOSE FATHER IS A VIETNAM VETERAN WAS BLATANTLY DENIED MUCH NEEDED FINANCIAL AID TO CARE FOR THEIR HANDICAPPED DAUGHTER, WHILE A FILIPINO IMMIGRANT WHO HADN'T EVEN UNPACKED YET RECEIVED EVERY BENEFIT REQUESTED. WHAT THE HELL IS WRONG WITH THIS SYSTEM?! It's no wonder some immigrants come here with no other motive than to live off the wide array of social programs our idiot government affords to them. Hell, I guess I really can't fault them. At what point do the elected dopes that are responsible for disbursing our hard earned tax dollars begin to fix the grossly flawed system they allow to exist?

On the bottom of the Statue of Liberty an inscription reads, "Give me your tired, your poor, your huddled masses yearning to breathe free …"

As many others have asked, and are increasingly asking, "What about OUR tired, OUR poor, OUR huddled masses?"

At some point things must change or America will gorge itself from the inside out. Something must be done to preserve our culture and our way of life. We can no longer stand by and allow the American heritage to take a back seat and continually be overrun by the cultures of other ethnicities and nationalities. In my opinion promoting cultural unity is the only way this country will stay strong. As long as things like multiculturalism, bilingualism and ethnic identity are encouraged the overall stability of this country will continue to erode. The United States of America will become the antithesis of its own credo. Instead of "E Pluribus Unum" from many, one, we will be a nation under a new credo: "E Unum Pluribus" from one, many.

Think something like this can't happen to our beloved country? Think again. It is currently happening and will continue to happen. The former governor of Colorado, Dick Lamm, has painted a frighteningly accurate portrait of how America can slip from its position of dominance and influence. At an immigration overpopulation conference in Washington D.C., the former governor gave a straightforward assessment of how, over the course of time, great civilizations seem to destroy themselves. According to Lamm this is how our society can be destroyed: "First, to destroy America, turn America into a bilingual or multilingual and bicultural country."

No nation which was not originally born a multicultural, multilingual country can survive the introduction of two or more competing languages and cultures and the tension, conflict, and antagonism that comes with it. It is a blessing for an individual to be bilingual; however, it is a curse for a society to attempt such an existence. Seymour Lipset, a recently deceased political sociologist and senior fellow at the Hoover Institution and the Hazel Professor of Public Policy at George Mason University, cited many bilingual and bicultural societies have, in his words, "histories of turmoil, tension, and tragedy." Among them are Malaysia, Lebanon, Belgium and even our neighbors to the north, Canada — who less than 40 years ago experienced Quebec French terrorists murdering a foreign government official to spark flames of unrest in an effort to encourage the province of Quebec to secede from the country.

Dr. Lipset also discussed the difficulties that Pakistan and Cypress have faced, as well as the many problems France has encountered with Basques, Bretons, and Corsicans. A day seldom goes by when a story isn't brought to our attention involving unrest as a result of some various ethnic or immigrant group protesting in some fashion or inciting some degree of violence. Biculturalism is a plague that will destroy America. Nearly 43% of California residents speak a language other than English at home, a proportion far higher than any other state, according to the U.S. Census' most current figures. Overall, between the 2000 and 2010 census results, the Hispanic population grew by 43 percent, or four times the nation's 9.7 percent growth rate.

Immigration to this degree is no longer "immigration" as we are traditionally familiar with. At this level it becomes outright colonization with far to many colonizers having little desire to mesh with their new surroundings. Instead, most merely seek to recreate an atmosphere that strongly resembles the places they have defected from.

Former Gov. Lamm offered another point for reducing America's power and influence in the world: "Second, to destroy America, invent multiculturalism and encourage immigrants to maintain their own unique culture. I would make it an article of belief that all cultures are equal that there are no cultural differences. I would make it an article of faith that the black and Hispanic drop-out rates are due solely to prejudice and discrimination by the majority. Every other explanation is out of bounds."

Lamm's third point in his "plan" for America's demise is to promote diversity rather than unity, "I would encourage all immigrants to keep their own language and culture. I would replace the melting pot metaphor with the salad bowl metaphor. It is important to ensure that we have various cultural subgroups living in America enforcing their differences rather than as Americans, emphasizing their similarities."

You need make no more effort than to simply take a casual drive to see what the former governor is speaking of. In nearly every city across this massive country areas of ethnic division are becoming more defined every day. Specific ethnic "regions" with moderately defined borders are becoming the rule instead of the exception throughout most urban areas. Most locals in such areas can tell you first-hand how the boundaries of ethnic divisions exist throughout their town. In my hometown of Atlanta, for example, I can tell you that almost the entirety of the Hispanic population lives in about a six-mile stretch up and down Roswell Road and about an eight-mile stretch up and down Buford Highway. The bulk of the Korean population mostly resides in an area called Doraville mainly in the Tilly Mill Road and Winters Chapel areas, while the large Indian population is heavily concentrated in the Dunwoody area, sometimes taking over entire apartment complexes and neighborhoods. To drive through these areas is to see a strong resemblance to the original countries of its inhabitants. Many signs are in the foreigner's native language while the majority of the goods and services provided are much more traditional to the local foreigner as opposed to the local American. It's as if these places are not just neighborhoods of people with a common bond, but etched-out colonies looking to become a self-sustaining recreation of a land left behind. Separation and not unity is fast becoming the normal order of things as it is rare to see persons of the individual ethnic group outside of their chosen region and mingling with the local population at large.

In addition, Lamm includes three other social pit falls for the undoing of the American fabric most of which are already well under way:

1. Make the fastest-growing demographic group the least educated.
2. Get foundations and businesses to invest in ethnic identity and establish the cult of victimology.
3. Promote divided loyalties and encourage dual citizenship.

Lamm's so-called plan isn't really a plan for the future, but an accurate description of what, in many places, we're experiencing today which in my opinion is a very frightening reality that reflects very little of the assimilating and contributing which immigrants of previous generations intentionally achieved.

From this country's founding until the early 20th century, the majority of the American population arrived as the immigrant seeking a better life and more opportunity. The influx of those ambitious, hopeful people was a huge asset to this developing nation. Just because massive immigration was once good for this country, however, doesn't mean that it still is. During the pre-modern period of the United States a language, culture and set of traditions and customs was established. English was determined to be our native dialect. Variants of Judeo-Christian ethics were dominant in everyday life — right down to saying grace before meals. And holidays such as the Fourth of July, Presidential birthdays, Thanksgiving and other religious observances helped shape our American heritage.

In recent years, however, the refusal of many immigrants to assimilate into the fabric of America, besides being blatantly disrespectful, in my opinion is diluting our culture. Many foreigners make no attempt to learn the language of the country that they have chosen to reside in while our government, through bilingual programs, fails to encourage or facilitate that much-needed transition to take place. (I'll get much more specific about my feelings on that subject in the next chapter.) Many of these foreigners don't respect our customs and holidays such as the Fourth of July and Memorial Day. These holidays, and many others, celebrated by all Americans were created to show appreciation to the men and women who made sacrifices so that we may enjoy the litany of freedoms America has to offer. To disrespect such a part of our heritage is to disrespect the men and women who through their sacrifice have given the unassimilated immigrant the opportunity to live in the greatest country on earth. Yet I feel that logic has probably never registered nor matters to some immigrants who are here merely as parasites on the body of our nation. Ironically, in many cases these unassimilated ingrates, while not respecting our local traditions, attempt to force their customs and culture onto us. It's almost silly to point out that the Fourth of July is not celebrated in Mexico, yet Cinco de Mayo has become a day of annual festivities here in America. Why should we as Americans observe a day commemorating a Mexican victory over the French? If Mexican immigrants truly wanted to be and become everything that is American, wouldn't it seem that our Independence Day would be more important to them than celebrating a holiday of a country so stifling that hundreds of thousands of its citizens to flee every year seeking a better life elsewhere? It would warm my heart to sit next to a Hispanic or Indian family at Piedmont Park here in Atlanta and watch the Fourth of July fireworks show as we collectively celebrate our Independence Day. When will it end? What's next? In a few years will Bastille Day become a National holiday? What about the Queen's birthday or the day the Berlin Wall fell? At what point as a society do we say, "When in Rome do as the Romans do?"

If immigrating peoples are so hell bent to retain their foreign identity then may I make a suggestion? As opposed to taking advantage of America's good fortune and prosperity, while often times giving nothing in return, yet forcing your culture upon us, instead, why don't you remain in your own country and attempt to improve the society of your homeland just as the many generations of Americans have done up to now? If the previous generations filled with so many great Americans possessed the same attitude as many of our modern day immigrants, America would be unrecognizable as we now know it.

Imagine if hundreds of thousands of the great Americans who fought for the preservation of the Union during the Civil War had instead fled to Canada or another country who was not engaged in bloody civil conflict. What state would our great nation be in had the "Martin Luther King(s) and Andrew Young(s)" of the civil rights movement chosen to abandon their fellow countrymen for a land with a much-less-tumultuous social atmosphere? Suppose the greatest generation had decided the path of least resistance seemed best and had not engage Germany and Japan during WWII? Had any of these events been met with the "easy-way-out" mentality of some of our modern day immigrants, the world as we know it would undoubtedly be unrecognizable and the good ole' U.S. of A. may not even be a shadow of its current self.

As I sit and write this book I observe with great admiration the tenacity with which the peoples of Libya, Egypt and Syria are standing and have stood against the oppressive regimes that have repressed them for decades. Everyone has an undeniable right to be free. For those, however, who do not desire to behave with the same courage and bravery that our Middle Eastern brothers and sisters have done and seek to enjoy freedom elsewhere in my opinion that freedom comes with strings attached.

So to the modern immigrant I say you have two choices: First, if you love your country of origin so much that you proudly display its flag, you still observe its holidays and are insistent upon speaking its language, then why don't you remain in the country of which you seem to be so fond and try to improve it for you and all of your fellow countrymen? Reinvest your pride in the heritage of your homeland instead of packing up and bringing it here.

However, if you choose to come here to benefit from all that America has to offer, then understand you will not fully enjoy all that is America until you assimilate yourself into the fabric of this country and the heritage that its people have established over many prior generations. I don't dismiss the fact that societies constantly evolve. A society must adapt to keep up with cultural changes, economic changes, social changes and political changes. Lawmakers constantly test society's temperature to find out what adjustments need to be made in order to keep up with changing times. New organizations adjust to ever-changing opinions and lifestyles of various members in a community. That's growth in the pursuit of prosperity. But things can be taken too far. There are adaptations we as a society must refuse to make if we expect the unique culture that already exists within our 50 states to continue to survive and thrive. We must stop giving away our American heritage under the guise of political correctness. Americans need to focus on the one driving force that has sustained and, in the many cases quite literally saved this country and freedom at large: Unity.

Countries rarely retain what they once were in the face of trying to survive the tension and conflict created by competing cultures. The color of one's skin or country of origin ultimately has little to do with a person's success or failure in America. But immigrants' refusal to dissolve cultural barriers and become immersed into American society will lead to frustration, failure and life's many hardships which is not the outcome sought by any immigrant seeking to make a better life in America.

If you do not choose, like generations of immigrants before you, to learn the language, adopt local customs and perpetuate our native heritage, the true American opportunity will pass you by. In situations such as these, an immigrant must depend more and more on other unassimilated immigrants for mere survival and in turn form separate sub-societies in the midst of a much larger culture. The path of assimilation is, as early American immigrants have proven, the only way to permanently succeed in a new and different place. Unfortunately, a path of least resistance is the preferred direction for a number modern immigrants, which in my opinion ultimately leads to ostracism from the very society in which they have chosen to live.

The dilemma facing this country doesn't have as much to do with the number of immigrants crossing our borders every year, but the lack of desire many of these people have to truly become and be able to call themselves Americans. One cannot look solely to the immigrant for blame, however. In large part it is our government and our society as a whole that is responsible for this defection from within. In my opinion our hapless government does little to encourage and guide today's immigrant towards realizing the unity and integration that is crucial to the sustainment of America. Without this the modern day immigrant cannot be entirely held at fault.

In contrast, currently in process, the Australian government is stepping up its proactive and aggressive stance on immigration and the way immigrants must assimilate themselves to Australian culture. In 2006, then-Prime Minister John Howard published a book in which he warned that Muslims were Australia's first wave of immigrants to fail to assimilate with the mainstream.

Five years later, government leaders in that country are coming forward to condemn radical Muslim clerics who have declared that husbands have a God-given right to beat their disobedient wives, force them to have sex and also for suggesting that women who expose their faces and show off the curves of their bodies deserve to be raped.

As this book goes to print, the New South Wales State government, which rules Australia's most populous cities of Sydney and Melbourne, where most Muslim immigrants live, will be voting on a new law that will force Muslim women to remove veils and show their faces to police on request or risk a year in prison and a $5,900 (US) fine.

Already in France, wearing a burka — the all-covering female garment that hides the entire body except eyes and hands — in public is punishable by a 150 euro

($217 US) fine.

Of course, there are liberal special interest groups along with left-leaning politicians and commentators who bemoan even proposing such a law in Australia as being culturally insensitive. But as New South Wales State Premier Barry O'Farrell said, "I don't care whether a person is wearing a motorcycle helmet, a burka, niqab, face veil or anything else — the police should be allowed to require those people to make their identification clear."

Surprisingly, at least to me, even the Australian Federation of Islamic Councils begrudgingly agrees that legal exceptions cannot be made for immigrants' religious or political beliefs, and that immigrants must respect the laws of their adoptive lands. "I wouldn't like to go and say this is Muslim bashing," said Ikebal Patel, president of the Islamic Councils in Australia.

The second key issue beyond immigrants assimilating, I believe, deals with the level of individual contribution versus the level of individual consumption. Here's where we get down to the nitty-gritty practicalities of the matter. You may not care about bilingualism and the like, but you better care about what's being taken out of your purses and wallets and spread around to those who consistently don't contribute to the systems they so grossly depend on.

Many times this glaring issue is blatantly ignored for fear of upsetting the political correctness police. In my opinion political correctness is nothing more than avoiding a problem for the sake of appearances and to protect the "fragile psyches" of those who may find themselves in the minority or guilty of whatever accusations are being made. It is nothing more than a fabricated mindset by which the majority is made to feel guilty for simply being the majority and in turn do whatever is necessary to bow to the whims of the minority and their enablers.

One topic at the top of the politically correct "off limits" agenda is the massive fiscal burden illegal immigrants are responsible for on a yearly basis. Rather than point out the factual financial weight with which illegal aliens yoke around the necks of the American tax payer, the media would rather chastise anyone who points out this obvious fact, and create a feeling of guilt for having the audacity to utter such "hateful" words. Many have claimed that without the cheap labor of illegal aliens, many things in this country would not get done, citing the presumed fact that local Americans won't do such jobs. Of course they don't/can't, because illegal-immigrants have driven labor costs down to such levels that the average tax-paying American citizen can't compete with a population that doesn't play by the same set of fiscal rules. Fact of the matter is the jobs that many illegals do now have always existed in this country and have always been done by the local American population. Jobs in agriculture, construction, hospitality and many other occupations existed long before the rampant influx of the illegal immigrant and were performed by hard-working native born citizens or legal immigrants.

The justification used by most has become so tired it's almost to the point of being an old cliché.

"Cheap illegal labor is necessary to allow various goods and services to remain affordable ..." is the standard defense of those who break the law by existing in this country. To respond to that I'll use another old cliché: "There's no such thing as a free lunch."

If you think you're saving so much on the back end due to cheap labor on the front, how about the increased cost of medical care due in large part to the many benefits that our inept government chooses to give to illegals? The increased cost of health insurance premiums that have become a national problem in recent years is in part created by the billions of dollars of unpaid health care service received by illegals. Or what about the cost of keeping illegal aliens in prison? What about the cost of welfare, of crime, additional burdens on the public school system ... All of these things cost money, and when an illegal enjoys any of these benefits or creates an additional burden, he's not going to pay for it. You and I are. Just remember the money you're saving today on cheap labor, you're simply spending somewhere else.

I'm not speaking in hypotheticals but, I admit, I am speaking in somewhat broad scenarios, based on what we read in the newspapers, see on television and hear in commentaries from politicos and pundits. Now let me speak of a more specific situation that will explain my point: Let me tell you a true, actual story, of which I am sure there are thousands just like it.

A Mexican kid connected to a gang in southern California is a suspect in a minor crime. He's an illegal immigrant — a teenager — and the authorities put out an offer: If he turns himself in for deportation (for the third time!) they WON'T deport any of the rest of his family, each of whom is also in the country illegally. He takes the deal, turns himself in and after a night in jail is shipped back across the border by bus.

Within weeks, he's back in the United States, new cell phone, new place to live, and back into his "quick cash" business — selling drugs.

In less than a month, he is arrested again. This time, however, they just cut him loose. The officers tell him that they're tired of arresting him for these same minor offenses and spending the time and money to put him through the system, imprison him for a few nights and ship him back to Mexico. They give up, deciding it's cheaper to just turn him loose on the streets rather than pointlessly running in circles. This is ONE kid. Imagine how many thousands of illegal immigrants who are not otherwise criminals who keep jumping the border time and time again until the authorities just give up?

In 1965, President Lyndon Johnson quietly signed into law the "Immigration Reform Act" which overturned America's traditional immigration policy and replaced it with the most liberal, "easy-access" immigration policy in our history. As a result as many as 1.8 million immigrants arrive on U.S. soil every year which is more than all other countries on the globe COMBINED! That's according to our federal government's Census Bureau. Immigration officials also admit that roughly 60 percent of foreigners who are granted temporary work or student visas never, in fact, leave the country when they're required to be law.

To say that illegal immigration is a problem in this country is a laughable understatement. In 2004 estimates were released declaring that nearly three million illegals entered this country on an annual basis. That's nearly 8,000 persons every day. What's even more frightening is that many experts predict the number of illegals currently residing in the U.S. at approximately 15 to 20 million. That is more than the population of Nevada, Oregon and Washington State combined. This situation permeates nearly every community from Miami to Seattle. It is not changing the face of America; it HAS changed the face of America. And in many ways not for the better. It's safe to say that, as sure as today turns into tomorrow, our American way of life is being steadily eroded with each rising sun. It's only a matter of time before the house our ancestors built WILL come crumbling down. U.S. Census projections indicate that if we stay on our current course, within 50 years our population will nearly double; non-Hispanic whites will account for less than half of all residents; and English will no longer be our predominant language.

As more and more illegal immigrants pour into this nation, the standard of living in many areas is on an accelerating decline. It's a simple fact. You can't expect someone who has spent two decades living in a Third World environment under conditions that are common in Third World countries to migrate to the United States and instantly assume a lifestyle and habits consistent with the standards of most Americans. It's simply not possible. As more and more illegal immigrants from these countries overrun our nation's cities, they will not raise their standard of living to meet ours. Instead the way of life in these areas will decline to the Third World expectations of these newcomers, finally coming to rest somewhere in a state of Second World mediocrity: an existence far less than what we've come to expect in this great nation of ours and grossly inferior to the standards we want our future generations to experience. The New York Times already saw this coming. In an article from August of 2005, the Times made this prediction: "U.S. Becoming Third World Country."

Steven Murdock, the state demographer for Texas, summed up his findings of current and future demographics with this statement: "In some sense Texas is a preview of what our nation will become in the long run. Our future in Texas is increasingly tied to our minority population. If their education and skills continue to lag, the state will be less competitive in the global economy."

Texas, Arizona, New Mexico and California are already suffering what the rest of the country will eventually face. Why else would voters in Arizona have approved the nation's strictest laws so far in an attempt to rein in its illegal immigration crisis — much to the chagrin of the ACLU and many others? Among a number of reasons, it's because they are already seeing a decline in their overall quality of life.

This country cannot survive and retain its "greatest nation" status with an overpopulation of ditch diggers and hotel maids. True, the world needs day laborers and I absolutely will never disparage anyone for the work they do in their lives. Anyone who works for a living, no matter what the task, is "A OK" in my book. I'm all for an honest day's work for an honest day's pay, but with approximately 8,000 illegal workers — or more — crossing our borders every 24 hours, and many more unskilled workers arriving legally, we are making a sharp right turn off the path necessary to build and maintain a prosperous and stable society.

The large number of foreign-born day laborers in this country suppresses the earnings of blue collar America by working illegally for far less than the average wage. Many times these immigrant workers are able undercut our native citizens by avoiding common living expenses such as health and auto insurance, as well as federal and state taxes, accurate amounts of property taxes, social security and Medicaid. On this uneven playing field, these day laborers can — and do — force local Americans out of work.

The suppression of wages is not the only economic problem created by this tidal wave of unskilled labor across America's borders, however. Perhaps much more frightening is the potentially devastating effect on tens of millions in regards to our extremely lethargic economy. Heaven help us if the housing market continues to fail, as well as other industries that depend largely on unskilled manual laborers. There will be far too many workers for the jobs at hand — so then what? According to reports in mid-2011, the American housing market is actually worse off than during the Depression of the 1930s. Welfare lines stretch around the corner as the job market struggles desperately to keep up with the enormous unskilled labor population. We see it every week as the weekly jobs reports indicate that new unemployment claims continue to rest at an alarmingly high number, and with such a large and growing population of unskilled laborers when and how will it ever end? Unfortunately it is not only the unskilled laborers who feel the pinch. Thanks to the "freeloading friendly" liberals and democrats, the rest of us will feel the burden as more and more tax payer dollars must be pumped into existing and newly created social programs. As you can see, when the economy is strong, the largely unskilled immigrant population is a benefit in some ways. Let the economy falter for a few years, however, and with an over abundance of manual laborers things have gotten real bad, real quick.

How many unskilled laborers does one country need? When our economy spiraled into a recession, the first ones out of work were the ones who could least afford it. Armed with only the skills of manual labor, these people are the first casualties of an economic slowdown. They will also be the ones finding it the most difficult to gain new employment. But not to worry, thanks to our country's bleeding-heart liberals, the unskilled and unemployed won't need to find new jobs. They'll get fat and happy living off the tax payers' tit. Something must be done to curb the consistent surge of day laborers into this country and maintain a proper balance between the skilled and unskilled labor pools.

Social programs provided to the newly immigrated population of this country total a staggering $346 billion annually, according to the National Research Council. I could break that down into what such a figure represents to each and every taxpaying citizen, but do I really need to? In short, it's staggering. I, for one, would rather pay a dime more for an avocado at the grocery store than continue to shell out thousands of dollars a year in taxes for a segment of our society that leeches off each and every one of us in some form or fashion.

The out-of-pocket pinch we all feel under the weight of ballooning social programs is by no means the only area of our daily lives that must withstand the undo burden created by our increasing illegal problem. Between 1993 and 2009, nearly 100 hospitals in California were forced to shut down because, like all hospitals, they were legally required to treat anyone who enters an emergency room, whether he or she has the ability to pay or not. In many areas it's quite common for illegal residents to receive emergency room medical attention for anything from a cold, to mental illness to a gunshot wound, and there is no recourse for the hospital if these services go unpaid.

As the Los Angeles Times reported, "Emergency room physicians say the closures have led to long waits, diverted ambulances and, in some extreme cases, patient deaths. The closures also make it necessary for patients in need of emergency care to travel much farther, delaying access to treatment."

California is by no means the only state affected by such a phenomenon. Fifteen hospitals closed in New York City alone during the past several years. It's said that although substantial there is no firmly agreed number of how many hospitals across the nation have closed in the past decade due to fiscal problems.

According to the Center for Immigration Reform, the medical treatment of illegal aliens costs this country about $2.2 billion each year. Unfortunately this number is not just a dollar figure; it is far more serious than that. The standard of health care will continue to decline as the resources of our nation's hospitals are spread dangerously thin in an attempt to care for an illegal population which is breaking the law by its mere presence in this country.

Health care, however, is just the tip of the iceberg when considering the negative impact illegals have had on certain aspects of our society which are integral to a great majority of our citizens. According to a report in the Washington Post, citing statistics from the Urban Institute, "About 65,000 illegal immigrants graduate from U.S. high schools every year, unable to work legally and often unable to afford college without access to in-state tuition or government-backed financial aid."

According to the Federation for American Immigration Reform (FAIR), a conservative advocacy group that favors tighter immigration laws, "the total K-12 school expenditure for illegal immigrants costs each state nearly $12 billion annually, and when the children born here to illegal aliens are added, the costs more than double to $28.6 billion."

Thanks to jackass politicians and groups like the ACLU, as a taxpayer in America there seems to be no relief in sight. California alone, while facing a budget deficit of $14.4 billion in 2010-2011, is burdened with an estimated $21.8 billion in annual expenditures as a result of their illegal immigration problem, according to FAIR. A 2009 study by the Center for Immigration Studies (CIS) generally concurs with Fairs' assessments of the various costs of illegal immigration on the American tax system.

So the next time payday rolls around and 15 to 40 percent of the money YOU earned is missing due to taxes, understand that a significant portion of that money is going to people who have no right to be here, and others who are simply here to take advantage of a system that has been set up to take care of you and your family in your time of need. Understand that next time the end of the month is here and you really could use a couple of extra bucks to make ends meet, those couple of extra dollars are being used to house an incarcerated illegal alien. When your credit card debt just won't seem to decrease, and you wish you could pay a little more on your Visa next month, understand that bill could be better managed if our government didn't force you to give away your hard-earned money so that an illegal uninsured immigrant could skip out on his emergency room expenses. When it comes down to it, the lower- and middle-class American workers are stretched thin enough financially without having to constantly overcome the economic incompetence and downright selfishness of many modern day immigrants. And what's perhaps the most angering and disheartening aspect of it all stems from the fact that is our useless elected officials who have consistently allowed them to live in this manner and most likely will continue to do so.

I have discussed many scenarios and cited several examples of the detrimental effects illegal immigrants pose to our economy, society and culture. So why then isn't something being done to stop our gradual demise at the hands of these foreign parasites? Why doesn't the American government negotiate with other foreign governments in an attempt to derive a formula, which will slow down this massive surge of foreign nationals pouring across our borders? This seems like a logical question which should have a logical answer. Correct? Well, here's your logical answer: The Mexican government, for example, which one would assume would be our ally in solving such a crisis, is actually one of the largest proponents at perpetuating this nightmare. In December, 2004, Mexico's foreign ministry created and began distributing millions of flyers chocked full of advice to Mexican border jumpers. The pamphlet read, in part: "This guide is intended to give you some practical advice that could be of use if you have made the difficult decision to seek new work opportunities outside your country."

The Mexican government educates its citizens on the most advantageous ways to illegally immigrate to the United States. Why isn't the Mexican government informing its citizens who want to "seek new work opportunities outside their country" how to immigrate to another country legally? It appears that the government of Mexico is just as selfish as many of its citizens. The illegal Mexican immigrant may tell you that he/she simply wants to make a better life for him or herself, but in reality many simply want to freeload off the good fortune that has been created in this country as the result of the back breaking efforts of the current and prior generations. Our forefathers with a lot of blood, sweat and calloused hands created prosperity; they created opportunity and our government has put measures in place for those of us who sometimes struggle. Yet as a result of spineless politicians and people who have become intoxicated with political correctness the foundation of this country and its government is being compromised. The Mexican government will never assist us in curtailing this matter. That's a laughable notion to even suggest. Mexico couldn't be happier about our illegal immigration problem. It has the good fortune of expelling an element of its society that is largely nothing more than an economic burden, and in doing so passing their burden onto us.

In fact, to make the transition as seamless as possible the Mexican government actually distributes identification cards to its citizens which it doesn't accept, but the government of the United States for some asinine reason actually does. These forms of ID are known as "Matricula Consular Cards." First of all, what the hell is that, and secondly, why do we depend on an identification card issued by another country to identify people living within OUR borders? The purpose of these cards is to simply create a way for illegal aliens to subvert the immigration laws of the United States. If this were not the case and these immigrants were in our country legally; they would have proper U.S. documentation and would not need identification issued by the Mexican government. What makes this whole thing even more absurd is that the Mexican government doesn't even recognize these cards as valid forms of identification. In Mexico the official ID is a voter registration card. If you are a Mexican citizen and received a matricula consular card and go back to Mexico, you can't use it as an identifying document; but somehow it's a valid form of ID here. Who is scamming who here? It's simply amazing that after the terror attacks of 9/11 the immigration policies of this country still remain so absurd. It truly is disturbing when you think about all of the ways our government and its officials allow our system to be subverted.

Now, I can live with some of the problems caused by many of the illegal aliens in this country. I can't say they won't always disgust me, but I can live with my hard-earned tax dollars funding social programs that our government allows these people to exploit. I can live (for now) with the metaphorical "middle finger" many immigrants give me by showing very little respect for my country's culture, language and heritage. I can live with these problems for now; I can't say I don't want to see them changed and I can't promise that at some point I won't be one of those who actively tries to change them.

Once upon a time, not having valid documentation such as a driver's license or birth certificate was simply a minor issue that many people chose to casually overlook. The events of September 11, 2001, however, have showed Americans that we can no longer take the requirement for proper documentation so lightly. The men who orchestrated the attacks of 9/11 had over a period of years accumulated some 63 driver's licenses. Two of the hijackers actually had a valid Virginia driver's license. Mohammed Atta, one of the masterminds behind the attacks of 9/11, was stopped by police but not detained because he possessed a valid license even though his visitor's visa had expired — which actually made him an illegal alien and therefore should have been deported. According to the 9/11 Commission's Report, "All but one of the 9/11 hijackers acquired some form of U.S. documentation; most by fraud. Acquiring these forms of identification would have assisted them in boarding commercial flights, renting cars and other necessary activities." In a roundabout way, the government of the United States and their flimsy incompetent policies had a hand in allowing those horrific acts to be carried out. Or maybe I should say it was the apathy of our government that ultimately played a large hand in the tragedy of 9/11. It wasn't, of course what our government officials did; it was what our government officials didn't do. This indifference in fact as has become a heated center for national debate in recent months as to why our government seemingly refuses to follow one of its very own laws. In section eight of the United States Code 1324 it's spelled out pretty clearly: A person (including a group of persons, businesses, organizations or local government) commits a federal felony when she or he assists an illegal alien she/he should reasonably know is illegally in the U.S. Had this simple law which governmental democrats are trying so hard to still ignore been followed, 9/11 might have been avoided.

Yet all but one of the September 11th hijackers had some form of fraudulent U.S. documentation. Here is, however, perhaps the most shocking realization. After everything this country went through as a result of 9/11 and the ease with which these illegal alien terrorists were able to move within our society, 14 states still issue driver's licenses to illegal aliens. What the hell are we doing? All it takes is one! Am I missing something or is this as obvious as it seems?

Of the possibly 20 million illegals in our country don't think that there is not at least one who is looking to destroy us from within. And thanks to our government, which can't seem to follow its own rules, those in this country who want to do us harm all but have the key to the city. You may ask yourself, "it can't be that easy, can it?"

Well just hear what writer Frosty Woodridge observed in a column written in 2004: "John Slaghe, a former 30-year border patrol officer, noted that among 37,000 captured illegal aliens in the Tucson, Arizona, sector, 7,500 of them were from terror-sponsoring countries. Since they catch only one in four, what if the ones who slipped through were able to gain driver's licenses? How about another 9/11 brought to you by your inept, political-correctness obsessed, spineless leaders? How do you think we suffered the first one?"

See, it's not just the poor, humble immigrant seeking a better life who is seeping through our porous borders. Our borders in their current condition along with the moronic method of documentation in this country serve as a welcome mat to terrorists from all over the globe looking to take their shot at the red, white, and blue. When will a logical move be made to remedy this problem so that the United States and its citizens don't feel like we're all just sitting ducks waiting for "someday?"

Over the years media has afflicted me with the label of racist among other not-so-flattering descriptions. The full conversation you have just read was quite similar to the one had with an SI reporter all those years ago, although not reported in nearly the same manner. Basically the last 20 pages were reduced to a simple, crude paraphrase of "I don't like foreigners." As you can see and I think many can relate, it's a bit more complicated than a broad, Neanderthal-like absolute, and if after reading the thoughts, feelings and logic I have cited in the prior pages you still consider me a racist then so be it. I guess that will just be a place where you and I differ.

The personal experience I've lived, in my opinion, is where media's stubbornness and unwillingness to give the American people both sides of every story that makes it so hard for us to move forward as a nation. In some cases and situations, as I've just discussed, I don't like foreigners. I admit; I have a problem with those who come to this country in any manner seeking to manipulate, exploit and harm the integrity of the land I love, but it is these immigrants and only these immigrants that I take issue with. I fully understand and fully support those immigrants who come to this country with the desire to do things the right way — to assimilate, to contribute, to strengthen the fabric of America for all of us. To those immigrants I welcome you and wish you luck. To those with selfish, self-centered ideas nothing would make me happier than to see you drag your parasitic ass back across whatever border you slithered across and recede into the hole from which you came. I truly hope the day comes where you and your kind are permanently prevented from infiltrating our country with the harm you bring.

As I write this it seems that my latter wish may be in the process of becoming a reality. I was thrilled to witness what happened in Arizona last year, when Gov. Jan Brewer signed into law the nation's toughest bill on illegal immigration aimed to identify, prosecute and deport illegal immigrants.

Simple.

Of course, the move unleashed immediate protests and reignited the divisive battle over immigration reform nationally and summoned a rebuke from President Obama, who said it threatened to "to undermine basic notions of fairness that we cherish as Americans, as well as the trust between police and our communities that is so crucial to keeping us safe," according to the New York Times.

Spoken like a true bleeding-heart socialist. What a moronically blind way to view this piece of legislation. Call it "racial profiling," say it's "racially insensitive" or even unfair and I will say again: stereotypes are there for a reason. If someone of Hispanic origin is worried about being unfairly singled out, I have a fool-proof way to combat your fears.

"HAVE PROPER DOCUMENTATION; SHOW IT TO WHOMEVER IS REQUESTING IT AND YOU WON'T HAVE A PROBLEM!" Why is this so @#$%ing hard to understand or deal with?

If you have the proper documentation then there is nothing to worry about. If you don't then here's your one way ticket via the State of Arizona. Either way, as a legal American citizen, I feel safer, which should be the ultimate concern here, not the fear of upsetting Manuel because he had to show his passport or visa. If Manuel has a passport then Manuel is free to go. But it's not only about the "Manuels" of Arizona. What if this measure allows police officials to apprehend the next Muhammad Atta? I can't speak for everyone, but personally I would much rather calm the irritation of a few people who feel they have been unfairly profiled than have to deal with or possibly be a part of another catastrophe like 9/11. Why is this even a debate considering the state of the world we live in? It's idiotic!

To make my point let me share a personal story with you. I was playing winter ball in Venezuela back in 2004 and had been living there for a few months. One night while driving home after a game, I had to go through a random police checkpoint. There were approximately 20 cars ahead of me, and as we approached the checkpoint I noticed only one other car had been asked to pull to the side of the road. Well, when it became my turn; the officer asked me and the three other gringos inside to pull our vehicle off the road.

Now let me tell you something about the Venezuelan Policia. They wear army fatigues and carry automatic weapons (vastly more threatening than an Arizona police officer). At any rate I pulled over. My girlfriend, two other teammates and I were asked by a man in camouflage carrying an AK-47 to get out of the car and produce our car registration and passports. Guess what? I had my car registration; I had my passport and so did everyone else in my car. I've traveled enough to know its just part of the protocol to carry those things with you. We were only held up about five minutes while the officers reviewed our documents and then were allowed to leave, no harm, no foul. Had I been racially profiled? You're damn right I had, but you know what? When you're in a car with four white folks in a country with very few white folks there are a lot better odds that I'm not supposed to be there than someone who looks like they're from Venezuela. Was it a problem? Do I want to sue the Venezuelan government for unfairly profiling me? That's what some idiots in this country would suggest, but hell no.

These Venezuelan officers did absolutely the right thing. They were looking for people who looked suspicious or out of place. Once again, stereotypes are there for a reason, and stereotypically I was someone that looked out of place and maybe should not be in Venezuela. These officers were simply doing their job attempting to protect the citizens of Venezuela from people who are not in the country legally and therefore may not have the best of intentions. What's the big deal? I proved that it was "OK" for me to be in the country; I proved I was not doing anything wrong and I was free to go. It was as easy as that.

Well, enough about me. Let's get back to the Arizona immigration law that is now being mimicked by numerous other states which in turn is doing nothing more than mimicking a federal mandate that already exists. The law is simply making the failure to carry immigration documents a crime and giving the police broad power to detain anyone suspected of being in the country illegally. If I had been unable to produce proper documentation at the police check point in Venezuela;

I possibly would have been detained and rightfully so. Opponents have called it an open invitation for harassment and discrimination against Hispanics regardless of their citizenship status. I had proper documentation and wasn't harassed in a country where I was in the overwhelming minority; so why is there an automatic assumption that our legal Hispanic residents will not be treated in the same manner. With tongue in cheek, opponents to the Arizona immigration bill seem to be calling the brave law enforcement men and women of that state racists, but as we all should know by now that's generally the standard "go to" for all gutless libs looking to promote the social agenda. You would think by now they would have come up with a strategy that's a bit more creative.

While police demands of proper documents are common on subways, highways and in public places in an ever-increasing number of countries, Arizona is the first American state to demand that immigrants meet federal requirements to carry documents legitimizing their presence on American soil.

Ms. Brewer acknowledged critics' concerns, saying she would work to ensure that the police have proper training to carry out the law. But she sided with arguments by the law's sponsors that it provides an indispensable tool for the police in a border state that is a leading magnet of illegal immigration. She said racial profiling would not be tolerated, adding, "We have to trust our law enforcement." Why do all detractors of this law assume that law enforcement officers are going to naturally behave with racial bias? Isn't that a bit insulting?

It hasn't been and isn't going to be a smooth ride. The law is contentious, even as additional states are considering similar measures and other states are invoking bans on trade with Arizona or any state that enacts similar legislation.

Its proof of what a divisive issue immigration is in this country and the potential it has to create massive disruption where I don't believe it should exist.

This bill will require police officers, "when practicable," to detain people they reasonably suspect are in the country without authorization and to verify their status with federal officials, unless doing so would hinder an investigation or emergency medical treatment. It also makes it a state crime — a misdemeanor — to not carry immigration papers (put them in your wallet, the glove compartment of your car, wherever, just as I did my passport). In addition, it allows people to sue local government or agencies if they believe federal or state immigration laws are not being enforced.

The Atlanta Journal-Constitution's Cynthia Tucker wrote that the law "Harkens back to apartheid," while the New York Times' David Brooks wrote that it's "Terrible … an invitation to abuse." My rebuttal is that the way the system currently exists gives illegals an invitation to abuse America.

But as conservative columnist and frequent TV commentator Byron York, says:

"Has anyone actually read the law? Contrary to the talk, it is a reasonable, limited, carefully crafted measure designed to help law enforcement deal with a serious problem in Arizona. Its authors anticipated criticism and went to great lengths to make sure it is constitutional and will hold up in court. It is the criticism of the law that is over the top, not the law itself."

The law requires police to check with federal authorities on a person's immigration status, if officers have stopped that person for a legitimate reason and come to suspect that he or she might be in the U.S. illegally. The heart of the law is this provision: "For any lawful contact made by a law enforcement official or a law enforcement agency … where reasonable suspicion exists that the person is an alien who is unlawfully present in the United States, a reasonable attempt shall be made, when practicable, to determine the immigration status of the person …"

So it's hardly a law aimed to be a mass civil rights violation of Hispanics. Remember the statistic citing the number of illegals apprehended from terror sponsoring countries in the Tucson area alone. This law is designed to curb their infiltration as well. According to the law, a police officer must already be "engaged in some detention of an individual because they have violated some other law," says Kris Coach, a University of Missouri- Kansas City Law School professor who helped draft the measure. "The most likely context where this law would come into play is a traffic stop."

I strongly agree with Byron York, who asks, "Is having to produce a driver's license too burdensome? These days, natural-born U.S. citizens, and everybody else, too, are required to show a driver's license to get on an airplane, to check into a hotel, even to purchase some over-the-counter allergy medicines. If it's a burden, it's a burden on everyone."

Of course, the Arizona law is just the tip of the iceberg with immigration, which will more than likely always be a polarizing issue which political parties will strategically use to their benefit when courting voters.

Senator Harry Reid of Nevada has been key in the effort among Washington politicians to use the immigration debate to energize Hispanic voters to help Democrats, but given the rebounding of the Republican Party in November of 2010, it's apparent that immigration can also energize conservative voters as well.

One thing is for certain – and it's probably the only thing I agree with Senator Reid on, when he proclaimed, "The system is broken."

CHAPTER NINE

Speak English

While obsessing about the problems we face as a nation with regard to national security, the state of our borders, our faltering economy, immigration and many other polarizing issues that this country must confront on a daily basis there is one significant aspect that I feel stands out as the most obvious, yet the most simple, characteristic which has the ability to circumvent many of our differences and ultimately bond us together as a nation. In my opinion that unifying quality is our English language.

As I've said in the previous chapter with regard to the need for immigrants to integrate, assimilate and then contribute to their new adoptive country, it's clear that for the past five or maybe even 10 years, our language is losing its power as a unifying element.

A 2010 report from the U.S. Census Bureau shows that the number of non-English-speaking households in the U.S. has increased significantly. According to the report, which uses data collected in 2007 as part of the American Community Survey, 55.4 million Americans speak a language other than English when they are at home. This represents a 140 percent increase since 1980.

At the time I first started thinking about it however, I wondered what I could do personally to draw attention to what in my opinion is and will continue to be an enormous detriment to America: residents who not only don't but can't speak

English.

One day I called my assistant and told her I wanted some plain white T-shirts made up with bold, black lettering that simply said, "Speak English."

It's not that I wanted to go into the business of selling T-shirts. I merely wanted to create a focal point to help spawn dialogue and discussion about something that I think is crucial to this country's future and the unity that is ultimately needed to keep it strong.

Now, before I go any further: I want to stress I don't think people should be forced to speak English – in fact I think it's amazing if you have the ability to speak a number of different languages; more power to you. But I DO think that if you live in America, plan to raise your family here, as well as seek to prosper on American soil, I feel very strongly that one of those languages should be English. I don't think any hospital in the country should have to employ Spanish (or any other kind of) translators just in case the ER finds itself with patients that its doctors and nurses can't communicate with. Above anything else, I think it's inherently dangerous for patients and their families if they can't communicate with the people trying to save their lives. Furthermore, I feel a wedge is being driven between the cohesiveness of young Americans when entire high school curriculums are taught in the foreign language of that student. The most basic way we communicate with one another is verbally and when that simply ability does not exist unity as a people will not either.

The more I enjoyed being involved with something I truly believe in and the more I promoted this idea through media interviews; the more it evolved into a clear concise effort of what I simply like to call "The Speak English Campaign."

I feel that further elaboration on the immigrants' involvement in the creation of this great country is not necessary at this point, but I do feel, however, that I need to repeat or even risk belaboring the point that our unique heritage and culture that has been established over the last several hundred years by these first immigrants and their first-generation American children is like no other on earth. It is a culture full of customs, traditions, dialects and religions that are our own and unites us as Americans. It was immersion into this culture that the early American immigrant knew would be vital to his success in this new country. It is this heritage that I and so many others who have had a hand in its creation and sustainment would like to see protected and supported so that future generations of immigrants can continue to realize their dreams of living in the greatest country on earth.

The mission statement of the "Speak English" campaign is to encourage people to promote and support the endurance of the American heritage and the American culture at its most basic level, the language we speak. Many people over many generations have invested blood, sweat and tears as well as lives, into creating an America that affords all of us opportunities that are not available anywhere else in the world. Out of respect to these past generations, the least we can do as the present generation is to promote the longevity of the culture that our forefathers created.

This campaign is in no way intended to degrade or demean the cultures or heritages of another's nationality or race. There is never an excuse to show disrespect to anyone based simply on the diversity of his or her culture. However, this is a two-way street.

"English is the key to full participation in the opportunities of American life." So said the late senator Samuel Ichiye Hayakawa, who was a Canadian-born American academic and political figure of Japanese ancestry. He was an English professor, and served as president of San Francisco State University and then as a United States Senator from California from 1977 to 1983.

His words certainly resonate with me and in 2005 I was compelled to write what I call the Speak English Campaign Mission Statement. I wanted to get a lot more involved in promoting the English language not as an exclusionary block to a portion of the heritage of our current or future generations of American immigrants, but to help create awareness and understanding that, as Senator Hayakawa pointed out, possessing the ability to speak English is a crucial element needed to get the most out of being an American and to truly realize everything this great country has to offer its citizens.

I wrote this statement when I began doing media interviews and promoting this "campaign." It has been successful in every way I could imagine. Despite many in the media assuming and insisting that this effort is nothing more than an endeavor created through racial motivations, the truth could not be further from the media's preconceived judgment.

To this day my views remain the same. Perhaps more steadfastly than ever, as I observe on a daily basis what appears to be a consistent fracturing of my country's culture and heritage. Here is an abridged version of my Speak English Campaign Mission Statement. I've abridged it because in its full form I repeat and addressed many points I've already made and cited sources which have already been addressed.

SPEAK ENGLISH CAMPAIGN MISSION STATEMENT: "Over the last several years, immigration, whether it be legal or illegal, has been an enormous issue of national debate in this country. Undoubtedly, it will continue to be addressed by liberals and conservatives alike, well into our future. Immigration is obviously not a new concept to this country. We all, at some point in our lineage, have immigrants that make up our ancestry, and who are responsible for giving us the opportunity to live in the greatest country on earth. Immigration, to a large extent, is what gives America its uniqueness and allows this country to thrive in so many different ways. I myself am a fourth-generation descendant of German immigrants, and am very thankful for the courage and fortitude, which my ancestors possessed, that has ultimately allowed me to enjoy life as an American. I hope everyone in this great country understands how they got here and appreciates those immigrants who made it possible."

"The fact that this country was founded and sustained by immigrants doesn't need much elaboration. A point I feel that is not focused on nearly enough, however, is the unique heritage and culture that has been established over the last several hundred years by these early American Immigrants. Immigrants that have come from all corners of the world with dreams and desires of a more prosperous, and fulfilling life for themselves and their families. Over the course of many generations, these brave men and women have established a culture that is like no other on earth. It is a culture full of customs, traditions, dialects and religions that are our own and unite us as Americans. It was the immersion into this culture that the early American immigrant knew would be vital to his ultimate success in this new country. It is this heritage that I and so many others who have had a hand in its creation and fulfillment, would like to see protected and supported so that future generations of immigrants can continue to realize their dreams of living in the greatest country on earth."

The mission statement of the "Speak English" campaign is to encourage people to promote and support the sustainment of the American heritage and the American culture. Many people over many generations have invested blood, sweat, and tears into creating an America that affords all of us opportunities that are not available anywhere else. Out of respect to past generations, the least we can do as the present generation is to promote the longevity of the culture that our forefathers have created.

This campaign is in no way intended to degrade or demean the cultures or heritages of other nationalities or races. There is never an excuse to show disrespect to anyone based simply on the diversity of his or her culture. However, this is a two-way street. When immigrants vote with their feet and migrate to this country with the intent to live, work, raise a family and enjoy all of the incredible advantages that America has to offer, but make no attempt to learn the language, observe the customs, or celebrate the holidays, these people, in my opinion, are showing a tremendous amount of disrespect to their hosts. They are showing a tremendous lack of deference as well to the men and women who over the course of history have sacrificed much to make this country great and in turn have afforded them the ability to seek opportunity here.

In my own personal experiences, I have collectively lived abroad for over a year of my life, three different times in Puerto Rico and once in Venezuela. During my time in these countries, I did my best to speak their language even though my Spanish was barely adequate. I still attempted to speak the language whenever the situation presented itself and worked to become more adept at communicating in their language in order to avoid the "ugly American" stereotype. I went to numerous local holiday celebrations such as events which centered around the Puerto Rican holiday "Three Kings Day," as well as numerous other festivals and gatherings. My life during the time I spent abroad was certainly much easier trying to conform to local society rather than asking local society to conform to me.

In my opinion assimilating to local society is a concept that is being lost on many of today's immigrants. Every current and future immigrant should realize what all early American immigrants knew, that immersing oneself into the American culture is the only way to truly realize and enjoy all that this great country has to offer. Countless numbers of pre-modern immigrants went to great lengths to intertwine themselves into the fabric of their new country. Many newcomers did things such as change their last names in order to seem "more American." They also understood that the adoption of local customs as well as learning the language was critical to their survival. In the last generation however, we are seeing a much more unassimilated immigrant who seems to care more about recreating the culture of his/her homeland than accepting the culture of his/her current place of residence. This attitude of many of today's immigrants, in my opinion, is not a healthy one if we are to retain a strong, cohesive and united America.

Generation after generation, people from all over the globe have made their way to the United States to be absorbed under the common brotherhood of American nationalism. Whether from Japan, Denmark or Italy, immigrants have arrived for centuries with a desire to eventually enjoy a common bond shared with their countrymen based on language, traditions, customs and similar beliefs. It is this common bond, felt by the citizens of this country that has made America a beacon of hope around the world. Unfortunately, there are forces that have been introduced into this country over the last decade that are threatening that common bond and our national unity.

This campaign, as I have said before, is not to demean or degrade other cultures or nationalities, but instead to bolster American nationalism and promote pride in the American culture. This country was made strong by the influx of immigrants and will continue to be a great nation with the help of new ones. These new immigrants, however, will strengthen America and realize genuine prosperity for themselves and their families only to the extent with which they are willing to integrate themselves into the fabric of this country and truly become Americans.

This country was made great and will continue to be such only through assimilation and unity not through dissimilation and separation. Without assimilation, America will grow more and more divided; and a country divided against itself cannot stand. As Americans, we need to band together against the forces that encourage division and help new immigrants blend themselves into our culture. It is only with this that America will stay united and strong.

To those of you who have always supported me, I thank you. On the contrary, I know there are many of you who are reading this that have disagreed with me over the years, and I truly appreciate you taking the time to hear what I have to say. I love this country and I will use my voice to help make it a better place for all of us to live. It's time to stop feeling guilty for living in the greatest nation on earth, and start standing up for America."

In many ways, my "mission statement" and my drive for the Speak English campaign was rather late to the table when it comes to the whole issue. The late Sen. Hayakawa, who I found so inspiring, started the nation's oldest and largest non-partisan citizens' groups dedicated to keeping America OFFICIALLY English. In 1983, he started U.S. English, Inc. (www.usenglish.org) which now has more than 1.8 million members.

Since 1812, the voters of 31 states have approved legislation making English their official language.

In Tennessee and Montana, legislators have introduced legislation requiring that all drivers' license exams be conducted in English. A 2009 survey by U.S. English, Inc. showed that eight states have limited their license exams to English only while 14 states have increased the amount of languages for the tests.

"The 2010 elections showed legislators the consequence of neglecting the will of their constituents," said Mauro E. Mujica, the current Chairman of U.S. English, Inc. "The American peoples' support for official English legislation is at an all-time high. The new legislators were elected in part for their support of policies that bring people together and don't divide us along linguistic lines. I look forward to working with the new legislators and passing common sense measures that unite us and promote sensible government."

During the 2009/2010 legislative session, official English measures were introduced in 15 states. This includes the successful passage of a U.S. English bill in Oklahoma that sailed through both the House and Senate in April of 2009. The voters overwhelmingly voted in favor of the referendum in November 2010 adding Oklahoma to the list of 31 states that have made English their official language.

A Washington state legislator, Jim McCune, introduced legislation to make English the state's official language and require all official government actions to be conducted in English.

"Washington has long been one of the most diverse states in the nation. Yet, the numbers of those who are trapped in linguistic isolation continues to grow at an alarming rate," said Mujica. "The role of government is to lead people towards success and self-sufficiency, not handicap them through failed multilingual polices. We must maintain a common language through which we can share the ideas that are necessary for a vibrant and diverse society."

With the introduction of HB 1769, Washington became the fourth state to have an official English measure pending in 2011. Legislators in Texas, Wisconsin and Minnesota have already introduced bills to make English the official language of the state while a measure in Indiana will strengthen the existing official English law if enacted.

As Oklahoma's official English law was filed a Tulsa law professor sued to block the implementation of the measure. State Question 751, which was passed by more than 74 percent of Oklahoma voters made English the official language of the state. In my opinion it is individuals such as this along with various "action groups" hiding behind the guise of civil rights infringement and accusations of racism that do the most harm to efforts of a cohesive American population and ultimately damage the ones they are attempting to "protect" in the long run.

"Official English was passed by the voters in Oklahoma by one of the greatest margins we have ever seen," said Mujica. "This lawsuit is nothing more than a distraction that will ultimately end up costing the taxpayers who will foot the bill defending a law that is not only constitutional, but overwhelmingly supported by the voters in the state."

In April of 2011 the case challenging Oklahoma's Official English law was dismissed – yet the attorney claims he's going to keep fighting to the Supreme Court if he has to.

In 2007, the Alaska Supreme court upheld the state's official English law, rejecting claims that it violated the state constitution. The court ruling followed a long trend of judicial decisions in favor of official English laws, including the requirement that English be the official language of government documents.

"As in other states, Oklahoma's official English law will withstand this assault from radical fringe groups that are more interested in dividing the nation along linguistic lines instead of uniting us under a common language," said Mujica.

As is readily apparent by voter reaction, official English legislation is something the vast majority of Americans think is necessary.

As Mujica says, "This isn't a new or radical proposition. In most developed countries around the globe, newly arrived citizens are expected to deal with the official language. Learning English does not take away from your individuality and your ability to grow independently in whatever other foreign language you choose to speak."

With that in mind I would like to share a story about a close personal friend, Jonah Easley. Approximately four years ago Jonah and his wife, Cathy, moved to China as English teachers in the Dongguan, Guangdong, province of that country. After living there for a couple of years Jonah and Cathy decided they liked it and were making no plans to return to the U.S., but instead for the foreseeable future were going to live and raise their family in China. Over the last two years Jonah has purchased a coffee shop, and he and his wife just had their first child.

I had a chance to spend a few days with Jonah last year over the Thanksgiving Holiday on a hunting trip. As a result of his family's decision to remain in China, work in China and raise their family there, Jonah now speaks fluent Mandarin Chinese. Also, he, his wife and his new son all have Asian names and he says he does everything he can on a daily basis to live as "Chinese" as possible, understanding full well that is the only way for he and his family to truly thrive in their new surroundings.

Jonah chose to move to China. No one put a gun to his head. If Jonah is going to make that decision and intend on establishing a life for himself and the rest of his family there, Jonah needs to live like the Chinese if he expects to survive and prosper which is exactly the way it should be. Jonah would not last very long in the environment where he lives if he insisted on everyone conforming to him. My friend Jonah gets it; why is his attitude such a hard concept for many American immigrants and the enablers on the left to grasp?

English is the key to opportunity in this country. It empowers immigrants and makes us truly united as a people. Common sense says that the government should teach people English rather than provide services in multiple languages. What would happen if our government had to provide services in all 322 languages spoken in the U.S.? Without a common language, how long would we remain the "United" States?

According to the Canadian government, it spends $260 million annually to perform government business in both of the nation's official languages (English and French). This figure was 0.16% of the Canadian federal budget. If the U.S. was to spend 0.16% of the federal budget to do government business in two languages, the cost would be $3.8 billion!

That among other reasons is why Speak English campaigns — and legislation mandating English as the country's "official" language are so important. The most recently proposed legislation was House Resolution 997 — The English Language Unity Act of 2009.

It started out as the English Language Unity Act of 2005. Sponsored by Rep. Steve King (R-Iowa), H.R. 997 garnered 118 co-sponsors, making it one of the most widely supported bills before Congress.

K.C. McAlpin, executive director of The ProEnglish Advocate, cited a national poll finding that 87 percent of American voters support declaring English the official language of the country.

But in 2005, 2007 and again in 2009 the bill was held up in committee, or blocked from going to a floor vote by House Speaker Nancy Pelosi, (D-Calif.).

Representative King hasn't given up and, alongside Senator Jim Inhofe, introduced the English Language Unity Act of 2011 on March 10, 2011.

As reported by CBS News, King defended his proposition by saying "A common language is the most powerful unifying force known throughout history. We need to encourage assimilation of all legal immigrants in each generation. A nation divided by language cannot pull together as effectively as a people." Inhofe added: "This legislation will provide much-needed commonality among United States citizens, regardless of heritage. As a nation built by immigrants, it is important that we share one vision and one official language."

I believe chances are strong that, considering how many states are declaring themselves "officially" English, federal legislation will eventually make it over all the hurdles. Just as I hope legislation passes that stops President Bill Clinton's Executive Order 13166 in its tracks. On Aug. 11, 2000, Clinton signed into law an act making the federal government officially multilingual, requiring any entity receiving federal monies to provide services in any language. Private physicians, clinics, and hospitals that accept Medicare and Medicaid must provide, at their own expense, translators for any language spoken by any patient. As I noted earlier, there are 322 different languages spoken in the U.S. The mere concept of this order is absurd and the actuality of its requirements on various organizations and groups is mind-boggling.

In a report to Congress in 2002, the U.S. Office of Management and Budget (OMB) reported that forcing physicians to provide multilingual outpatient services would cost $180.8 million annually. In addition, inpatient services in multiple languages would cost hospitals $78.2 million, while the bill for multilingual emergency room services would tally $8.6 million, pushing the burden absorbed by health-care total to $267.6 million. And we all wonder and obsess at the massive surge in health –care related costs in recent years. Mandates such as this plays a large role in the increased value of health services which we the patient/consumer ultimately must bear. Don't think for a minute that a physician is going to allow government policy to decrease his/her overall earnings. He/she is simply going to charge the consumer more for the services they provide.

There has already been one House Resolution to repeal Clinton's Executive Order and hopefully it won't be long before its termination.

According to the U.S. Census, the number of Americans who are incapable of speaking English on any level jumped from 1.22 million in 1980 to 3.37 million in 2000, a 176 percent increase over 20 years. During the same time frame a similar increase has occurred in the number of U.S. residents who display a glaring inability to speak the English language at a competent level. California leads the nation in the number of persons who are limited in English proficiency, with 6.3 million, or one-fifth of the population of the Golden State. Texas is second with 2.7 million, followed by New York, Florida and Illinois while New Jersey, Arizona, Massachusetts, Georgia and Pennsylvania round out the top 10.

This has certainly been a rallying point during immigration-law reform demonstrations which began on May 1, 2006, when then-President George W. Bush said, "I think people who want to be a citizen of this country ought to learn English and they ought to learn to sing the national anthem in English."

For those of you who just rolled your eyes at the inclusion of this George W. quote; he was not the only U.S. president to speak out concerning the overall assimilation of the immigrant. Theodore Roosevelt's ideals on immigration and what it means to be an American were voiced as follows in 1907: "In the first place, we should insist that if the immigrant who comes here in good faith becomes an American and assimilates himself to us, he shall be treated on an exact equality with everyone else, for it is an outrage to discriminate against any such man because of creed, or birthplace, or origin. But this is predicated upon the person's becoming in every facet an American, and nothing but an American …"

"There can be no divided allegiance here. Any man who says he is an American, but something else also, isn't an American at all. We have room for but one flag, the American flag."

"We have room for but one language here, and that is the English language ... and we have room for but one sole loyalty and that is a loyalty to the American people."

It is with this attitude and intent that the American immigrant during the time of Roosevelt behaved, and it is with this attitude that the early 20th-century immigrant built the greatest nation the world has ever known. It is my strong opinion, however, that many of today's immigrants unfortunately do not possess the same mindset as our ancestors. I feel that the disrespectful and ignorant behavior displayed by many along with moronic policy by our civic leaders is slowly but surely dissolving the fabric of this great nation.

I hope people can see that despite how the media has tried to portray me, I am not a radical racist, "foreigner-hating" redneck with an obnoxious yearning for every citizen of America to speak English. I am simply one of millions of American citizens who are echoing the words that two of our presidents spoke more than 100 years apart: "Speak English."

CHAPTER TEN

A Few of the Kings

Ok, enough political ranting; let's get back to baseball.

In every season and within every generation of Major League Baseball there are players who find their way into the hearts and souls of the fans.

There are players who are placed on pedestals and looked upon not only as great athletes but as ambassadors for the game. These icons have not only been given a responsibility by their respective teams to try and bring glory to their individual organizations but they have been given a much greater responsibility: to protect and enhance the legacy of Major League Baseball.

Since the inception of the game, each generation has produced a few special athletes who have been designated to carry the torch of baseball greatness, to sustain the county's love for its national pastime and be there as role models to inspire and recruit the next generation of players and fans alike. During and after each era it's pretty easy to identify who the torchbearers are and were. Most times it's easy to recognize and acknowledge the positive impact these players had on the game as a whole.

Baseball, however, has not survived and thrived for more than 120 years on the shoulders of great players alone. In addition there have been and are many other icons behind the scenes that have been a foundation to the sustainment of our signature sport. Some, while never putting on a uniform, should be recognized all the same with greats like Mantle and Ruth for their accomplishments in sustaining the heritage of the game. While still there are others who have bolstered Major League Baseball in ways few will ever know, but whom I feel deserve a substantial amount of gratitude. These great men may never have received the glorious accolades of a Joe DiMaggio or a Nolan Ryan, but when it comes to the enrichment of our game, their involvement was and is no less important. I would like to recognize a few of these great men.

BOBBY COX

It seems fitting that as I'm writing my account of this great man; Bobby is in the midst of his farewell "retirement tour" around Major League baseball. I am extremely proud to see the level of respect with which other teams and players throughout the league are treating him. Although Bobby has been around the game for over 50 years there naturally are many players and coaches from other organizations who have never had the pleasure to be in his presence. It gives me a great deal of pride to witness these members of my fellow baseball fraternity paying their respects to a man that has done so much for this game we all love which ultimately has benefited us all.

A tribute as the one I've seen Bobby receive in no way is warranted by pure statistics alone, however. Although Bobby will always be remember most for his managerial prowess by the lay fan, the ones paying their parting respects so graciously to him know there is much more to Bobby than just a flattering won/loss record, and this is why we, the players, pay homage.

Often in this "all about me" society in which we live, men and women of integrity and character are tough to come by. Unfortunately, the world of Major League Baseball is no different. Professional sports are simply a microcosm of secular society when it comes to the search for honest and forthright people. Luckily, there are exceptions. For me I was one of the fortunate few who have the ability to say I had the privilege to play for one of the most genuine, respectful, "man of integrity" in baseball history, Bobby Cox.

Bobby Cox, myself and childhood friends Ryan & Butch Wiggins at a charity golf event.

As a player, Bobby didn't make much of a mark on the game of professional baseball. He was traded from the Milwaukee Braves to the New York Yankees where he played a few seasons at third base. Hindered by bad knees which eventually gave way to his signature hobbled walk from dugout to mound; Bobby's career as a player ended much sooner than I'm sure he would have liked. This may have been a disappointment for Bobby, but undoubtedly the baseball god's knew what they were doing. Bobby's loss was an enormous gain for many thousands who can say that in some way, shape or form they are better off for having known Bobby Cox. I am one of those privileged ones who can safely and thankfully make that statement.

To say Bobby was a great manager would be a gross understatement. He won manager of the year four times, led the Braves to 14 straight division titles, 5 national league pennants and won the '95 World Series. He also led the Toronto Blue Jays to an American League East title. It may seem to some that Bobby was merely a great manager, a field general blessed at manipulating the Xs and Os of the game.

Many critics will tell you he was simply a fortunate recipient of a wealthy, passionate owner who had a desire to win at any cost. Still others will claim that with all of the outstanding players Schuerholz bought with Turner's money winning more than 2,500 games was inevitable. Maybe so, but I've witnessed many situations with huge payrolls and Hall of Fame lineups where the team can barely play .500 ball. So the question therefore is this, "What is the difference between a "Bobby Cox" managed team and so many others?"

Sure, Bobby knows the Xs and Os and all the managerial strategy, at that level everyone pretty much knows what everyone else knows. In my opinion the difference is the intangible attitudes with which Bobby infuses within his teams and players which in turn gives them the overwhelming desire and expectation to win. This fire possessed by many of his players was generated in large part because of the respect we all had for him which was spawned from the integrity and character he carries himself with daily. And through this phenomenon Bobby often made the poor player mediocre and the mediocre into a champion. So for all those who so naively criticize Bobby in the ways I've just described let me give you a quick two sentence education: Turner's money and the players Schuerholz bought with it were the fortunate recipient of Bobby Cox not the other way around. He made 'em all look like geniuses.

It may seem a bit "hoakie" to credit respect as a dominant vein present in someone's enormous success. The level to which he was endeared, however, went far beyond what is commonly seen. I played for quite a number of managers in my 13 years of professional baseball, and I never met a manager, or a coach, for that matter, who was more respected by his players, as well as every member of an organization than Bobby. To some their respect was derived from a simple shallow appreciation for his numerical achievements. To most, however, they were simply treating him as they had been treated.

It never seemed to matter who Bobby was dealing with —a player, a fan, member of the media, the front office, a bat boy or the team owner, everyone got the same hand shake, look in the eye, genuine attention and forthright answer. This may not sound like much, but in a game where the pecking order is so rigidly defined, it's something unique to behold when a man of Bobby's stature responds the same way to Tommy the bat boy as he does to Greg Maddux the Cy Young winner.

Bobby truly cares about his players as people, which is a rarity in the meat market atmosphere of professional athletics. Players are used to being treated with a "what have you done for me lately attitude." Most times it's like night and day regarding the reception a player may receive from certain coaches after a good performance versus a bad one. Often one may wonder if it a demonic possession had taken place from the time you left the dugout to the time you returned in respect to certain members of a coaching staff. It's the bad times as a player that make you realize very quickly which coaches have integrity and understand that you and your mistakes are human, as opposed to the ones who view your self-worth on a night-to-night basis. You never got that feeling from Bobby Cox. As a player, you knew Bobby might be disappointed with you the player but never with you the person, and as a person would treat you no differently. Every player no matter what he'd done on the field was always treated with the same consistent degree of dignity.

As with any position, however, where you are the boss; there are always going to be situations where issues need to be address. Perhaps the trait about Bobby his players appreciated the most was the inevitable discussion of these issues always taking place behind closed doors. No airing of embarrassing grievances in public. I've played for managers that would threaten a player with his job in front of the entire team on the bus ride back to the hotel. Now I'm a man and you're a man, and just because you're my manager doesn't mean I don't deserve to be treated like one. It was things like this about Bobby's character that endeared his players to him for three decades. Bobby Cox will go down in history as the legendary manager for the Atlanta Braves. Overall he was responsible for 2,504 wins. Bobby Cox, however, did much more for the game of baseball for the man he is rather than the manager he was than many people will ever know. Thanks Bobby.

JOE TORRE

If there is one other manager in Major League Baseball who commands the same amount of respect as Bobby Cox not only for his winning ways but also his staunch personal integrity, in my opinion it would be Joe Torre.

Unfortunately, I never had the honor or pleasure of playing for Joe, but certainly know enough men who have. I played against Torre-managed teams and received quite an education observing the actions and attitudes of one of the game's all-time great men.

Before becoming a World Champion manager, Torre forged quite an impressive career as a player. Playing 18 seasons with a career batting average of .297; he played in 9 all-star games and was the 1971 NL MVP.

These numbers, as impressive as they are, are not the reason most people know the name Joe Torre, however. The average and especially the educated baseball fan knows the name "Torre" as being perhaps the greatest manager during the storied history of the legendary New York Yankees.

Before Torre the tenure of most Yankee managers lasted about as long as a lunar phase. From Lou Piniella to Buck Showalter and Billy Martin (who are/were all fine managers and men in their own right), it seemed no one could keep the Yankee dynasty consistently performing at the level of excellence the City of New York had grown to expect. That is no one until the reigns were finally handed over to Torre.

To me, managing the New York Yankees would be the toughest job in baseball. With a "short-leashed" owner for the past several decades — just because George is no longer with us, don't think that leash is going to get any longer — and piranha-like local media, it doesn't take many games in the loss column for a platter to be constructed that's about the same size as ones head. This proud organization went through an extremely turbulent time during the 1980s. Something had to be done. That something was Joe Torre. During the following 15 years Torre took the Yankees to the post season each year winning 10 American League East Division titles, six American League pennants, four World Series titles, and overall compiled a .605 winning percentage.

Similar to Bobby Cox, Joe Torre also has Hall of Fame managerial numbers. But as with Bobby one does not achieve to that level on knowledge and ambition alone. Being involved in many conversations over the years with numerous former Torre players, I have heard the same adjectives and analogies used to describe Joe which I also attach to Bobby. If these accounts are true (and I have no reason to believe they are not) it's easy to see why Joe enjoyed so much success where so many others failed.

While not forgetting the many feats and tremendous accomplishments Torre collected during his Hall of Fame career, I would like to recognize Joe for the personal integrity and character with which he conducts himself along with the respect and dignity I believe he treats everyone in all facets of the game. As great as the career accomplishments are it is these things that will be passed down to future generations of players and fans alike and will forever enrich the game we all love. Thanks Joe.

MARK SHAPIRO

I've been, quite appropriately, praising two of baseball's most-decorated managers. Not simply for their many accomplishments but for their internal make up as men ... which, ultimately translated into two extremely impressive on-field careers. Although the success which Bobby Cox and Joe Torre enjoyed appears obvious to fans, the underlying reasons behind their triumphs might not be so obvious. The same goes for baseball's general managers. These men who usually remain behind the scenes and in the shadows, wear suits and ties while sitting around board room tables in offices with mahogany walls, playing the chess games that will ultimately have a large impact on determining their team's successes and/or failures. The shrewd, wily generals whose board-room maneuvers result in on-field success are seen as masterminds of manipulation and negotiation, while others who lack the proficiency required for such a job will likely find themselves scouting in the New York Penn League the following spring.

These men often have large checkbooks handed over by team owners along with the orders to win or ... well, you know. With responsibility like this, unethical and borderline-dishonest practices have almost become the norm with GMs trying to keep their precious jobs, spend the boss's money wisely and, above all, win. During my 12-year career I had dealings with a number of general managers and heard stories both good and bad about many more. Some of them I would trust with my last dollar; others I wouldn't turn my back on for all the money in the world.

Many GMs unfortunately don't see players as actual human beings with wives and children and futures that hinge on solitary decisions which ultimately are theirs to make. Instead, most general managers simply see players as a line item on a budget that will pay dividends if the player performs well, or will be a liability if they don't.

Mark Shapiro, current team president of the Cleveland Indians, was poised to assume his first GM role during my time with the Indians. Fortunately for me Mark is one of the few men in baseball front offices that understands the "human factor" of his job and possesses the integrity which many lack. His word actually means something. In this world of cutthroat deals and high-dollar players finding someone in his position who is as honest and forthright as Mark is a rarity.

To illustrate my point here is a little story about ... me. When I was traded to the Cleveland Indians in June of 2001 the GM was John Hart, who was in his last season with the team. He'd taken the Cleveland organization from a laughing stock to a perennial contender and by most standards was considered a very talented GM. It was during my time there that John began the process of handing the reins over to a young and inexperienced Mark Shapiro.

During most of my time as a Cleveland Indian I was mired in a frustrating "closer by committee" situation with fellow reliever Bob Wickman. Bob is a great guy and a very talented pitcher in his own right, and before my arrival had been handling the closing responsibilities quite handily. Once I arrived though it became apparent that the Cleveland bullpen wasn't big enough for the both of us.

Based on the successes each of us had enjoyed during our respective careers we both had a legitimate claim to being king of the bullpen mountain. From the beginning we collectively coveted the "top dog" spot, but instead found ourselves in somewhat less than a routine situation. One day Bob would close. The following day I would. The next day Bob would. The day after I would get the call. It was as if you were pitching for your job each and every night instead of just trying to win.

I found that I was always at my best when I knew precisely what my role was and could prepare accordingly each day. If my role changed, my approach would change; but knowing what situation to prepare for was always key. If I was going to be the one responsible for getting the last three outs in Yankee Stadium, my mental preparation would begin accordingly from the first pitch. If I would likely be called on in another scenario my preparation would need to adjust accordingly. That disciplined knowledge always made me more comfortable and in my opinion a more effective pitcher. This new circumstance in which I found myself was unorganized at best and seemed to have me constantly searching for some solid direction.

As the irritation surrounding my situation continued the season was drawing to a close. With the end of the year fast approaching I requested a meeting with the incoming Shapiro to discuss my options for the following season. I was concerned the organization was going to re-sign Bob and I would spend another season mired in discombobulated frustration.

I was still an above-average pitcher with my fastball consistently reaching the upper 90s. I felt I could certainly add value in the closer's role with another organization, and wanted the Indians to explore that option on my behalf. Understanding the dynamics that exist in most front offices, I knew my request was a long shot, but wanted to make it none the less.

A meeting was scheduled during which I asked Mark if he would trade me if they re-signed Bob during the off-season. He spent a few moments pondering the idea and reluctantly promised that he would. The key word there being "promised." To most GMs, doing what's best for the team, not for some random player sitting across from them asking for a favor, would have been top priority. Most organizations and most general managers would have promised the moon in order to pacify me during the short term. After the fact, however, my request would have been ignored like yesterday's newspaper had it not fit with the team's overall wishes and desires. "You don't like it, John? Deal with it" would have been their response to my complaints. To say the least I would have been an expendable commodity. Not for Mark, however.

Even though I was a 27-year-old left-hander who could still throw 95 to 100 miles an hour, when the Cleveland Indians re-signed Bob in December of that year, Mark Shapiro made good on his promise and traded me to the Texas Rangers. That maneuver showed me a lot about the integrity and character of this rookie GM. At the time the trade was made, I did not make a lot of money by Big League standards, still had great stuff and had reached veteran status, already having played in two league championships and one World Series. On paper it was not that good of a move for the Indians. But Mark honored his word and showed me a lot about his ethics.

Unfortunately, behavior like this is a rarity among front office personnel in professional sports. In this rare case, however, a general manager did what was best for the player and maybe not best for the team, simply because he said he would.

Although not commonly seen or experienced in this game, Major League Baseball and organizations like the Cleveland Indians benefit to an immeasurable degree when men of such character emerge. Thanks Mark.

MARVIN MILLER and DON FEHR

If you aren't familiar with Marvin Miller and Donald Fehr, yet consider yourself to be a devout fan of America's greatest pastime then you need to listen up while I tell you why the game you love wouldn't be nearly so lovable without the painstaking work performed by these two men over the last four decades.

I could be wrong, but I doubt that Don ever had much of a fastball, and I would be very surprised if Marvin could have hit a curve. Yet despite what I presume to be a shortage of on field talent, these two men have done more for this great game of ours individually than every Hall of Famer has collectively. It's safe to say that I and every other player over the last 40 years owe our entire baseball experience to these two men. And if you love and respect the game as we do … then you do, too.

Much of the look, feel and function of today's game is a result of the persistence of these determined individuals, Miller and Fehr. Consider things such as the establishment of free agency that ended a stranglehold which stronger organizations once possessed, thereby creating parity giving every team renewed hope that can be fulfilled during each off-season. Additionally, provisions such as a luxury tax were developed under the careful watch and skillful negotiations of Fehr and

Miller. These and many other conditions have gained acceptance over the years ushering in what many people — certainly I — believe has been a golden era of baseball.

It is difficult to dispute the manner in which the game has flourished over the last 30 years. Parity exists year over year in large part due to the new relationship between players and management created by Miller and perpetuated by Fehr. Games in today's era are not just games, they are events. Ballparks are like cathedrals, and from the product on the field to the entertainment in the stands, satisfying the fans' love for the game is the focal point.

Some will argue, but in my opinion and experience Marvin Miller and Donald Fehr have taken the game we love, and in many ways need, from the dark age to the new age.

Marvin Miller was elected in 1966 as the first full-time head of the Major League Baseball Player's Association. He is basically the creator of the game as you and I know it. The excitement every fan feels during the winter when a team signs a new big name free agent who could be crucial to propelling that team to the World Series — has Miller to thank. The game was not always as it is today. Today teams spend the winter months embattled in a strategic game of organizational chess between general managers collectively trying to make that one special move which will send their team over the top and into championship contention. Before Miller the owners had total control over a player for his entire career. If a player was not happy with his situation for a variety of reasons the only way out was simply to retire or beg for a trade, which did not have to be granted. Owners of Major League Baseball teams not only owned the team, they owned the players as well, literally.

And then along came Marvin Miller. Through many years of hard-fought negotiations he restructured the Major League player contracts to allow the player to become a free agent after six years in the game. Traditionally, contracts contained something called the "reserve clause," calling for the automatic renewal of every player's contract at the end of each season. This condition, when implemented by the owners, did much to hinder the improvement of the league. It kept salaries so low that almost all players had winter jobs to offset their incomes. Travel, field and clubhouse conditions left much to be desired as owners had no reason to improve facilities in order to attract the game's best players. At one point the league minimum salary was $6,000, and had not been increased in 20 years. During Miller's first year on the job he negotiated to raise the average annual salary to $10,000. This was the beginning but by no means his greatest achievement. This was merely the first in a long line of successes against an oppressive group of owners who were guilty of oppressing players under their thumbs for decades.

In 1970 Miller negotiated and won what would prove to be a monumental case for player's rights, and in the end changed baseball forever. It was in this year that Miller and the Major League Baseball Player's Association was awarded the right to have disputes between players and management settle through binding arbitration. Seems harmless enough, doesn't it? Well, this ruling served as a springboard in 1975 for Andy Messersmith and Dave McNally to challenge the "reserve clause" in the player contract, which bound them to one team for the life of their career. The two players won their arbitration case behind the shrewd skills of Miller. The fight wasn't over, however. The arbitrator's decision was appealed by the owners and ended up in federal court. Once again, Miller proved victorious and the modern game of baseball was born.

Miller, through his tough-mindedness and intense negotiating abilities, took a loosely organized players' union and organized it into one of the strongest and most respected unions in all of America. And in my opinion doing so almost single-handedly created the stage for baseball as we know it.

Miller stepped down in 1982 after 19 years as the head of the MLBPA, paving the way for the next in line to carry his torch in the battle for players' rights against an all-powerful, group of Major League owners. Donald Fehr assumed the helm of the players' association in 1986 and quickly let league ownership know that, as with Miller, it was going to be no picnic dealing with him if they had ideas to take advantage of players.

No sooner had Fehr taken office when he was faced with a grievance of extreme proportions. It was discovered that in the 1985, '86 and '87 seasons the Major League owners engaged in a conspiracy against the players and their agents in order to keep salaries low. The collusion that ensued involved owners collectively deciding not to bid on certain high-priced free agents in order to keep salaries below market value, and if teams were to bid on a player's services, the owners agreed not to bid over a specified dollar amount. The purpose of this action was to keep salaries low and money in the pockets of the owners. Fehr put up a tremendous fight for player's rights and all of capitalism for that matter and in 1990 won an extremely lucrative settlement against the owners. The arbitrator's decision, influenced by Fehr's astute negotiating, solidified the state of free agency and helped preserve the game as we know it.

Although this case helped Donald Fehr make his mark on Major League Baseball, it is not the only time he has stood against a cutthroat group of owners looking to take food off the players' tables to further line their own pockets. In 1994, during the negotiation of the collective bargaining agreement, the owners were asked to accept a luxury tax on the 16 richest teams in order to level the financial playing field between the large-market and the smaller-market organizations. Predictably, the owners wanted no part of it. They instead offered the solution of a salary cap which would take money away from the players and not themselves. Fehr fought this resolution tooth and nail. After an eight-month strike which had some damaging short-term affect on the game, the players prevailed and, again Fehr, like Miller before him, protected Major League Baseball from the historical exploitation at the hands of ownership.

As fans of the game, people can say what they want to about Donald Fehr. By some who possess a different opinion than I, Donald has been painted at times in a negative light. I know it can be difficult to sympathize for either side during the many conflicts that have arisen between ownership and players. Who do you feel sorry for, the millionaires or the billionaires? The bottom line is, however, that Feher was hired as the head of the MLBPA to protect the rights of players against the sometimes-tyrannical efforts of management and ownership. As a former player I will tell you in many ways Donald has gone above and beyond to protect the integrity of the game and has ultimately stabilized and enhanced its overall future.

As previously discussed the establishment of a luxury tax and the solidification of free agency has done more for the game than the lay fan probably realizes. I understand on the surface it simply looks like a bunch of rich greedy people fighting with a bunch of other rich greedy people over the last dollar on the table. In reality those two monumental achievements by Fehr have honestly changed the game as we know it forever. In the last decade fans of the game have had the opportunity to enjoy watching the success of such small market teams as the Oakland A's, Tampa Bay Rays and Minnesota Twins. True, these small market teams can't compete with the Bostons and New Yorks of the league year in and year out, but I guarantee that a fan of the Tampa Bay Rays or the Minnesota Twins has definitely enjoyed watching playoff baseball over the last few years in which their respective teams are participating. And whether critical fans or media alike want to admit it, teams like the Rays, Twins ands A's have been given the ability to field talented teams and compete in playoff baseball in large part because of the Donald Fehr negotiated luxury tax.

In addition, free agency and the dynamics surrounding it may seem like nothing more than some spoiled brat athlete holding out for an extra million because he's tired of driving his old Ferrari and wants a new one. In some cases that may be true, in large part, however, the concept of free agency has done an overwhelming amount of good for the game as it currently exists.

"That's ridiculous" you may say. "How can giving a bunch of guys who played a child's game for God's sake the ability to manipulate the system for more money ever benefit that system?" Well let me give you another angle which will possibly reframe your opinion.

First of all, "free agency" is nothing more than just good old fashion American capitalism where by any product, good, or service will seek the highest value for that product, good, or service which the market will bear. I don't care if you're talking about bread, beef, cars or professional athletes at the end of the day they are all products that will be paid for in the amount to which the free market will allow. Ok, enough economics 101 let's get back to free agency. The free agent concept established by Marvin Miller and solidified by Don Fehr has become the backbone of professional baseball. Before Miller "created" free agency a team owner had a player for life; could pay him whatever he wanted to pay him and basically had most aspects of that players existence and future in the palm of his hands. Salaries were extremely low and the opportunity for a player to negotiate a better position didn't exist.

Question: If Major League Baseball ownership still had a stranglehold on players and if salaries were still grossly suppressed do you really think that Ichiro Suzuki would have left Japan to come play 10 years with the Seattle Mariners? Do you think Sammy Sosa would have left his homeland of the Dominican Republic to come play baseball in America for six thousand dollars a month? Would Bobby Abreu have left his native Venezuela to play for a team owner that had a stranglehold on him for the entirety of his career? The answer to each of those questions is not only no; it's HELL NO!

There are undoubtedly a variety of factors which have brought each of these players and many, many more like them to Major League Baseball. No matter what the numerous underlying factors may be, however, the one key central driving force is money. And that's not greed my friends; that's life. Some may say, "I came to America to play professional baseball because I wanted to compete against the best in the world." Guess what, without a system in place for the best in the world to be paid like they are the best in the world; the best in the world do not come to America to play in our Major League. There would be no Ichiro Suzuki, there would be no Sammy Sosa, there would be no Ivan Rodriguez, no Rafael Palmeiro, no Dennis Martinez, no Vladimir Guerrero, no Andruw Jones and the list goes on and on and on. Make no mistake about it, Marvin Miller and Don Fehr's establishment and solidification of free agency is what has brought the best of the best from around the world. Imagine what Major League Baseball would be like without the world's best coming from all parts of the globe seeking everything it offers. The dynamic of Marvin Miller and Don Fehr's free agency has given you, the fan, the ability to watch and enjoy the best players from around the world every night.

My own personal experience as a member of the institution of Major League Baseball as well as a lifelong fan will forever be enhanced and sustained by the sacrifice, accomplishments and unwavering integrity of these two men. No pun intended, but Marvin Miller and Donald Fehr, are and truly have been "game changers" for all players and fans alike. And as a member of each group I say "Thank you Marvin; thank you Don." You're the best.

BUD SELIG

Hopefully within the previous pages you have gained some behind-the-scenes insight into the lives and characters of whom, in my opinion, are some of our game's greatest men. It is an understatement to say that without the character and dignity with which these men and numerous others carry and conduct themselves, this game that is loved by so many would be nothing more than a shadow of its current state.

I've made an effort to show my appreciation and gratitude to those in our game who have always remained steadfastly on the side of "Good." Unfortunately, just as in life where there is good, "Bad" is generally lurking somewhere close by. And in Major League Baseball there's at least one man who seems to personify a healthy dose of the bad in Major League Baseball, Mr. Alan H. (Bud) Selig.

From my perspective this single man stands far and above anyone else I can describe as merely "bad." In better words, a true cretin. The Commissioner of Major League Baseball — the man, the myth, the idiot.

To narrow down all Bonehead Bud's blunders into just a few pages may pose as an effort in futility, and after this attempt I will probably find it to be as such. In all good conscience, however, I wouldn't be doing justice to the game I love if I didn't at least make the effort. Just as many are or should be unaware of the strong moral fiber of the few men I have previously noted, the same goes for the lack of such fiber within Mr. Selig, I believe. It would be tough, dare I say, impossible to educate the lay fan concerning all aspects which categorize Bud as the despicable person he truly is. I estimate it would take a court reporter from now until the next passing of Halley's Comet to transcribe all of the gross transgressions that have befallen Major League Baseball and its players on account of his grotesque character and flimsy personal will. So with that in mind I will simply do my best to just hit the high (low!) points.

Selig was, and for all practical purposes, is the owner of the Milwaukee Brewers. He owned and operated the team from 1970 through 1992 before "officially" stepping down and turning the team ownership over to his daughter. Nepotism at its finest. People inside Major League Baseball in general and members of the Brewers organization more specifically aren't dumb enough to think for a single second that Selig didn't continue his involvement in the ownership of the Milwaukee Brewers despite what his claims may be. Whether it be from a monetary stand point or spear heading such efforts like the construction of Miller Park (at the taxpayers' expense, to at least some degree, of course) no one inside MLB takes for granted that at least on some scale, Selig is still the "wizard" behind the curtain of the Milwaukee franchise. Let's face it if you want something like a new stadium for your team, it's not a bad thing to have Daddy as the Commissioner of the League. If that whole situation doesn't scream conflict of interest I don't know what does. But as you will see, when it comes to the dealings of this commissioner, a simple conflict of interest is the least of his transgressions. From my personal experience and informed opinion, Bud Selig is moron of extreme proportions and an appalling detriment to the game of Major League Baseball.

In 1992 Selig manipulated his way into the Commissioner's role after helping oust Fay Vincent, who had served as the Commissioner for nearly seven years. Coming to power after the death of Bart Giamatti, Vincent, a former entertainment attorney, was not one of the "boys" and had a history of conflict with several owners around the league. The owners wanted to make a move and saw their opportunity to take advantage. Selig and five other owners, dubbed "The Great Lakes Gang," cleverly conspired to undo Vincent, who eventually resigned under pressure created by the political strong arming. With Vincent out of the way Selig resigned his post as owner of the Milwaukee Brewers in favor of his daughter and then received a unanimous vote from the rest of the owners (including his own daughter) to become the ninth commissioner of Major League Baseball. The "boys club" was securely in order, and since his grand victory Selig has been at the helm of nothing more than a puppet regime.

The team owners of Major League Baseball say "jump" to which Bud replies, "Certainly sir! How high and in which direction?" To say he is a spineless, gutless turd, I believe, would probably be the most accurate statement in this book. It was no coincidence in 1994, just two years after Selig took office, that baseball suffered its first strike in 90 years. This grueling work stoppage, which resulted in the first cancellation of the World Series in baseball history, might have been avoided had Selig not been naturally partial to protecting the interests of his fellow owner comrades instead of properly upholding the duties of the office of the commissioner and aligning his loyalties with the overall good of the game. It's obvious to see when a crucial situation such as this arises precisely why baseball's ownership put Selig, an owner, in this position to begin with. With Selig in place, the owners have someone working from the "inside" to protect their rights in any dispute that may surface. The Office of the Commissioner should be impartial to say the least, and as long as Selig remains in place the institution of Major League Baseball will consistently have to find a way to thrive despite his detrimental effect.

During the course of Selig's tenure as head dummy in charge, he has orchestrated some magnificent blunders. Most were just idiotic miscues of an unqualified pawn, but in one instance the former owner's personal relationships, which got him the commissioner's job in the first place, landed him in the face of some pretty serious allegations. In 2001 when the baseball world was still celebrating a World Series for the ages, Bud rained on the festivities by announcing the contraction of two of the leagues teams.

On the surface this event doesn't seem out of the ordinary, but if you are familiar with Bud Selig's history, however, and his rather questionable motives regarding a few certain scenarios, then this situation is anything but routine. Especially considering all of the relationships that were undoubtedly forged during his tenure as a team owner something as complicated and sensitive as his suggestion of contraction just stinks of conspiracy. Let me explain what I mean.

Most fans and students of the game remember the crudely timed announcement during World Series play 2001in which it was revealed that Major League Baseball would potentially be contracting two teams, one of which was the Montreal Expos. Shortly after this announcement was made the proverbial excrement hit the fan when a lawsuit was filed by the minority owners of the Expos against Jeff Loria (majority owner) and Selig for conspiracy and racketeering. Now in my estimation, if someone has the stones to file a lawsuit making such bold accusations as conspiracy and racketeering against the COMMISSIONER'S OFFICE you had better have the proof you need to back it up. Intelligent people don't just go around suing the Commissioner of Major League Baseball on a whim.

It was alleged that an agreement had been reached between Loria and Selig in which Jeff Loria would purposely neglect specific areas of team management in order to drive the value of the team so low an eventual sale would be forced. When the sale finally did take place in 2002 the purchaser of the organization was Major League Baseball itself. This transaction was designed to spawn a chain reaction which would allowed Loria to purchase the Florida Marlins with financing dollars acquired from (of all sources) Major League Baseball. Upon the sale of the Marlins, John Henry, another possible Selig crony and former Marlin's owner, orchestrated a purchase of the Boston Red Sox, even though his group was not the highest bidder for the ball club.

Of course Bud and Loria denied any wrongdoing and put up a fight. In the end these accusations could have cost Major League Baseball nearly $300 million dollars in punitive damages. But as the investigation and litigation wore on eventually the Selig/Loria defense settled out of court for an undisclosed sum of money. I don't know about you, but I don't believe innocent people "settle;" they prove their innocence. It would certainly appear that the commissioner's involvement in this situation was suspect enough to warrant a payoff before the circumstances pertaining to the case became any more public and the ugliness of their truth was unveiled. As to be expected, Loria and Bud Selig have never, and will never, admit to doing anything wrong; but with the conditions surrounding these events being as puzzling as they are, the average monkey can figure out that there is much more to this story than we will ever know and certainly much more that the Commissioner's office will reveal.

The debate over contraction not only raised questions concerning Selig's ethical standards; they also brought into serious doubt about the man's IQ. When an issue as serious as contraction gets raised in the baseball world, naturally all hands on deck are looking to the Commissioner's Office for some answers and direction. Unfortunately in this situation those answers were being delivered from the mouth of a boob.

During the debate over this subject Selig revealed the possible teams for termination as small-market teams, which had a smaller fan base and were centered in relative proximity to larger market teams. His suggestions for possible contraction based on these criteria were the Kansas City Royals because of their closeness to St. Louis (as well as other organizational struggles resulting from a small fan base).

The same logic was also applied to the Minnesota Twins and the Montreal Expos with respect to their nearness to the larger markets of Chicago and New York. Now this logic may seem appropriate until you realize the team his "daughter" owns, the Milwaukee Brewers, fits the exact same qualifications as the other three teams which were being considered for termination. When Selig was asked if the Brewers were a consideration for the chopping block his response was negative, citing that Minnesota was closer to and more of a satellite to Chicago than Milwaukee. Is he serious? Does he really think that most people are dumb enough to fall for the banana in the tailpipe trick? (Don't answer that.) For the record Milwaukee is only 91 miles from Chicago, roughly an hour and 30-minute drive while the home city of the Minnesota Twins is nearly 400 miles away. Why doesn't he just admit that there is no way in hell the Brewer's would ever be considered for contraction because his "daughter" owns the team? Did he really think he was fooling anyone?

Although it would seem from the previous accounts that Selig may have a slight problem regarding his ethics as a businessman, these issues are just the tip of the iceberg when it comes to character flaws, which consistently undermine the foundation of Major League Baseball. In addition to the ethical questions surrounding some of the events during Mr. Selig's tenure as commissioner, there are several other situations in which their handling by our esteemed commissioner could be referred to as nothing less than "what the @#$%".

At the top of that list ranks the decision to allow the 2002 All Star Game to end in a 7-7 tie. Upon completion of the 11th inning Bud grabbed a microphone, called the crowd's attention, and announced to the sold-out stadium in his hometown of Milwaukee, Wisconsin nonetheless, that there would be no winner, the game was over, and they all had to go home. Real creative you idiot! As you can imagine this announcement went over like a turd in the punch bowl, and Selig had to be escorted off the field under a title wave of boos.

As stated earlier these aren't all of Bud's borderline/outright despicable activities perpetrated against Major League Baseball since his tenure began, but they are a few of the more idiotic points. These scenarios, though certainly not flattering, are perhaps not as harmful as one notable transgression that seems to consistently exist within Bud's personality. In my opinion Selig is possibly and consistently the most spineless, gutless, easily manipulated, "yes man" that has ever brown nosed his way to the top of anything. Over the years it has become increasingly evident that Bud's ability to stand his ground in the face of opposition and handle things as he sees fit is completely nonexistent. There is a litany of scenarios I personally know of in which Bud has sheepishly cowered to whatever faction or specific interest group bangs on his door the loudest. If there is one thing that Commissioner Selig hates, it's to be personally accountable for anything, and the sooner he can pass the burden of responsibility to someone else the better.

I have been directly involved in three situations personally, and can speak from a very educated perspective as to Mr. Selig's cowardice: The situation which I am most familiar with, of course, is the one pertaining to the fallout from media and special interest groups centering on my feature article in Sports Illustrated during the winter of 1999-2000. This article, which contained several accounts of disturbing text, which surprised even me when I saw the context in which these comments were used, created a massive media and social backlash. As a result that winter was an extremely difficult one for me, the Braves Organization, and baseball, at large.

Everyone embroiled in this controversy was going to great lengths to save face amidst an onslaught of hazing from the media, as well as several special interest groups and liberal activists who acted as if my mere existence was a detriment to mankind as a whole. They couldn't wait to sink their teeth in and make a "politically correct" example of me, and one of the first places they started was the Commissioner's office.

"Off with his head!"

Were the daily cries from the mob outside Bud's door.

Everyone involved could have greatly benefited from a strong and forthright leader to divert the daily assault not just on me but the Braves organization and Major League Baseball as well. In my and the opinion of many others, a leader was needed who could have asked for the respect to allow this issue to be dealt with from within, and away from the circus atmosphere which had evolved. A stronger man would have assured the observing public that the situation was under control and the only statement that would be issued was going to be when a resolution had been reached in an appropriate manner and time frame. Instead however, we got Bud. A small, weak, little man, Bud immediately tucked his tail and looked for the nearest desk to hide under.

After only a few short days Bud crumbled under the barrage of scrutiny which I'd managed to create and issued a punishment so ridiculous it was like killing an ant with an anvil. The sentence handed down by Selig, which he knew good and well violated a number of provisions set forth in the collective bargaining agreement, included a 60-day, 28-game suspension, a $50,000 fine and two months of "sensitivity training." If enforced this action would have constituted the worst punishment ever levied by the Commissioner's office on a player.

At the outset, Selig knew this punishment would never be enforced. He was fully aware that based on the collective bargaining agreement which existed at the time; the maximum fine the league could administer on a player was $5,000 in such a scenario and he also understood there was no precedent for a player to be suspended nearly twenty-percent of the season for an "off field" transgression. He was fully aware it would never stand, and was equally aware that levying such an outrageous punishment would silence any criticism that was being aimed at him. Which if you've observed Bud that is generally goal number one.

Undoubtedly, Selig's intent was to have the Player's Association fight all aspects of his "self-deflecting" reprimands, by sighting the obvious violations of the bargaining agreement and complete lack of precedent and in doing so would have the penalties reduced to a more realistic level, in the process shifting the burden of criticism from him squarely to the shoulders of Donald Fehr and the Player's Association. At the end of the day when the dust settled, Bud would have the ability to answer all criticism with, "Don't blame me. I tried."

As the player at the other end of Bud's duck-and-run strategy, I witnessed firsthand the cowardly approach, which in my opinion has become second nature to this man. Do you really think that in his heart of hearts Bud Selig actually gave a rat's ass about the misguided, misreported ramblings of some 24-year-old, hot-headed baseball player? Of course he didn't care personally. How do I know this? Because as soon as the Commissioner's office handed down the sentence in grand publicized fashion the media's attention immediately shifted from Bud bashing to the chastisement of the Player's Association and the grievance they filed on my behalf.

The plan worked like a charm and Bud had wiggled off the hook, and as expected the reprimand was reduced to a 14-day suspension, $5,000 dollar fine, and two weeks of sensitivity training. Following this decision Selig and the Commissioner's office did not take one step to ensure the punishment which was ultimately administered ever got enforced. I know this because I never paid one dime of that fine and attended only 15-30 minutes of "sensitivity" training and was excused after the trainer informed me I really had no business being there. The only part of the penalty which was ever enforced was the suspension. If Bud was so concerned about teaching me a lesson and making me a more "sensitive" person then why was the Commissioner of Major League Baseball's reprimand so easy to ignore? I'll tell you why. It's because this man is nothing more than a paper tiger whose only interest lies in deflecting as much attention as possible away from himself with the hope it will be refocused somewhere else. As far as Bud was concerned all was right with the world.

Now, you may think I have a twisted view that can't possibly be impartial given my central role in this whole affair. Yet, the same scenario almost as if it were scripted played out in the 2006 season with Chicago White Sox manager Ozzie Guillen and Chicago Sun Times reporter Jay Mariotti. In this situation Guillen referred to Mariotti as a "fag" in retaliation for some of Mariotti's criticisms concerning Ozzie's managerial decisions. As you can imagine, it didn't take long for the journalistic fraternity to rally the troops against Ozzie in support of their fellow gossip whore. And naturally they went the extra mile to incite the gay community against all involved, especially the Commissioner's office. Like "déjà vu all over again," Selig quickly shirked all responsibility by frantically issuing a reprimand similar to mine — one so outrageous that the Player's Association would have no choice but to come to Ozzie's defense in an effort to reduce the punishment to a more legitimate status.

Once again Bud threw the Players' Union and a member of Major League Baseball under the proverbial bus to avoid any confrontation or consequence for himself personally, confirming once again that he doesn't actually care one way or the other about politically incorrect statements, but simply runs for the nearest fallout shelter to avoid any personal effects or responsibility.

Recalling another instance during the 2005 season, beloved manager of the Chicago Cubs, Dusty Baker, ruffled a few feathers with some moderately charged comments of racial overtone. When asked about the virtue of night games over day games at Wrigley Field, especially in the summer heat. Baker responded, "Personally I like playing in the heat. Most Latin people and minority people do. We were brought over here because we could work in the heat. Isn't that history? Your skin color is more conducive to heat than it is to the lighter skinned people." I personally didn't see what the ensuing fuss was all about. Dusty is a black man and commands a wide range of respect throughout the league. I thought his comments were simply based on his logical opinion. As such the media made a meager attempt to create some negative momentum surrounding these comments, and even though there were some who took offense the effort never really took hold.

In comparison it was a similar comment that got Jimmy "The Greek" Snyder dismissed as a football analyst back in the 1980s but Baker's comments, although interpreted by some as being racially biased, barely cause a blip on the radar. With the lack of media attention and therefore personally scrutiny, Selig, who has claimed time and time again that he will not tolerate racial insensitivity from anyone, did nothing. To me these situations make the glaring argument that Selig does not operate based on personal conviction, but simply along the lines of self-preservation.

Bud has talked tough about offensive speech and wants special interest groups and the media to think he carries a big stick. The only catalyst, however, for Bud's actions have always been in direct proportion to how much pressure is being put on him to react. So the truth is — no outside pressure, no reaction, and personal convictions be damned.

Unfortunately, these hand-picked accounts citing Bud's questionable ethics and internal fortitude (or lack thereof) while bruising the integrity of the game to varying degrees are mere blips on the radar screen compared to the public relations catastrophe created with the discovery of rampant steroid use in Major League Baseball. This debacle of epic proportion has left a long-lasting if not permanent scar on the game while pitting some of the game's most legendary players in a knock-down, drag-out fight to preserve their legacies and in some cases their freedom.

As I sit back and assess the damage which the steroid scandal inflicted upon the game it amazes and confuses me at what a truly monstrous situation it became. For nearly three years Congressional hearings, player confessions, and supplier arrests were almost daily news which was not confined to just sports media, but spilled over on a regular basis to secular mediums as well. It's safe to say the "steroids in baseball scandal" was/is the greatest PR disaster in the history of sports and is extremely unlikely that any of us will witness anything during the rest of our lifetimes remotely similar.

It's only fitting and not too surprising that such a calamity would befall the league during the tenure of Bud Selig. It would be unfair to say (even for me) that Bud had a hand in creating this extremely unfortunate situation which has ruined the lives of so many because he certainly did not. In my opinion, however, his severe lack of integrity, lack of fortitude and lack of character contributed significantly to the severity with which this situation played out. The poorly handled accounts of political correctness and questionable ethics I've discussed previously merely left temporary bruises on the game. The handling of the steroid scandal by Selig has left a mark that will never fully heal.

During the heat of it all Selig behaved like vintage Selig. Ducking, dodging, blaming, and deflecting it seemed his greatest concern as always was to preserve his own personal image and all others could fend for themselves. Numerous times during this tumultuous saga it was requested that Selig turn in his resignation and give way to someone with more astute leadership skills. Bud, however, wrapped up in his own delusional world naturally refused, and continued to dowse kerosene on the flames of turmoil. It seems drastically obvious that a commissioner better able to bridge the gap between the Player's Association and the Commissioner's Office, as well as, more capable of dealing with outside third parties who attempted to deal with MLB's internal affairs would have been invaluable in keeping the situation under control. Perhaps had the reigns changed hands in time two legends of the game, Rafael Palmeiro and Roger Clemens, wouldn't have faced charges regarding their testimonies before a Congressional committee, while many others such as Alex Rodriguez and Mark McGuire will forever have an "asterisk" of doubt beside their legendary careers. Think about that statement for a minute. It actually got to the point where not once, but numerous times, players were subpoenaed to Washington D.C. to testify before CONGRESS! When the reality of that fact sets in, I hope we can all appreciate how absolutely ridiculous that whole scenario was. But such is the downward spiral created by Bud's ineptness which landed Major League Baseball and many of its players as the central attraction in the three-ring circus.

As the years of scrutiny and embarrassment dragged on, Selig was consistently unable to thwart the onslaught of outside intervention. From the "Mitchell Report," to Congressional hearings and FBI investigations the credibility of the game and its players was increasingly tarnished with each passing day. True to form, Bud blamed the Player's Association in every instance where it seemed fitting to do so while attempting to avoid any personal responsibility by claiming no prior knowledge or awareness that such an issue even existed as if in some way he had been the victim of a surprise personal attack. I don't find Bud to be a genius by any means, but I don't think he is dumb enough to be that naive.

To the first count I will actually come to Bud's defense. One provision of the collective bargaining agreement the Association has always adamantly defended is the right of all players to not be subjected to drug tests of any kind without the existence of any prior issues (i.e. if a player had never failed a minor league drug test or had ever had an off-field incident with drugs then a test could be forcibly administered). Even as a player during this era I thought the MLB testing policy was a little suspect. If I'm the owner of a Major League franchise with tens of millions of dollars tied up in my athletes you can bet your "you know what" I want to make sure none of them are doped up on marijuana, cocaine etc. Steroids obviously is an entirely different scenario as they are intended to enhance your performance, but nevertheless, even as a player I feel that some form of drug testing should have been in place; so concerning Bud's criticism of the MLBPA I can't totally disagree. I do take exception, however, with Bud's negotiating skills and lack of ability to come to an acceptable drug-testing resolution with the Association before Congress and the FBI felt it necessary to intervene in the affairs of Major League Baseball. In my opinion much of the circus affair was created after it became evident to the U.S. Congress and others that Selig was incapable of keeping order. Had he been more adept it's quite possible that many of the game's greatest players of the past 20 years would not have had their legacies irreparably smeared.

In one brief breath I actually support Bud's position pertaining to the PA, in the next, however, I will never buy into the notion he was oblivious to the fact that steroids existed in baseball. Why do I have such strong feelings in regards to Selig's insistent lack of knowledge? A situation that involved me directly should help explain.

In early January of 2000 the fallout from my Sports Illustrated article was consuming me. I was in conversation with my agent and the Player's Association on a daily basis speculating at how to best deal with my very difficult situation as it pertained to public relations and the Commissioner's Office. Based on these conversations I was made aware that the Commissioner's Office was extremely irritated and looking to take swift, firm action against me. Years later I gained a more clear understanding of why the Commissioner's Office was seeking to treat me with such a heavy hand which I've discussed at length in this chapter. At the time, however, I knew a heavy blow was on its way and wanted to soften it as much as possible.

During one of those early January conversations my agent informed me the Commissioner's Office had requested I take a drug test for steroids. Knowing I didn't have to take the test and being fully expectant I would fail, I told my agent there was no way in hell I would succumb to such a measure. A few days later my agent again asked me if I would consider taking the drug test. I was told the Commissioner's Office was insisting on it, and he didn't feel they would let up until I agreed. I let him know I would think about it. A few more days passed and again I was approached with the same question. This time my agent literally begged me to consent.

"The Commissioner's Office is adamant you take this test, John," he pleaded with me. "They are already extremely angry with this situation and I would not recommend irritating them further."

So after a series of insistent requests, I finally agreed to take the test. By this time it was mid-January and I was contacted by a man from Comprehensive Drug Testing, Inc. and we discussed where we would meet to have the test administered. After the drug test was taken it was clearly explained to me that I would be contacted directly by someone from Comprehensive Drug Testing, Inc. to discuss my results and that everything would remain strictly confidential. Well, a few days passed and I received the results of my test. Not directly from Comprehensive Drug Testing, Inc. as I had been told, but instead was informed by my agent that I had given a positive test for steroids. Doesn't sound real "confidential" does it?

Now at this point I'm not so surprised at my positive test; I'm mainly shocked and confused that the news was being delivered to me by my AGENT. I had been told this test was going to be confidential! If my agent knew then who else knew?

"What if the media finds out?" was the first terrifying thought that went through my mind. "That's all I need is one more thing for the media to bury me with."

As I obsessed about the lack of presumed confidentiality concerning my drug test I was hit with another horrifying thought.

"If my agent knows then there's no way the Commissioner's Office doesn't know. They hounded me for a week to take the thing; so why in the world would they not want to know what the results are?" After all, the entire point of taking a test is to ultimately learn the results is it not?

Now, I've already publically accused the Commissioner's Office once about knowing steroids existed in Major League Baseball long before 2004 based on this experience, and understandably they denied it. I have little doubt when this book comes out they will deny it again, but let's lay out the facts and let you, the reader, form your own opinion:

• The Commissioner's Office was extremely angry and hostile toward me over the SI article.

• The Commissioner's Office requested to the point of insisting that I take a drug test for steroids.

• The Commissioner's Office had someone from Comprehensive Drug Testing, Inc. contact me to have the test administered and assure me the results would remain confidential between the testing organization and I.

• When the results of the test were revealed, my AGENT, who probably had the least amount of involvement in this whole process was the one who gave me the results.

So with those facts in mind, I'm suppose to believe that a very angry Commissioner's Office, who insisted over the course of a week and a half that I take a drug test, didn't know the outcome of the very test they insisted that I take, but my "agent" did?

Really?

I might have been born at night, but it wasn't last night.

So how and why is this even relevant? The relevance lies in the place where Bud stood in the face all media, and most of America denying any prior knowledge to the existence of steroids in the game and thereby placing the burden of blame and all consequences as squarely as he could on the backs of the players of Major League Baseball and its association. In my mind this constitutes perhaps the grossest, most cowardly, spineless act of his embarrassing career.

To me there is no way this Commissioner of Major League Baseball did not know I was using steroids during January 2000. Firmly believing that statement, wouldn't it be prudent to assume that a qualified, astute leader of an organization as massive as Major League Baseball would have had the sense and foresight to have taken my positive steroid test and presume that out of the 750 or so players in the Big Leagues I was not the only one taking steroids? Wouldn't one figure that the man who had been "commissioned" with upholding the integrity and legacy of Major League Baseball would have taken my positive drug test as a tip that maybe some further investigation need be done concerning the existence of other players around the league using steroids? At this point, in my mind there really are only two possible explanations concerning Selig's lack of initiative in handling the steroid issue until it was too late and neither one of them are very flattering. Either he was just too stupid to figure it out, or he simply didn't care. I really can't come up with another logical explanation.

In my opinion, had a man with more foresight and integrity been available then perhaps Major League Baseball would have been able to handle its affair with steroids in house, and avoided the catastrophe that ensued. Perhaps Barry Bonds would not have had to go through an embarrassing and damaging perjury trial, as did Rafael Palmeiro and Roger Clemens. Perhaps Mark McGuire, Jason Giambi, and Alex Rodriguez wouldn't have a permanent stain beside their amazing careers and accomplishments.

Instead, Bud ran for the hills, blamed the Players Association, denied personal knowledge and hoped it would all just go away. We would have all been much better off had he just gone away.

In stark contrast, Roger Goodell, the commissioner of the National Football League, has had some equally challenging issues to confront. In my opinion and from all personal observation and conversations I've had Roger is the "stand up," "backbone-possessing man one expects to see in such a position. His handling of extremely volatile situations such as the Michael Vick dog-fighting issue, the Ben Roethlisberger and Brett Favre "sex scandals" and even the currently ongoing labor disputes, portray him to be a man of substantial fortitude.

As a resident of Atlanta I distinctly remember the fire Goodell underwent when the accusations of Michael began and the truth about that terrible situation came to light landing Michael in some serious legal trouble, in addition to the public relations storm not dissimilar to the one I experienced. As in my situation, many special-interest groups such as PETA were steadily launching grenades at the Falcons' Organization and more specifically Goodell himself demanding harsh, immediate action be taken. Standing in the face of that fire Goodell seemed to calmly and coolly address these special-interest groups with an attitude that seemed to say, "Look, I'm in charge here. I don't pander to your whims and demands. I will get to the bottom of this in due time and administer judgment as I see fit. I will let you know when I have made my decision. Now it's time for all of you to go home and let me do my job. Thank you."

I was equally impressed with his handling of the situation when Michael requested re-entry into the league. Facing similar scrutiny from the same special-interest groups who wanted an additional pound of flesh from Vick, Goodell stood tough, calmly assessed the circumstances according to his schedule and in his best discretion allowed Michael to resume his career. I have no doubt based on my personal experience with Bud Selig, faced with a similar situation; he would have looked for the nearest hole in which to stick his head.

Goodell, however, faced his critics, stood his ground and did what he thought was right by Michael. Personally, I'm extremely happy for Mike and hope he knows how fortunate he is to have a commissioner who behaves and reacts based on his own code of morals and ethics not according to the direction of the winds of criticism. Michael to a great degree has gotten his life back, which is great to see. I shudder to think what Mike's current reality might be had his life been in the hands of Bud Selig.

Hopefully one day soon Major League Baseball will be blessed with a forthright commissioner to lead it into the next generation.

After playing Major League Baseball for six seasons and becoming directly involved with Selig on more than one occasion, I can honestly say that the state of America's greatest pastime would be in much better position without the detrimental influence of this man, and his penchant for bowing to and being manipulated by whoever squeezes him the hardest.

Whether it's steroids, a case of politically incorrect speech, or player/ownership disputes, it seems that matters are always made worse by Bud's consistent cowardice and pandering behavior. How could baseball not be in a better position with a commissioner of a more stand up and forthright variety who does not cower so easily to the tides of manipulation?

From the problems created during the 1994 strike to the issues around contraction, steroids, and political nonsense, baseball has received numerous black eyes during the inept tenure of Bud Selig. During every one of these "scandals" serious PR damage could have been avoided had the game simply possessed a commissioner with a vertebra. Time and time again Major League Baseball could have evaded the circus atmosphere created around each of these situations had Bud simply had the guts to stand up for his players and his League while letting the public know that Major League Baseball would handle its own affairs. Instead of panicking at criticism and cowering to scrutiny, had Selig shown firmness and determination to not air baseball's dirty laundry in the forum of public opinion, much of the damage which has been done to baseball's image over the past twenty could have undoubtedly been avoided.

By this time next year he won't be the Commissioner of Major League Baseball. Or so he says. We can only hope.

CHAPTER TWELVE

A Few of the Stupid Moments ...

So, what's it like when the cameras are off, the reporters are gone and it's just the guys in the locker room or on the team bus?

It's almost impossible to describe — but I'll give it a shot! The most important thing to grasp when attempting to appreciate the off field atmosphere of Major League Baseball is that you kind of have to know the personalities of the people involved, so I'll do my best to give you a little look behind the scenes at some of the "Stupid Moments".

One question almost all athletes in every sport get asked by fans and media alike is about superstitions and rituals practiced by players.

I can't tell you what a lot of the other guys did — I really don't know. But I'll tell you mine: I don't know how or why my superstitious routines came about, but every game I played I would have to step over the chalk line entering or leaving the field with my left foot (this one is actually quite common among many players especially the "cock-eyed" lefties). This superstition went for pregame, postgame, intragame, whenever. In the first inning I would have a banana, and in the fifth I would have to eat four Nutter Butter cookies. In addition, I also only used two jockstraps during my entire 12-career. They would only get washed about once a year when one of the clubhouse guys would forcibly make me put it in the laundry. When I retired, the jock which I still have to this day was being held together with safety pins! So, I would say as silly superstitions went; I probably had some of the milder neurosis I came across during my career.

In addition to getting the commonly asked "superstition" question, many people also want to know what were some of the greatest moments I had in the game. Of course my first Big-League victory, first Big-League save, first time in some of the great ballparks such as Wrigley Field, Yankee Stadium, and Fenway Park along with memories of NLCS's and the World Series top the list. In addition, however, and probably what I miss most about the game, is the off-field camaraderie I experienced with many of my teammates. We had some truly great times in those clubhouses, team buses, team planes, and various other venues we would gather in when the game was done. It certainly can get entertaining when you put 25 dudes together ranging in age from 18 to 40 and ask them to spend 12 hours a day with one another for about 200 days a year. To this day, I'll spend time with people who have known me since childhood engaged in a conversation. I'll let loose with some "baseball clubhouse-esque" type comment, and they'll just stare at me with a confused look on their face and simply ask, "Where do you come up with this stuff?" Well, I'm going to give you a sneak peak into the baseball life that only those who have played the game at its highest level know about.

I hope you fans will get as big a kick out of reading these short stories as I did living them and now telling them. They're pretty much G-rated — the participants in some of the R-rated ones may not appreciate such things being told (!). I also hope to reveal the camaraderie, fun, respect and affection I still have for all the guys I'm telling these stories about. I'm pretty certain (well, hopeful!) they won't mind me revealing these little quips, and I hope you enjoy.

TED TURNER

I've always liked and respected Ted a great deal. I've done a fair share of slamming ownership during this book, but don't include Ted in that camp. Ted was truly a players' owner, and I don't know of a player who would claim otherwise. Not to say he wasn't concerned about the bottom line, but he was always a great owner to play for. I'd bet that at one point in his life Ted would have traded many of his millions for the chance and ability to have put on a uniform and head out to centerfield himself.

When I started with the Braves, Ted also owned World Championship Wrestling and would often tease me on his strolls through the clubhouse, shouting over to me in the corner, "Hey, Rock, when you gonna come out and wrestle for me?!"

I'd always answer back, "If you can get it OK'd with John (Schuerholz); I'll be there. What'll be my wrestling name?" We both knew that wasn't actually going to happen and of course never did.

Now, Ted's obviously a man of wealth, power and influence yet he also has a wonderful eccentricity and sense of humor about him. We'd see him come through the clubhouse two or three times a week during the season; he'd usually come through and say hello and make pleasantries but normally didn't hang around too long, instead heading down to the owner's box for the game.

Of all the stories I like to tell about my time in Atlanta, this is one of my favorites mainly because of Ted's "giggly" since of humor and lighthearted nature. It was early in the 2000 season, sometime around April or May and Chipper Jones had just signed a big contract with the team — $90 million for six years.

One day Ted started his usual stroll through the clubhouse, but didn't cruise on through as usual, and instead made a hard left to join about 15 of his players in the food, media and entertainment room for some "guy time". It was actually kind of sweet. At the end of the day I think he just wanted to be one of the boys.

Before most games in Atlanta it was usually a very low-key atmosphere which was a direct influence of Bobby's personality along with a few of the veterans. Generally, most Major League teams will take on the personality of their manager and a few of the most tenured players. After batting practice it was common for this food/media/entertainment room to be full of guys playing cards, watching TV, playing video games or fixing a pregame meal. As it was, this particular day was pretty typical with the exception of being joined by Ted.

"Hey guys," Ted announced in his usual jovial voice as he walked over and sat down beside me on a big couch in front of a huge TV screen.

"Hey Rock. When ya gonna come wrestle for me?" He humorously asked once again.

We exchange a few words and then he began to look around the room to see who else he could start in with. As he glanced around he saw Chipper sitting just to our right playing cards. All of a sudden Ted perked up and said, "Hey, Chipper, how about that big contract I just gave ya? You better not screw it up. I thought about bringing some roses with me; one for every million I'm givin' ya. Eh, but that's too many damn roses!"

Then Ted sat quietly for a second, at which point I'm sure Chipper thought he was off the hook. But then Ted popped up again, "Hey Chip. You know I gave one of those big contracts to Dale Murphy too. I told him not to screw it up either. He did pretty good. You better not screw it up!"

Now, Chipper was one of the top dogs in that clubhouse, and no one really gave him too much grief. What do you do though when it's not another player diggin' at you; it's your boss, and your boss just so happens to be international mogul Ted Turner? There wasn't really much Chipper could do except chuckle a bit with all the humility he could muster and hope Ted would just move on.

Again Ted got quiet, looked around the room for a minute and spoke to a few other players who were hanging out and relaxing.

Then he got a second wind. "Hey Chipper, how are your wives doin?"

I think everyone in that room, especially Chip, thought to himself, "I can't believe he just said that!"

It had only been a few months since Chip had come out publicly concerning extramarital affairs and disclosed that one of them had resulted in a child. The mother, a Hooter's waitress, had moved to Atlanta with the baby and Chip was looking after them. I always had a lot of respect for Chip regarding that decision. That was certainly not the easy way out, but it sure did show some backbone and character. It came at quite a cost for Chip, naturally. He ended up getting divorced and had to endure quite a bit of public hazing for the first few months of that season. During many road games that year some of the home fans would show up wearing Hooter's T-shirts and chant "HHHHHOOOOOTTTTEEERRRRSSS, HHHHOOOOTTTTEEERRRRSSS" when Chip would come up to bat. That must not have been easy for him.

And here he had his boss, Ted Turner nonetheless, trying to be one of the boys and wearing him out about it. If any of the rest of us had made that comment there would have been an instant fist fight, but it's Ted, so here again what are you gonna do? We all just sat there waiting for Chip's reaction which was nothing more than a half-hearted chuckle while keeping his head down and trying to focus on his cards.

Just when we thought Chipper's hazing session was over Ted got another silly look on his face and blurted out, "You know, every time I go to Hooter's I ask myself, 'what would Chipper do?' "

At this point the crowded media room was battling to hold back its inappropriate laughter on one hand and just feeling sorry for Chip on the other. I don't know what was going through his head, but we could all see the confusion on Chip's face as if wondering what he had done to warrant one of the most powerful men in the world to sit in a crowded room and roast him.

It was absolutely priceless. Ted is certainly not a mean-spirited guy. He was definitely teasing Chip in jest and as I said earlier it always seemed like Ted just wanted to be one of the boys. At times, being around Ted it even seemed that HE was actually jealous of US. I simply don't think Ted was familiar with the etiquette of clubhouse hazing. There's definitely a code to ragging on people in a baseball clubhouse and by the time you've played in the league for 8-10 years you know it backward and forward. Ted was just unaware of the rules of engagement, which made Chipper squirm all the more, and the whole scene that much funnier.

BOB WICKMAN

Bob is a great dude, a fun-loving, happy-go-lucky guy that was very good at doing two things: throwing a baseball and drinking beer, and he did both of them pretty much every day. Bob loved beer (and probably still does). A large "Norseman" looking fellow, Bob was from Wisconsin and finished most sentences with "Eh" or "Use guys" and was often directly referred to as "hoser" by most of his teammates. Bob would be a shoe-in for the Friar Tuck role should he ever have the desire to be in a Robin Hood production.

Bob had a great career. He played about a dozen years with the Yankees, Brewers, Indians and Braves. He made a few all-star teams, went to a few post seasons, and was well respected around the league as being one of the top closers for quite a few years. Bob used to give the credit for his unhittable sinker to the fact that he only had about half of an index finger on his throwing hand (from a farming accident when he was a kid) which was just one more thing that made Bob a true character of the game. I mean what pitcher only has half a finger on his throwing hand? Bob swore it was his deformed digit that made his sinker so devastating.

As I've already said, Bob loved beer. I can remember most games sitting in the clubhouse watching Bob polish off a couple during the first few innings and then putting two more in a "to go" cup before we made our walk to the bullpen. As a fan you may think that's outrageous or irresponsible, but when your sporting a 2.00 ERA and have converted 28 of 30 saves; you just keep doin' what your doin'. Some guys drank protein shakes, some guys used creatine, others took steroids; Bob drank beer. In my opinion it's guys like Bob who add so much character and spice to the game of baseball, and it's the time I spent with the Bob Wickmans of the game that makes me so fondly reflect back on the years I played and miss it the most.

One story I'll never forget took place on a trip from Cleveland to San Fran to play a series against Oakland. Now, on most team charter flights there's access to pretty much whatever you want (within reason) on the culinary and beverage side of things. It's like a restaurant went into the charter flight business. From beer and wine to steak and salmon and whatever snack you may want in between, there is always the opportunity to sit back and stuff yourself.

Being the beer-loving gentleman that Bob is, a four-hour plane ride offers a substantial amount of time to get in plenty of reps on the 12-ounce curl machine. Needless to say, by the time we touched down in San Francisco Bob was hammered! But here again, don't go judging Bob. Bob was a veteran player having yet another stellar season. Bob could do pretty much whatever Bob wanted to.

After the plane landed and we filed onto the two buses that had been awaiting our arrival, it became quite evident that Bob was in a really, really good mood. The buses got under way for the 30-minute ride to the team hotel. During our ride Bob proceeded to get out of his seat and "entertain" his travel-weary teammates with some jokes, harassment of some of the younger players, and I even think he sang a little. As we got closer to the hotel the entire bus was hysterically laughing at Bob's dumb ass.

As the buses got closer to the hotel, like a stage performer not wanting to disappoint the crowd, Bob took it up a notch. And by "take it up a notch" I mean he got naked! I'm not talking about underwear and undershirt naked; I'm talking completely naked! Now Bob is not a tan fellow; nor is he hairless, so let that image sit in your head for a while! It wasn't just enough to be naked either. He began cruising up and down the aisle messing with everyone. To this day it was one of the funniest sights I've ever seen. Imagine big ole' 6'4", 280-pound Bob Wickman standing buck naked beside Ellis Burks trying to have a conversation like everything is normal … then acting like he dropped something and bending over in front of Charles Nagy. You can imagine the looks on Charles' and Ellis' faces. They weren't sure if they should keep laughing or get ready to defend themselves. He then continued down the aisle and tried to sit in my lap. Do you have any idea how hard it is to keep a 280-pound naked fat guy from sitting on you? What's the protocol there? You don't want to touch him, but you sure as hell don't want him sitting on you, either!

Luckily Bob didn't make much of an effort and we soon arrived at the four-star team hotel in downtown San Francisco. By this point the whole team was thinking, "What the hell is Bob gonna do now?" The bus lights came on. We were parked right next to a busy sidewalk in downtown San Fran and Bob was still naked. Well I, of course, thought this whole situation was hysterical and wanted to get in on the comedy, so I looked around and saw Bob's clothes which I was closer to than he was. Before Bob could beat me to them, I grabbed them and took off running. I stood on the sidewalk in front of the hotel for about two minutes holding Bob's clothes — with him looking and swearing at me through one of the bus windows. For a few seconds, I thought of continuing into the hotel, but was talked into giving Bob his clothes back; just as well! What an idiotic night!

Sure, the game itself is fun, but its stories and memories like that along with the people that helped create them that I cherish and miss the most about playing in the Big Leagues.

JIM THOME

Man-child, Baby Huey, Gently Jim are just a few of the endearing nicknames Jim's teammates have tagged him with over the years. As the reader, I would like to give you a task. Ask high and low; question as many people as will give you an answer, and find one person to say a negative word about Jim Thome. In short, Jim is simply just a good dude, the best of sorts. I was fortunate to have had the opportunity to play with Jim — though unfortunately for just half a season. In that half season, however, I gained a lifelong friend. Jim is just that kind of guy though. He endears himself to everyone; dislikes no one, and all that have the good fortune to be around him are better off for having done so. To sum the man up into one phrase would be to simply say, "Jim's a beauty."

Those who have played with Jim and know him best will whole heartedly agree with my perception. But what about Jim the player? With wrists like ankles and forearms like calves, Jim has been one of the most prolific home run hitters of our generation. Having a career that's spanned two decades and racking up more than 600 home runs in the process, Jim will undoubtedly be enshrined in Cooperstown as one of the game's all-time greats.

I'm very proud to say I once played with Jim Thome, and this next story is simply classic "Jim." Let me first start off by saying when it comes to physical ability Jim is as natural as they come. Some would refer to him as just being "country strong." To the best of my knowledge when Jim and I were playing together he took no supplements what so ever. He didn't need to. He'd simply go home, eat himself some mashed potatoes and collard greens and then come out the next day and blast a couple of dingers. Jim just kept it simple.

As uncomplicated as Jim's dietary routine was; he couldn't have taken any supplements even if he wanted to for simply not knowing what he was looking for, or what to do with it even if he found it.

In the Cleveland clubhouse after batting practice one day Jim and I began talking about how tired we were getting late in the season. It was the middle of August and the dog days of summer were really beating down. As we were discussing how fatigued and lethargic we had become, Jim asked if I knew of any supplements that would perk up his weary body. Well, it's me he's talking to here, and of course I knew many things he could take to help a worn-out body. In fact I was probably on some of the "good stuff" at that particular time, but Jim isn't that kind of guy and such a suggestion wouldn't have been received very well.

In the meantime, a few lockers away, our third baseman, Travis Fryman, and one of our utility guys, Russ Branyan, were listening to our conversation. As Jim and I were complaining and exchanging advice Travis popped up, "Hey Jim. Are you guys talking about supplements?"

"Yeah," Jim answered.

"I gotta find something to get my energy level back up. I'm draggin' ass out there."

Now Travis was a great player in his own right, and like Jim was a straight-laced fella. Whatever advice he was going to give Jim was going to be strictly on the up and up. So to answer Jim's question Travis and Russ walked over and joined in the conversation.

"Well Jim," Travis started. "I've been taking creatine for the last few months and I think it's really helped my strength and stamina."

Like an overgrown kid, Jim's eyes got real big as he began intently listening to what Travis had to say about this "wonder supplement." So Travis went into about a two-minute lecture on the benefits of creatine, how to use it, where to get it, and with about every other comment Travis made, Russ and I would chime in with our own two cents. After about three or four minutes the look on Jim's face was similar to that of a 13-year-old boy who's just hearing about sex for the first time. He was listening as closely as he could manage and becoming more intrigued with every word.

When the conversation was nearly over, Jim, with an almost relieved demeanor, nodded his head a few times and said, "Yeah … yeah … that's what I'm gonna do. I'm gonna get me some of that creatine. It sounds like that's what I need."

After hearing Jim's decision Travis responded, "Well Jim, if you're going to start taking it just make sure you hydrate with it. That's very important."

"All right Travis, I will. Where can I get some of that hydrate at?"

And he asked the question just as intently and sincerely as he could. Travis, Russ, and I looked at each other, dropped our heads, turned around and just walked away. At that point what else could we do! What a beautiful moment. Jimmy, you're a beauty, buddy, thanks for all the great memories.

WALT WEISS

Walty, perhaps taken from the same mold (although a much smaller one) as Jim, is another teammate that's just a true-blooded, genuine, good soul. I was fortunate enough to have played with some great dudes during my career and Walt is right up there as one of the best of them.

I'd like to tell you that so much of the overall experience one derives during a Major League career is based on the collection of guys you are fortunate or unfortunate enough to be lumped in with for 200 days a year. Pat Corrales, the ex-Atlanta bench coach, would say during an early spring training meeting every year, "Get used to it guys. You won't be able to pick your own friends for the next six months. I hope everybody likes each other."

Many more hours are spent together as a team off the field than on it. Long hours in the clubhouse, on the team plane, team buses and hotels with a bunch of guys who don't necessarily get along can be downright miserable. And that mood absolutely affects a team's performance. On the other hand, those same long hours spent with a collection of guys who entertain each other, laugh with and at each other, as well as just enjoy each other's company, can be some of the best times of your life.

The years I spent in the Atlanta Braves organization include some of the most enjoyable experiences I've had and probably ever will. I look back on those times with a great deal of fondness for obvious reasons, but there are many not-so-apparent things that will forever endear me to that period of my life.

As I've already said, Walt is a good cat. From Tuxedo, New York, Walty possesses one of those genuine gruff New York accents that makes pretty much everything he says a lot funnier than it probably should be. Don't get me wrong though, Walt is an absolutely hilarious dude; it's just that most of the dry and straight-faced stuff he would say and do would have the entire clubhouse laughing at his dumb ass probably a lot harder than if I had said the same thing. Always saying something ridiculous, Walt was one of the guys that consistently kept a light-hearted atmosphere in the clubhouse and made all of those long hours at the ball park much more enjoyable. Over a 200-game season a guy like that is integral in keeping team morale high.

One of the funnier stories I can recall during my career involved Walt, a gullible USA Today journalist, and one of Walt's idiotic pranks. So you can have full appreciation of this story I need to bring you up to speed and give you a bit of insight concerning sports journalism from a "behind-the-scenes" perspective.

First of all there is no bigger clown in the world of journalism than the majority of "sports journalist". Not all of them, but a great many. Most times he, but sometimes she; is usually a frustrated "never was" in the world of athletics. More often than not these folks have been blessed with the type of bodies that function best while sitting on the couch. A gross lack of physical ability did not squelch these people's desire to be a part of the sporting community, however, so many of them did the only thing they knew to do: they started writing about it. Unfortunately it's not quite that simple. Can you imagine how hard it would be to try and convey to hundreds of thousands of people what it's like to play a sport at the pinnacle of that sports existence of which you haven't played since the seventh grade. That would be like taking one year of high school Spanish and then trying to teach it to college seniors. That's sort of like what most sports journalists do.

So much of sports is mentality; it's instinct, as well as physical ability. There is a huge bridge to gap between those who do it for a living and those who haven't done it since they were 12. I can't tell you how many articles I've read over the years where I know the details of a specific story intimately, only to read the article and wonder if the author is not trying out his hand as a fiction writer.

Phrases like, "What the hell is he talking about? Is this article about the same game I was at? Or simply, "That never happened!" are extremely common among athletes in clubhouses who were the actual participants in various events that some journalist has butchered the details of in the next day's paper. So just for future reference — reader beware!

It was this mentality and lack of true understanding that made this next story possible. It was September 1999 and Atlanta was in a very heated playoff race with the Mets. We had been clinging to a small lead in the division for several weeks, and just couldn't seem to put the Mets away. It was the last week of the season when we traveled to New York for a crucial three-game set that could ultimately decide the season for each club.

Walt, who had signed a substantial contract the previous off-season, had begun the year as our starting short stop. Unfortunately, 1999 had been an injury-plagued season for Walt, requiring him to spend over half of it on the DL. Ozzie Guillen had been signed mid-season and had done an unbelievable job filling in during Walt's absences. In fact it's my strong opinion that we wouldn't have made it to the World Series that year and maybe not even the post-season had it not been for the tremendous year turned in by Ozzie. He was truly great for us that season.

Anyway, we won the first two games of this pivotal series with New York, which put us in the position to pretty much secure the division title with a win on Sunday. Walt had been on the DL for quite a long time, and after the game Saturday night, he met with the team physician in the training room. After the examination Walt was finally cleared to play, which meant he would be in the lineup for this crucial game on Sunday. No sooner had Walt emerged from the training room than the media got wind of his diagnosis and surrounded his locker.

With tape recorders, microphones and note pads blazing the media began hammering him with questions about his status.

"How do you feel?"

"Will you be in the lineup tomorrow?"

"Is the injury fully healed?"

"Will you be at full speed?"

I was about two lockers away listening to all the commotion along with some vintage Walt Weiss sarcasm. After hearing Walt's responses to a few of the questions I knew he was screwing with them. But keep in mind, with the blatant disconnect that exists between most journalists and players, they had no idea. I, on the other hand, knew exactly what was going on, and had to turn around and face my locker so that my snickering wouldn't give the whole thing away.

One poor goat from USA Today asked Walt: "Do you think you're 100 percent?" Legitimate question, right? Walt's answer, in his typical New York accent was, "Aaahhh, I duknow. I'd say I'm probably 'bout 90 percent right now, but ya know; my 90 percent is as good as most guy's 60 percent."

Overhearing his answer I just hid my face. There we were, the biggest series of the year, Walt has been hurt for over a month; he's getting ready to come off the DL for the biggest game of the season and he's playing grab-ass "zinging" the media. A couple of them were able to pick up on it; most of them didn't. I knew exactly what he was doing, however, and was having hard time keeping it together.

After the interviews were over we had a couple of private laughs at some of the answers he'd given then headed out to get on the bus back to the hotel. The next morning rolled around and the team slowly began filling the clubhouse for our 1 p.m. start when Walt burst through the front entrance, USA Today in hand, shouting at the top of his lungs.

"I GOT 'EM! I GOT 'EM! I WENT DA UDDER WAY ON 'EM, AND I GOT 'EM! I TOLD 'EM MY 90 PERCENT WAS AS GOOD AS MOST GUYS' 60 PERCENT AND HE PRINTED IT. I GOT 'EM!"

A few of us who had been within earshot the night before knew exactly what he was talking about and just started shaking our heads and laughing at some more vintage Walt Weiss. Some of the other guys needed an explanation. By the end of Walt's account regarding the previous night's interview most of the clubhouse was in hysterics. What a way to lighten a tense clubhouse atmosphere just hours before our biggest game of the year. But that was just Walty. What a tremendous guy.

Truly, my career and many of the best experiences I had during that career were enhanced by my friendship with Walt Weiss. It was truly an honor to have had the opportunity to play with him.

ADAM BUTLER

Adam Butler is not a household name, but he is definitely one beautiful dude. This world is full of characters, and I think the level of entertainment, happiness, laughter, excitement and enjoyment you have in your life is directly proportionate to the amount of true "characters" one runs across. And, boy, have I run across more than my fair share of them.

And Adam Butler is near the top of a very long list.

Butt (as he was endearingly referred to) is by no means short on distinctive qualities that made his persona uniquely his. First and foremost Butt's a rather large fellow with towhead blond hair, bearing a strong resemblance to the professional golfer, John Daly. Often times it was his physical prowess that made so many of his antics much funnier than they perhaps should have been. Let's face it: sometimes things are just funnier when a fat guy does them, especially when it's a guy as eccentric as Adam. Like the times during spring training when he would run off the field and into the clubhouse during work outs to get band aids for his chapped nipples because his wet T-shirt was be rubbing them raw. Don't put on a dry shirt! Get band aids for your nipples instead! Only an eccentric fat guy does that. I'll never forget getting back from a two-day road trip and the first thing Adam did when he walk into the apartment was start eating a pizza that had been left sitting out on the coffee table from the night before we left.

And I lost count of the times I sat at the Palm Beach Ale House watching the NCAA Basketball tournament while Butt knocked down a double order of hot wings covered in nuclear sauce, which would routinely run down his arm as he was screaming at the TV if a player on the team he had bet on missed a shot. And if a crucial shot was missed, particularly one that jacked up the point spread, it was not uncommon to see a few of those chicken bones take flight toward whatever TV was being yelled at. The whole thing might be ridiculous or even obnoxious, were it not for Adam being Adam which always made it hilarious and just beautiful.

I soon discovered after meeting Butt that his eccentricities probably stemmed from the fact that he is a genius. Before passing up a job offer as an actuary for the government to play independent league baseball, Butt received two degrees from William and Mary, one in math and one in accounting. Who passes up a guaranteed six-figure job to play INDEPENDENT league baseball? There's just something about people who are walking around with 160 IQs that just makes them different from the rest of us; and Adam is certainly no exception.

Independent ball over a guaranteed six-figure income would certainly seem like a poor choice to most, but Adam did things with a different level of logic, however. As it turned out though, Adam did the right thing. He was one of the best minor league pitchers I ever saw. To look at him, his appearance would convince you he was probably a nose guard. To watch him throw in the bullpen you would swear he couldn't get anyone out; but the rules that apply to the rest of us just didn't seem to apply to him. I sat behind home plate many times with a radar gun charting pitches when Butt would come in to close a game. The gun would never register higher than about 87 mph. He would literally throw about two breaking balls a month; yet every league he played in until he spent a short stint in the big leagues, he led in strikeouts per inning, saves, and would be near the top of the league in ERA. No one knew how he did it and I'm not even sure he could tell you. Night after night he threw 86 mph fastballs (which came to be known as the "phantom ball") by everyone. I routinely watched him have 11-pitch innings while racking up three punch outs. It truly was one of the damndest things I've ever seen on the field.

And off the field … well, let me tell you one of my favorite stories I have from all my 12 years in professional uniform. It's classic Butt.

We were nearing the end of one of those long, hot, mundane minor league seasons with the Double-A Greenville Braves. We had a great group of guys on the roster that year and always had a lot of fun together on and off the field. One day we were sitting around after batting practice, wasting the standard two hours before game time and as usual were bored to tears. By this time in each season the card games have become stale, we're sick of the three channels we got on the clubhouse TV and so we'd start to look for new and different ways to entertain ourselves.

On this one particular day, there were about 10 of us just sitting around engaged in a stupid conversation that our center fielder, Mike Warner, had brought up. Mike said that he'd read somewhere that it was impossible for the human body to consume an entire gallon of milk in one sitting. Where Mike got such a random piece of trivia, and why, I'll never know.

Overhearing Mike's statement, our little fat buddy Adam spoke up.

"Dude, there's no way that can be true," he said. "I love milk; I guarantee you I can do that."

And so began the challenge. Mike and Adam argued this idiotic point for a couple of minutes until finally someone said, "Just go get a gallon of milk and let's see if he can do it."

Of course Adam's all in, talking trash to Mike about how he is gonna prove him wrong.

Someone grabbed a gallon of milk out of the fridge and the challenge was on: Adam started chugging while Mike stood in front of him yelling that he better not spill any and taunting him that there was no way he was going to finish.

Every time Adam would take a breather he would give it back to Mike and let him know how it was going to be, while the rest of us just stood around being stupidly entertained by this whole scene. As this thing played out for a couple of minutes Adam was actually making serious progress toward the bottom of that gallon. I looked over at Mike and he appeared to be getting worried. I looked at Adam and saw his concentration and confidence as he neared the three-quarter empty mark.

We started to believe the big guy was actually going to prove Mike and biology wrong.

on, Adam's demeanor suddenly changed. I don't' think I've ever seen a 260-pound man move that fast as he dropped the jug and dashed for the large community shower.

The rest of us ran behind him with Mike shouting tauntingly all the way as Butt dove into the large clubhouse showers and blew that gallon of milk all over the place. I still have the crude visual of Adam Butler doubled over in that shower blasting a steady column of milk from his face. It was a briefly traumatic sight.

Well, when Butt finally stopped spewing and we all took a second to consider what we'd just witnessed; Adam said one of the funniest things I've ever heard even to this day. While doubled over in the shower with milk dripping off his face and Mike trash talking about his victory, Butt looked up at the entire team and said: "I know I could have finished it if I had just had some cake!"

Seriously, who says that? I guarantee to this day Adam would insist that he could have polished off that gallon if only someone had just gotten him some cake.

I'll say it again: Adam Butler is just one beautiful dude and another in a long list of very special people who I was fortunate enough to have had the opportunity to share many great life experiences with.

Playing professional baseball is full of many ups and many downs. The days can be very long as they melt into a season. The guys you play with, travel with, live with, laugh with and cry with become your family for eight months out of every year and leave you many years later with memories and thoughts of times so special they will always be a part of you within your soul.

Though times weren't always good, I can honestly say, as I sit and reflect back over it all, it was the greatest time of my life – and I ultimately never really had any other choice but to simply "Play Ball!"

CAREER STATISTICS

Pitching Stats:

Season	Team	W	L	ERA	G	GS	CG	SHO	SV	SVD	IP	H	R	ER	HR	HBP	BB	SO
1998	Atlanta Braves	1	3	2.13	47	0	0	0	2	--	38.0	22	10	9	4	3	22	42
1999	Atlanta Braves	4	5	2.49	74	0	0	0	38	45	72.1	47	24	20	5	1	37	104
2000	Atlanta Braves	1	2	2.89	59	0	0	0	24	27	53.0	42	25	17	5	2	48	77
2001	Atlanta Braves	2	2	3.09	30	0	0	0	19	23	32.0	25	13	11	2	2	16	36
2001	Cleveland Indians	3	7	5.45	38	0	0	0	4	7	34.2	33	23	21	2	3	25	43
2002	Texas Rangers	2	3	6.66	30	0	0	0	1	4	24.1	29	19	18	5	0	13	30
2003	Tampa Bay Devil Rays	0	0	9.00	2	0	0	0	0	0	1.0	2	1	1	0	1	3	0

Postseason Pitching Stats:

Year	Round	Team	Opp	WLser	G	GS	ERA	W-L	SV	CG	SHO	IP	H	ER	BB	SO
1998	NLDS	ATL	CHC	W	2	0	0.00	0-0	0	0	0	1.3	1	0	0	2
	NLCS	ATL	SDP	L	6	0	0.00	1-0	0	0	0	4.7	3	0	1	5
1999	NLDS	ATL	HOU	W	2	0	0.00	1-0	1	0	0	3.3	0	0	2	5
	NLCS	ATL	NYM	W	6	0	0.00	0-0	2	0	0	6.7	3	0	2	9
	WS	ATL	NYY	L	2	0	0.00	0-0	0	0	0	3.0	2	0	2	4
2000	NLDS	ATL	STL	L	1	0	0.00	0-0	0	0	0	0.7	0	0	1	0
2001	ALDS	CLE	SEA	L	1	0	0.00	0-0	0	0	0	1.0	1	0	0	1
4 Lg Div Series				2-2	6	0	0.00	1-0	1	0	0	6.3	2	0	3	8
2 Lg Champ Series				1-1	12	0	0.00	1-0	2	0	0	11.3	6	0	3	14
7 Postseason Series				3-4	20	0	0.00	2-0	3	0	0	20.7	10	0	8	26

Fielding Stats:

Season	Team	POS	G	GS	INN	TC	PO	A	E	DP	PB	SB	CS	RF	FPCT
1998	Atlanta Braves	P	47	0	38.0	7	1	6	0	0	--	--	--	1.66	1.000
1999	Atlanta Braves	P	74	0	72.1	11	1	10	0	0	--	--	--	1.37	1.000
2000	Atlanta Braves	P	59	0	53.0	7	1	6	0	0	--	--	--	1.19	1.000
2001	Atlanta Braves	P	30	0	32.0	6	1	4	1	0	--	--	--	1.41	.833
2001	Cleveland Indians	P	38	0	34.2	9	2	4	3	0	--	--	--	1.56	.667
2002	Texas Rangers	P	30	0	24.1	4	1	2	1	1	--	--	--	1.11	.750
2003	Tampa Bay Devil Rays	P	2	0	1.0	0	0	0	0	0	--	--	--	0.00	--
Career Totals			280	0	255.1	44	7	32	5	1	--	--	--	1.37	.886

Not quite big enough to dunk dad yet.

Childhood friends Barrett Daniels, Jake Fincher and Ched Smaha were the first three members. Had they been better organized it may have really taken off.

My high school baseball coach and mentor Jim Turner. An absolutely class individual who bent over backwards to help me realize my dream. YTB "JT".

Dad hassling me for an autograph. Between me and you, I think he sold them to the ushers.

Taking a quick break to pose with Mom during my first Big League spring training.

Kevin McGlinchy, Justin Spier, Mark DeRosa and myself doing a "boys night out" after a game.

Bullpen catcher Alan Butts and myself at Alan's house in Fort Walton Beach, Florida over the All-Star Break.

Evidently having a bad day and hearing about it from Leo. It looks like Javy just wants to go home.

Dad, my Uncle Ronald and his son Rodney after a game at Turner Field.

The Gambler and me before a game at Turner Field

One of my idols, the legendary Bob Feller, gives some much needed advice before a Braves/Cleveland spring traing game in Winter Haven, Florida.

Travis Tritt, Hank Williams Jr. and me at buddy Keith Brooking's house before Hank played a show at the Gwinett Arena.

Giving my cheesy grin.

Dad and me on my 30th birthday.

Travis Tritt and me doing a little King fishing in South Georgia a few weeks before what would prove to be my career ending shoulder injury.

Well it seems that I would get at least one vote.

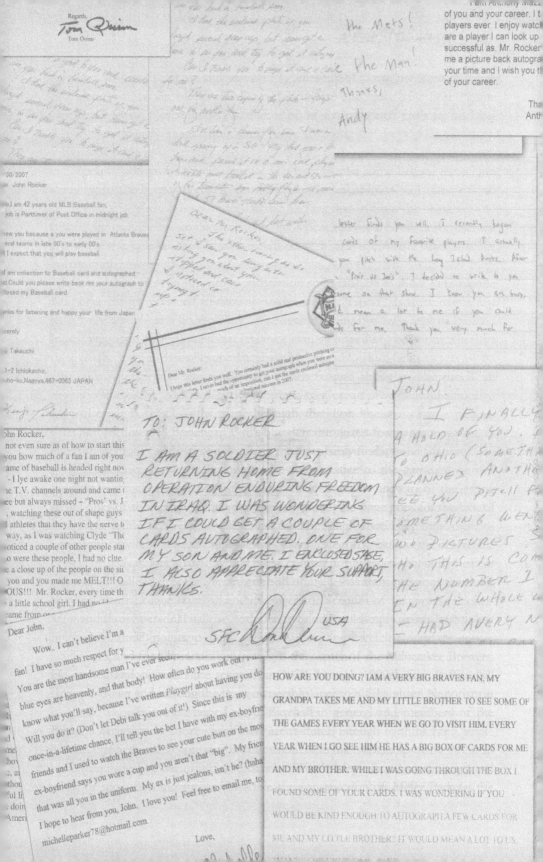